PA

FODOR'S TRAVEL PUBLICATIONS

are compiled, researched, and edited by an international team of travel writers, field correspondents, and editors. The series, which now almost covers the globe, was founded by Eugene Fodor in 1936.

OFFICES

New York & London

Fodor's Paris:

Area Editor: Dominique Sicot
Executive Editor: Richard Moore
Deputy Editor: Thomas Cussans
Editorial Contributors: Robert Brown, John Mayor,
   Vivienne Menkes-Ivry, John G. Morris, John Stokes, Tom Szentgyorgyi
Drawings: Lorraine Calaora
Cartography: Swanston Graphics

FODOR'S

PARIS
1988

FODOR'S TRAVEL PUBLICATIONS, INC.

New York & London

MANUFACTURED IN THE UNITED STATES OF AMERICA
10 9 8 7 6 5 4 3 2 1

CONTENTS

FOREWORD

One of Oscar Wilde's happier quotes runs "When good Americans die they go to Paris." But Oscar has been overtaken by modern travel. Good Americans now pour into Paris by every plane and train. Always popular with those who appreciate the better things of life, the sybaritic possibilities of Paris have acted as a magnet to generations of North Americans with a yen for the finer things. The British—who have eyed the French with a suspicion almost as deep at that with which the French have eyed them back for at least a thousand years—still have Paris very high on their list of popular foreign cities. It is *the* capital in which to relax, to eat up a storm, and where romance is in the air. As we unguardedly said in our *"1936 . . .On the Continent,"* when talking of Paris's feminine allure, "that indefinable something that gives Paris its famous animated, sparkling, vibrating air and, one might almost say, saturates the very pavements with an erotic fluid." Even when reading "sidewalks" for "pavements," the idea is still a bit flamboyant, though with a modicum of truth in it. We sincerely hope that we have outgrown the purple prose after more than 50 years.

This edition of our *Guide to Paris* has more practical information, maps to help you find your way around, things to do at night, and helpful coverage of how to spend those days out of the city, with sightseeing information and lunch spots.

*

We would like to thank the London branch of the French National Tourist Office, and especially Mrs. Pauline Hallam, for their help; our many friends in Paris who have contributed to this edition; Mr. John G. Morris, for kindly putting his 40-years experience at our disposal; and especially Dominique Sicot, for his help in updating our coverage of this ever-changing city.

*

While every care has been taken to ensure the accuracy of the information contained in this guide, the publishers cannot accept responsibilty for any errors which may appear.

All prices quoted in this guide are based on those available to us at the time of writing. In a world of rapid change, however, the possibility of inaccurate or out-of-date information can never be totally eliminated. We trust, therefore, that you will take prices quoted as indicators only and will double-check to be sure of the latest figures.

Similary, be sure to check all opening times of museums and galleries. We have found that such times are liable to change without notice, and you could easily make a trip only to find a locked door.

When a hotel closes or a restaurant produces a disappointing meal, let us know, and we will investigate the complaint. We are always ready to revise our entries for the following year's edition should the facts warrant it.

Send your letters to the editors of **Fodor's Travel Publications,** 201 East 50th Street, New York, NY 10022. European readers may prefer to write to **Fodor's Travel Guides,** 9–10 Market Place, London W1N 7AG, England.

FACTS AT YOUR FINGERTIPS

Planning Your Trip

SOURCES OF INFORMATION. The major source of information for anyone planning a vacation to Paris is the French National Tourist Office. **In the U.S.:** 610 Fifth Ave., New York, NY 10020 (tel. 212–757–1125); 645 N. Michigan Ave., Chicago, IL 60611 (tel. 312–337–6301); 1 Hallidie, Ste. 250, San Francisco, CA 94102 (tel. 415–986–4161). 9401 Wilshire Blvd., Suite 314, Beverly Hills, CA 90212 (tel. 213–272–2661).

In Canada: French National Tourist Office, 1981 Avenue McGill College, Suite 490, Montreal, Quebec H3A 2W9 (tel. 514–288–4264); 1 Dundas St. W., Suite 2405, Box 8, Toronto, Ont. M5G 1Z3 (tel. 416–593–4717).

In the U.K.: French National Tourist Office, 178 Piccadilly, London W1V OAL (tel. 01–491 7622).

They can supply information on all aspects of travel to and around Paris, from which type of vacation is best suited to your needs and purse, to the best and most economical ways of getting there from each of the countries. They will also have a wealth of material on hotels, restaurants, excursions, museums and so on. They produce copious amounts of information, much of it free and all of it useful.

TRAVEL AGENTS. The critical issues in choosing a travel agent are how knowledgeable that person is about travel and how reliable his or her bookings are, regardless of whether you are looking for a package tour or planning to go it independently. The cost will be substantially the same whether you go to a major tour operator such as *Maupintour, American Express, Thos. Cook & Son* and *Olson's* or to the small agency around the corner. Most commissions are paid by airlines, hotels and tour operators. In Europe there may be a small general service charge or fee-per-reservation; in the U.S. only out-of-the-ordinary telephone or telex charges are ever paid by the client.

The importance of a travel agent is not merely for the making of reservations, however. A good travel agent booking a flight for a customer will know what general discounts are in effect based on how long your stay will be, how far in advance you are able to make your reservations, whether you are making a simple round trip or adding extra stops and other factors. He or she will also likely be able to suggest suitable accommodations or packages that offer the kind of services you want.

In the case of package tours you want to be sure that the tour operator can deliver the package being offered. Here again, a travel agent can be helpful. Certainly the organizations named above have established their reputations based on reliability—the inevitable occasional foul-up notwithstanding.

Not all U.S. travel agents are licensed, as the laws vary from state to state, but membership in the *American Society of Travel Agents* (ASTA) is a safeguard. Similarly, reliable U.K. agents belong to the *Association of British Travel Agents* (ABTA). Members prominently display ASTA or ABTA shields.

 TOUR OPERATORS. From the U.S. Full details of the many operators offering trips to Paris are available from the French National Tourist Office, Air France and other airlines and, of course, travel agents. But such is the range of tours available from both North America and the U.K. that a summary of some of the more typical is of interest. All examples are meant to be representative of offerings that are regularly available. Details are as of mid-1987; check for more current information. Prices are per person, double occupancy.

Most airlines and tour operators offer independent city tours. They arrange your accommodations, a tour of the city, car rental if desired, with perhaps a bonus coupon or two. But you are generally on your own for sightseeing, shopping and relaxing.

One such tour is offered by *Pan Am Holidays*. "Simply Paris" is an independent package for 8 days, from $395. It features your choice of accommodations, including continental breakfasts, half-day city tour of Paris, and half-day tour of Versailles. *TWA Getaway Vacations* and *Air France* offer similar flexible packages.

For those interested in the art of Paris and France in general, *Maupintour* offers "Art of Paris and Southern France," 16 days, from $3,400. Included are visits to Paris, Dijon, Avignon, as well as several spots in between.

Barge tours stopping in Paris are offered by *Floating Through Europe*. These are luxury outings for small groups with full accommodations on board.

Among tour operators in the U.S. you may wish to consult are—

Air France, 666 Fifth Ave., New York, NY 10103 (tel. 212–247–0100).

American Express, 822 Lexington Ave., New York, NY 10021 (tel. 212–758–6510).

Bennett Tours, Inc., 270 Madison Ave., New York, NY 10016 (tel. 212–532–5060).

Caravan Tours, 401 N. Michigan Ave., Chicago, IL 60611 (tel. 312–321–9800).

C.I.E. Tours, 122 E. 42nd St. New York, NY 10168 (tel. 212–972–5600).

Cortell Group, 770 Lexington Ave., New York, NY 10021 (tel. 212–751–4200).

Cunard Lines, 555 Fifth Ave., New York, NY 10017 (tel. 800–223–0764).

Floating Through Europe, 271 Madison Ave., New York, NY 10016 (tel. 212–685–5600).

Four Winds Travel, 175 Fifth Ave., New York, NY 10010 (tel. 212–777–0260).

Globus Gateway/Cosmos, 95–25 Queens Blvd., Rego Park, NY 11374 (tel. 718–268–1700).

Hemphill Harris Travel Corp., 16000 Ventura Blvd., Encino, CA 91436 (tel. 818–906–8086).

Maupintour, 1515 St. Andrews Dr., Lawrence, KS 66044 (tel. 913–843–1211).

Olson Travelworld, P.O. Box 92734, Los Angeles, CA 90009 (tel. 213–670–7100).

Pan Am Holidays Tour Desk, 1901 N. Beauregard St., Alexandria, VA 22311 (tel. 800–221–1111; 800–722–3323 for the deaf).

TWA Getaway Vacations, 28 S. 6th St., Philadelphia, PA 19106 (tel. 215–925–7885).

From the U.K. Most British tour operators offer Paris deals, either through a travel agent or direct to the customer. The variety is enormous, from a £39 trip from *Paris Travel Service* lasting 3 days, to a full week of all-found accommodations plus a complete sightseeing program inside and around the capital. Between them the tour operators use the full impressive range of Parisian hotels and can offer almost anything you want.

Here are a few of the many operators to contact—

Air France Holidays, 69 Boston Manor Rd., Brentford, Middx. (tel. 01–568 6981).

Albany Travel, 190 Deansgate, Manchester H3 3WD (tel. 061–833 0202).

American Express, 19–20 Berners St., London W1P 3DD (tel. 01–631 4464).

French Leave Holidays, Travelpoint House, 21 Fleet St., London EC4Y 1AA (tel. 01–583 8383).

French Travel Service, Francis House, Francis St., London SW1P 1DE (tel. 01–828 8131).

Paris Travel Service, Bridge House, Ware, Herts. (tel. 0920–3900).

Time Off, 2A Chester Close, London SW1 (tel. 01–235 8070).

Westbury Travel/Just France, Westfield House, Bratton Rd., Westbury, Wilts. BA13 3EP (tel. 0373–826283).

 WHEN TO GO. The major tourist season in France stretches from Easter to mid-September, with the peak in July and August when the weather is hottest. But Paris is visited year-round and has much to offer at every season. Spring, once the favorite time to visit, is generally depressingly wet nowadays, but June is a delightful month, with good weather and plenty of cultural and other happenings.

July and August can be sultry and dusty and you should be warned that many restaurants, theaters and small shops close for at least four weeks during these two summer months. But you'll find a good choice of firework displays, fairs and the like, and even if there aren't too many genuine Parisians in town, at least you'll have the important bonus of much less traffic than usual.

September is a good month, with cultural life starting up again after the summer break and a good chance of sunny weather, which is also likely in the first half of October. November, as in most places, is a mixture of wet-and-cold and bright-and-sunny; the theater and ballet season is in full swing.

December is dominated by the "end-of-year festivities" *(fêtes de fin d'année)*, with splendid displays in food shops and restaurants and a busy theater, ballet and opera season continuing into January. February and March are the worst months, weather-wise, but with the coming of Easter Paris starts looking beautiful again as the chestnut leaves begin to unfurl.

Temperatures. Average afternoon temperatures in Paris are—

	Jan.	Feb.	Mar.	Apr.	May	June	July	Aug.	Sept.	Oct.	Nov.	Dec.
F°	42	45	52	60	67	73	75	75	69	59	49	43
C°	6	7	11	16	19	23	24	24	21	15	9	6

SEASONAL EVENTS. March, or occasionally April, *Salon du Livre,* a huge book fair open to the public. **Easter Sunday,** the *Prix du Président de la République,* a major race meeting held at Auteuil racecourse. Late **April** or early **May,** the *Foire de Paris.* The "Paris Marathon" is now a major event in May. Late **May** or early **June,** the French international tennis championships in Roland-Garros stadium. Air Show *(Salon de l'Air)* at Le Bourget airport (odd-numbered years only). **June** sees the start of the varied and exciting *Marais Festival* (music, dance and drama staged in the district's beautifully restored mansions). Weekend nearest to **24 June,** the *Fête du Pont-Neuf* and various firework displays to celebrate the Feast of John the Baptist.

The key date in **July,** as you would expect, is the 14th, when the storming of the Bastille is celebrated as France's National Day *(Fête Nationale).* The fun starts on the evening of the 13th, with open-air dances, some spontaneous (mainly near the Beaubourg arts center, in Montparnasse and in the popular districts in eastern Paris) but an increasing number organized by the local town hall—watch out for posters giving locations. Firework displays are another feature of the 13th and/or the 14th itself (it depends on whether the National Day falls at a weekend). On the morning of the 14th a solemn military parade draws huge crowds to the Champs-Elysées, with an impressive display of flags and bunting and a dramatic flypast set against the Arc de Triomphe. The Marais Festival keeps going in July, overlapping with the beginning of the Summer Festival *(Festival Estival)* of concerts, plays, ballet and other cultural events staged at various venues. The *Ile-de-France Festival* is another cultural feast, mostly staged in historic buildings both in Paris and in the surrounding area; it continues through the summer.

August is a fairly dead time in Paris, with many restaurants, theaters and shops closed, but the City Hall now stages a number of events designed to keep the place lively until the Parisians flock back for the *rentrée* (back-to-school-and-work) after the long summer break. There are no big happenings, but you'll find a number of local street festivals, firework displays and so on, many of them centered on **15 August,** Assumption Day and a major public holiday.

September sees major races at Vincennes and concerts in historic buildings continuing. The *Festival d'Automne,* with concerts, theater and dance performances all over the city, starts in September and continues for three months. The new season doesn't get truly underway until **October,** when the theaters open new shows, major art exhibits are staged, the Auto Show *(Salon de l'Auto)* takes place (even-numbered years only) and the city is full to bursting, with fashion aficionados flocking to see the latest *couture* and ready-to-wear collections. The sports highlight is the *Prix de l'Arc de Triomphe,* held at Longchamp racecourse on the first Sunday of the month. The *FIAC,* an important contemporary art show, is held in the Grand Palais, and may continue until November. The ballet season reaches a peak in **November,** with many of the world's leading companies appearing in Paris. On the 11th Armistice Day is celebrated with a number of moving ceremonies, the most important being that held at the Arc de Triomphe and attended by the President of the Republic and his government.

December offers the attractions of magnificent shop windows ready for the Christmas and New Year festivities, mouthwatering food displays everywhere and elegant street lighting near the Madeleine and in the avenue Montaigne, with rather more garish displays around the big department stores near the Opéra. The key meals are dinner on Christmas Eve and New Year's Eve *(Saint-Sylvestre* in French), when restaurants lay on lavish, and very expensive, menus with the champagne flowing freely and everyone dressed up to the nines.

Public Holidays. January 1; Easter Monday; May 1 (Labor Day); May 8 (VE Day—a new holiday and not observed as extensively as the others); Ascension Day (5 weeks after Easter); Whit Monday; July 14 (Bastille Day and National Holiday); August 15 (Assumption); November 1 (All Saints); November 11 (Armistice); Christmas Day. If a public holiday falls on a Tuesday or a Thursday, many businesses and shops and some restaurants will close on the Monday or Friday too.

 WHAT TO PACK. Porters are hard to find in France and although baggage trolleys are in theory available at airports and rail stations, in practice you may well have difficulty finding one. So we advise you to travel as light as possible, making sure that you can carry your baggage yourself. Motorists should bear in mind that thefts from cars are common, so don't take more baggage than you can hide away in your trunk during daytime stops and take to your hotel room at night.

Weather in Paris is very variable, so be prepared for all eventualities, with a raincoat and umbrella essential at all times of year. The French are still fairly formal, and we therefore advise you not to wear the jazzier and more casual items in your wardrobe if you're going to be visiting French families, going to good restaurants, the theater and opera and the classier stores. Jeans are of course worn universally these days, but a jeans-and-sneakers outfit will cause raised eyebrows in such establishments, as will wildly patterned shirts worn over shorts. Both men and women wearing shorts will probably be refused admission to churches and cathedrals, whether or not they are attending a service or mass, but you need not cover your head or arms (though beach-style décolletés are frowned on).

Unless you are planning to attend gala performances at the Paris Opera you do not need formal evening dress: in fact, people are dressing less and less for theaters and concerts. But if you're invited to a dinner party in a private home, the golden rule is: "If in doubt, dress up rather than down." French women take a great deal of trouble with their appearance and tend to dress up (except in very young or bohemian circles). As a result you won't feel silly even if you're dressier than most of the guests, but you will feel awkward if you're in casual clothes and no one else is. Long dresses and skirts are rarely worn in France, even for dances, so your best bet is a smart cocktail dress or a really pretty silk or chiffon blouse or shirt with a fairly dressy black skirt.

Practical, low-heeled shoes may be less flattering than dainty pumps, but they're better suited to wet weather, cobbled streets and long hours on your feet. Don't on any count bring your best suede shoes, as they're bound to get spoiled in Paris, where large areas of the sidewalks are made of a mixture of clay and gravel that turns into a sea of mud when it's been raining. A pair of soft slippers may be a lifesaver during long plane or train rides. You may need one pair of dressy (but not evening) shoes.

Handbags can be another problem. While it's wiser to select a model big enough to hold your passport, travelers checks, sunglasses, tickets, cosmetics, and other necessities, something really outsized may seem like a millstone after you've carried it day after day for weeks or months. We recommend you not to carry bags over your shoulder, where they are an easy prey for bag-snatchers; sling them across your body, bandolier-style, as most French women do. A handbag with enough interior pockets (at least one with a zipper closing for your money) to keep things in some kind of order makes life easier. Something with a positive fastening is protection against pickpockets. Take along another smaller flat bag for daytime sightseeing and leave money and other valuables in the hotel safe (but keep your passport as you're supposed to have some form of official identification on you at all times in France). A pretty evening bag will be handy if you're intending to go to dressy functions. Men used to carrying a shoulder bag should bear in mind our advice about bag-snatchers too. Either sling it across you, or go instead for the small type with a long handle you can loop over your wrist.

COSTS IN PARIS. Paris, like most capitals, is basically an expensive city. But, again like most capitals, it has such a wide choice of sleeping and eating places that you can find both hotels and restaurants at reasonable prices in most districts. See our *Practical Information* section for details.

Restaurants are basically good value at all price levels, as long as you avoid the tourist traps, since the French set such store by good eating. Snacks work out expensive. Hotels are good value for two (room charges are for the room itself, not per person), but as in many cities, those traveling alone tend to lose out.

Transport is good news in Paris. Public transport is frequent and efficient and costs are reasonable, since distances are not great within the city limits. Taxis, too, are less expensive than in many European capitals. What's more, many of the places you'll want to visit are close together, so a lot of your traveling can be free, gratis and for nothing—on foot.

Not much comes free in Paris, with admission charges for all museums and most exhibits, and even for some gardens. But most places charging admission do have certain days (often Sunday) or periods when charges are reduced, and offer reductions to some categories of visitors (see the *Practical Information* section).

Shopping is one of the delights of Paris but don't expect it to be an inexpensive pastime. Our shopping chapter gives you some hints on what to look out for.

YOUTH PASS. Good news for those under the age of 26 is the special youth pass *(Carte Jeune)* enabling them to obtain a large number of reductions on various services, including travel. The pass is available from youth information centers, or from the Crédit Mutuel and CIC banks, and is valid for a year. In 1987 it cost 50 frs. It may be bought by anyone in the under-26 age group, whether or not they are resident in France (take your passport to prove your age). A guide listing over four thousand services offered at reduced rates will be given to you when you purchase your pass. Here are just a few to whet your appetite: reduced rates in all state-owned museums; reductions in some hamburger or self-service restaurants; reductions at certain times of year in the upmarket Frantel and PLM hotel chains; 50 per cent reimbursement by Air France and Air Inter on the first air trip you do within France; access to university restaurants even to those without a student card; and 10 per cent reduction on already-reduced youth fares on French trains.

TAKING MONEY ABROAD. Traveler's checks are still the standard and best way to safeguard your travel funds; and you still usually get a better exchange rate in France for traveler's checks than for cash. In the U.S., many of the larger banks issue their own traveler's checks—just about as universally recognized as those of *American Express, Cooks* and *Barclays.* In most instances there is a 1% charge for the checks; there is no fee for Barclays checks. Some banks also issue them free if you are a regular customer.

The best-known British checks are *Cooks* and those of *Barclays, Lloyds, Midland* and *National Westminster* banks. The *Eurocheque* scheme, which many British banks participate in, is an excellent alternative to traveler's checks, as it allows you to write a check on your own bank account for an amount of foreign currency. However, Eurocheques are particularly attractive to pickpockets, so keep your card and checkbook separate, as one is no use without the other.

It is also always a good idea to have some local currency upon arrival for immediate needs. Some banks will provide this service; alternately, contact *Deak-Pererra,* 630 Fifth Ave., New York, NY 10111 (tel. 212–757–0100, call for additional branches).

Credit Cards. Major credit cards are accepted in most large hotels, and in some restaurants and shops. Our hotel and restaurant listings give the four major cards when they are accepted—American Express (AE), Diners Club (DC), MasterCard (MC), and Visa (V). You should be warned, though, that many thrifty proprietors are damned if they see why they should pay over their hard-earned cash in a percentage, and so refuse to accept *any* kind of credit card. Check very carefully to avoid acute embarrassment.

 FRENCH CURRENCY. The basic unit of currency in France is the French franc, which is divided into 100 centimes. At the time of writing there were 6 francs to the U.S. dollar and 9.88 francs to the pound sterling. But exchange rates change frequently, so it is important to check the latest position when planning your visit and again when you reach Paris.

The following coins are in circulation: 5, 10 and 20 centimes, all copper-colored; 50 centimes, 1 franc, 2, 5 and 10 francs, all silver-colored (note that the 2-franc coin is multi-sided, whereas all the others are round); 10 francs, which is a dark copper color and is thicker and heavier than the other coins. The bills are 50, 100, 200 and 500 francs. Watch out for telephone slugs or tokens, which are similar to 20- and 50-centime coins.

Visitors to France may take in an unlimited amount of foreign currency or French francs, but may only take out 5,000 francs or the equivalent in other currencies. There are no restrictions on taking out traveler's checks.

PASSPORTS. U.S. Citizens. Apply in person at U.S. Passport Agency Offices, local county courthouses or selected Post Offices. If you have a passport not more than eight years old you may apply by mail; otherwise you will need:

1—proof of citizenship, such as a birth certificate;

2—two identical photographs, 2 inches square, in either black and white or color, on non-glossy paper and taken within the past six months;

3—$35 for the passport itself plus a $7 processing fee if you are applying in person (no processing fee when applying by mail) for those 18 years and older; if you are under 18, $20 for the passport plus a $7 processing fee if you are applying in person (again, no extra fee when applying by mail);

4—proof of identity such as a driver's license, previous passport that includes a photo and signature, or any governmental ID card.

Adult passports are valid for 10 years, others for five years; they are not renewable. Allow four to six weeks for your application to be processed, but, in an emergency, Passport Agency offices can have a passport readied within 24–48 hours, and even the postal authorities can indicate "Rush".

If you expect to travel extensively, request a 48- or 96-page passport rather than the usual 24-page one. There is no extra charge. When you receive your passport, write down its number, date and place of issue separately; if it is later lost or stolen, notify either the nearest American Consul or the Passport Office, Department of State, 1425 K St. NW, Washington DC 20524, as well as the local police.

Canadian Citizens. Apply in person to regional passport offices, post offices or by mail to Bureau of Passports, Complexe Guy Favreau, 200 Dorchester West, Montreal, P.Q. H2Z 1X4 (tel. 514–283–2152). A $21 fee, two photographs and evidence of citizenship are required. Canadian passports are valid for five years and are non-renewable.

Note: All U.S. and Canadian citizens are now required to obtain a visa before entering France. To get a visa, send an application form, your passport, one passport-sized photo, and a self-addressed, stamped envelope to the French consulate nearest you. Application forms and consulate addresses are available from the French Government Tourist Office. Fees are $3 for a 72-hour transit visa, $9 for a 3-month multiple entry visa, and $15 for a one-year multiple entry visa.

U.K. Citizens. Apply for passports on special forms obtainable from your travel agency or from the main post office in your town. The application should be sent to the Passport Office in your area (as indicated on the guidance form) or taken personally to your nearest main post office. It is advisable to apply for your passport 4–5 weeks before it is required, although in some cases it will be issued sooner. The regional Passport Offices are located in London, Liverpool, Peterborough, Glasgow and Newport. The application must be countersigned by your bank manager, or by a solicitor, barrister, doctor, clergyman or Justice of the Peace who knows you personally. You will need two photos. The fee is £15. A larger, 94-page passport can be obtained for an extra charge.

British Visitor's Passport. This simplified form of passport has advantages for the once-in-a-while tourist to most European countries (Yugoslavia and Eastern European countries presently excepted). Valid for one year and not renewable, it costs £7.50. Application may be made at a local post office (in Northern Ireland at the Passport Office in Belfast); you will need identification plus two passport photographs–no other formalities.

HEALTH AND INSURANCE. Travel insurance can cover everything from health and accident costs, to lost baggage and trip cancellation. Sometimes they can all be covered with a blanket policy; other times they overlap with existing coverage you might have for health and/or home; still other times it is best to buy policies that are tailored to specific needs. It is easy unwittingly to end up with redundant coverage.

Generally, it is best to take care of your insurance needs before embarking on your trip. You'll pay more for less coverage—and have less chance to read the fine print—if you wait until the last minute and make your purchases from, say, an airport vending machine or insurance company counter. Consult your regular insurance agent first.

Flight insurance, which is often included in the price of the ticket when the fare is paid via *American Express, Visa* or certain other major credit cards, is also often included in package policies providing accident coverage as well. These policies are available from most tour operators and insurance companies. While it is a good idea to have **health and accident insurance** when traveling, be careful not to spend money to duplicate coverage you may already have . . . or to neglect some eventuality which could end up costing a small fortune.

For example, basic Blue Cross-Blue Shield policies do cover health costs incurred while traveling. They will not, however, cover the cost of emergency transportation, which can often add up to several thousand dollars. Emergency transportation is covered, in part at least, by many major medical policies such as those underwritten by *Prudential, Metropolitan* and *New York Life.* Again, we can't urge you too strongly that in order to be sure you are getting the coverage you need, you check any policy carefully before buying. Another important example: most insurance issued specifically for travel does not cover pre-existing problems, such as a heart condition.

Recently, several organizations have appeared which offer coverage designed to supplement existing health insurance and to help defray costs not covered by many standard policies. Some of the more prominent are:

Carefree Travel Insurance, c/o ARM Coverage Inc., 120 Mineola Blvd., Box 310, Mineola, NY 11510 (tel. 516–294–0220) offers insurance, legal and financial assistance, and medical evacuation arranged through Inter Claim.

International SOS Assistance Inc., P.O. Box 11568, Philadelphia, PA 19116, has fees from $15 a person for seven days, to $195 for a year (tel. 800–523–8930).

IAMAT (International Association for Medical Assistance to Travelers), 417 Center St., Lewiston, NY 14092 (tel. 716–754–4883 in the U.S.); or 188 Nicklin Road, Guelph, Ontario, N1H 7L5 (tel. 519–836–0102).

Travel Assistance International, the American arm of Europ Assistance, offers a comprehensive program providing medical and personal emergency services and offering immediate, on-the-spot medical, personal and financial help. Trip protection ranges from $35 for an individual for up to eight days to $220 for an entire family for a year. Full details from travel agents or insurance brokers, or from Europ Assistance Worldwide Services, Inc., 1333 F St., N.W., Washington, D.C. 20004 (tel. 800–821–2828). In the U.K., contact Europ Assistance Ltd., 252 High St., Croydon, Surrey (tel. 01–680 1234).

Baggage Loss. Another frequent inconvenience to travelers is the loss of baggage. It is possible, though often a complicated affair, to insure your luggage against loss through theft or negligence. Insurance companies are reluctant to sell such coverage alone since it is often a losing proposition for them. Instead, it is usually included as part of a package that would also cover accidents or health. Remuneration is often determined by weight, regardless of the value of the specific contents of the luggage. Should you lose your luggage or some other personal possession, be sure to report it to the local police immediately. Without documentation of such a report, your insurance company might be very stingy. Also, before buying baggage insurance, check your homeowners policy. Some such policies offer "off-premises theft" coverage, including the loss of luggage while traveling.

Trip Cancellation. The last major area of traveler's insurance is trip cancellation coverage. This is especially important to travelers on APEX or charter flights. Should you get sick abroad, or for some other reason be unable to continue your trip, you may be stuck having to buy a new one-way fare home, plus paying for space on the charter you're not using. You can guard against this with "trip cancellation insurance," usually available from travel agents. Most of these policies will also cover last minute cancellations.

 HINTS FOR HANDICAPPED TRAVELERS. The French authorities are now very aware of the need to cater for handicapped travelers and the SNCF (French rail system) is progressive in providing for them. Ask a French National Tourist Office for information about facilities available at main rail stations and on main-line trains.

A very useful guide to Paris, *Access in Paris,* lists carefully researched details about access to major buildings, with plans, and gives general information needed by handicapped visitors to France. Obtainable from Mr. Gordon R. Couch, 39 Bradley Gdns., West Ealing, London W13, free of charge, but a donation to cover postage would be appreciated. You might like to contact the *Association des Paralysés de France,* 17 blvd. Auguste-Blanqui, 75013 Paris, which can supply details of hotels with facilities for wheelchairs. The official Paris hotel list also has a symbol indicating hotels with rooms "accessible to the disabled with help." Free babysitting for physically and mentally handicapped children is provided by an organization called *Volontaires pour Enfants Handicapés,* 42 rue du Louvre, 1er (tel. 45–08–45–15 between 2 and 6 P.M.); service available day or evening, weekdays or weekends.

More information is available from the *Travel Information Center,* Moss Rehabilitation Hospital, 12th St and Tabor Rd, Philadelphia, Pa 19141 (tel. 215–329–5715); the *Society for the Advancement of Travel for the Handicapped,* 26 Court St, Brooklyn, New York 11242 (tel. 718–858–5483); and the *Information Center for Individuals with Disabilities,* 20 Park Plaza, Rm. 330, Boston, MA 02116 (tel. 617–727–5540). *Mobility International,* 62 Union St., London SE1 (tel. 01–403 5688), is a good source of information on access facilities in Europe. A very useful book on the subject is *Access to the World,* by Louise Weiss, published by Facts on File, 460 Park Ave. South, New York, N.Y. 10016 ($14.95). The *International Air Transport Association* (IATA) publishes a free pamphlet entitled *Incapacitated Passengers' Air Travel Guide* to explain the various arrangements to be made and how to make them. Write IATA, 2000 Peel Street, Montreal, Quebec H3A 2R4 (tel. 514–844–6311).

Getting to Paris

FROM THE U.S. BY AIR. Air fares are in a constant state of flux, and our best advice is to consult a travel agent and let him or her make your reservations for you.

Agents are familiar with the latest changes in fare structures—ever more confusing despite "deregulation" among U.S. carriers who now allegedly base prices on distance traveled—as well as with the rules governing various discount plans. Among those rules: booking (usually) 21 days in advance, minimum stay requirements, maximum stay allowances, the amount that (sometimes) must be paid in advance for land arrangements. Lowest prices overall will, of course, be during the off-season periods.

Generally, on regularly scheduled flights, you have the option, in descending order of cost, of First Class, Club or Business Class, Economy Class, or APEX. APEX is by far the most used and the most useful of these categories. Some charter service is still available; again, an agent will be able to recommend which ones are reliable. Sometimes it is also worth investigating package tours even if you do not wish to use the tours' other services (hotels, meals, etc.). Because a packager can block-book seats, the price of a package can be less than the cost when a flight is booked separately.

If you have the flexibility, you can sometimes benefit from last-minute sales that tour operators have in order to fill a plane. A number of brokers specializing in such discount sales have also sprung up. All charge an annual membership fee, usually about $35–45. Among these: *Stand-Buys Ltd.,* 311 W. Superior, Suite 414, Chicago, IL 60610 (tel. 312–943–5737); *Moments Notice,* 40 E. 49th St., New York, NY 10017 (tel. 212–486–0503); *Discount Travel Intl.,* 114 Forrest Ave., Narberth, PA 19072 (tel. 215–668–2182), and *Worldwide Discount Travel Club,* 1674 Meridian Ave., Miami Beach, FL 33139 (tel. 305–534–2082). Sometimes, tour and charter flight operators themselves advertise in Sunday travel supplements as well. Try to find out whether the tour operator is reputable and whether you are tied to a precise round trip or whether you will have to wait until the operator has a spare seat in order to return.

Airlines specifically serving France from major U.S. cities (usually via New York) include:

Air France, 666 Fifth Ave., New York, NY 10103 (tel. 212–247–0100).

TWA, 605 Third Ave., New York, NY 10016 (tel. 212–290–2141).

Pan Am, Pan Am Building, New York, NY 10017 (tel. 212–687–2600).

A number of other carriers including *El Al* and *Pakistan International* stop over in Paris on their way to other destinations.

Typical fares as of mid-1987 for New York to Paris:

$3,562 roundtrip, First Class; $1,944 roundtrip, Business Class; $1,296 roundtrip, Economy; $667 APEX depending on season. Airport taxes and security add around $25 to these fares. Charter fares are about the same as, or slightly lower than, APEX.

From Canada, *Air Canada* and *Air France* operate regular flights out of Toronto and Montreal to Paris.

FROM THE U.S. BY SEA. Cunard's *QE2* is the only luxury liner that makes transatlantic crossings on a regular schedule—four roundtrips annually that stop at Cherbourg. Rates vary by season, but "intermediate" season (July) fares range from $1,600–$6,800 as of mid-1987, per person, double occupancy, each way. Contact *Cunard Lines, Inc.,* 555 Fifth Ave., New York, NY 10017 (tel. 800–528–6273).

Currently *Polish Ocean Lines* is operating a freighter vessel with passenger accommodations for 6 (3 double cabins). From U.S./Canada these vessels call at the ports of Halifax, Nova Scotia; Port Newark, NJ; Baltimore, MD; and Wilmington, NC to Le Havre, France; Rotterdam, Holland; and Bremerhaven, Germany on a weekly basis. Information and ticket sales in the U.S. are handled by Gdynia America Line, 39 Broadway, New York, NY 10006 (tel. 212–952–1280).

For details on the possibility of other freighter travel to or from France, consult *Air Marine Travel Service,* 501 Madison Ave., New York, NY 10022 (tel. 212–371–1300) publisher of the *Trip Log Quick Reference Freighter Guide.*

FROM THE U.K. BY AIR. As you would expect, Paris has an excellent service from both London airports, Heathrow and Gatwick. *British Airways* and *Air France* between them operate some 14 flights daily from London (Heathrow) to Paris (Charles-de-Gaulle/Roissy) airport. The flying time is one hour. *Air France* and *British Caledonian* fly from London (Gatwick) to Paris (Charles-de-Gaulle/Roissy) and between them they offer up to nine daily, the departures approximately every 2 hours. The flying time from Gatwick is slightly shorter, at around 55 minutes. This, coupled with the efficiency of the Gatwick Airport Express service operated by British Rail from London (Victoria) to the in-terminal station at Gatwick and the swift Roissy Rail Service (Line B) from Charles-de-Gaulle/Roissy airport to the centre of Paris (both journeys taking around half an hour) makes Gatwick–Paris the quickest and easiest route.

There are also direct air connections from other parts of the U.K. to Paris, though not all operate daily, including Birmingham *(British Airways),* Bristol *(Air France),* East Midlands *(British Midland),* Manchester *(British Airways/Air France)* and Southampton *(Air UK).*

Fares. Air fares have been artificially high for this short hop—in 1987 APEX fares rose again to around £82 after falling the previous year. Club Class, with its superior accommodations and service was still around £190 return. "Scheduled charter" flights are now available to Paris (Orly) from London (Gatwick) on three days a week at £59 return. There should be more flights in '88. Details in the U.K. from *Nouvelles Frontières*, 1–2 Hanover St., London W1R 9AB (tel. 01–629–7772); in the U.S. from *Nouvelles Frontières*, 19 West 44th St., New York, NY 10036 (tel. 212–764–6494).

Don't forget that many tour operators run short-break holidays to Paris. These are very good value when compared with the flight-only prices. Ask for the brochures produced by *Time Off, French Travel Service, Thomson Paris, Nouvelles Frontières,* or *Air France Holidays* for a start. All offer accommodations ranging from the basic to the luxurious.

FROM THE U.K. BY CAR. Travel to Paris by car is so easy! The closest channel crossing to London is the route from Newhaven (some 9 miles east of Brighton) to the beautiful French port of Dieppe. This is a quiet route even in high summer, but its drawback is the length of the crossing—about 4 hours. From Dieppe it is possible to drive along less busy roads to Paris, avoiding the motorways.

For the motorist the shortest sea crossing is from Dover to Calais. This 22-mile stretch of water can be crossed by hovercraft in 35 minutes or by conventional ferry in around 75 minutes. The port of Dover has excellent access from London via the M2/A2, which takes you right to the Eastern Docks. Both Calais and neighboring Boulogne are served by *Hoverspeed* hovercraft and by the fast ferries of *Townsend Thoresen* and *British Ferries.* Departures are frequent, rather like a city bus service, so that it is only really necessary to book for the peak weekends. *Sally Viking Line* operate from Ramsgate to Dunkerque.

Getting to Paris from these French Channel ports is equally easy with disembarkation and customs checks usually quick and efficient. Calais and Boulogne are served by the A26 motorway which now commences at Nordausques, only a few kilometers from the coast, and goes all the way to Paris (260 km.). The roads leading to the motorway are—from Calais take the N43, from Boulogne the N42 and from Dunkerque follow the signs for the A25 which runs to Lille then the A1 which connects with the A26 near Arras. Don't forget that tolls are charged on French motorways, so be sure to have some small denomination notes and change ready for toll booths.

Other crossings which are useful for Paris are the services from Portsmouth to Caen by Brittany Ferries, and to Le Havre operated by Townsend Thoresen. The daytime sailing to Le Havre takes around 5½ hours, while the night service takes longer, berthing at seven in the morning local time, allowing a comfortable overnight crossing.

Ferry Fares. Fares vary widely according to both the season and the convenience of the timing. Away from the peak weekends in high summer the ferry companies offer a wide range of special deals for motorists, with or without accommodations in France. Even in high summer it is possible to save substan-

FERRY SERVICES FOR TRAVEL TO PARIS FROM BRITAIN

	SALLY VIKING	SEALINK BRITISH FERRIES	HOVERSPEED	P&O EUROPEAN FERRIES	BRITTANY FERRIES	DIEPPE FERRIES
RAMSGATE – DUNKIRK	●					
DOVER – CALAIS		◆	●	●		
– BOULOGNE			◆	●		
FOLKESTONE – BOULOGNE		◆				
NEWHAVEN – DIEPPE		◆				◆
PORTSMOUTH – LE HAVRE				◆		
– CAEN					●	
– CHERBOURG		●¹				
POOLE – CHERBOURG					●	
WEYMOUTH – CHERBOURG		●¹				

◆ Route especially suitable for rail passengers easy interchange between train and ship.

● Only really suitable for motorists.

1) Seasonal service operates April to September only.

tially by traveling mid-week. To give an idea of costs: for two adults and a small car (under 4.5m. long), the crossing from Dover to Calais works out at around £90 peak single, falling to around £80 mid-week in summer. On the longer overnight Portsmouth–Le Havre run, expect to pay around £120 single including cabin accommodation.

FROM THE U.K. BY TRAIN. As we go to press (mid '87) there is still a wide range of routes to Paris by rail and ferry/hovercraft. We will take them in order of speed.

For those in a hurry Paris can be reached in under 5½ hours by the Citylink rail–hovercraft–rail service run by *Hoverspeed*. There are up to four through services on weekdays—five at weekends—during the summer. The journey, an experience in itself, is in three stages. First by train from London (Charing Cross) by special train to Dover, then across the Channel by hovercraft in around 35 minutes to Boulogne (Aéroglisseurs), and finally by express Turbo-train direct to Paris (Gare du Nord). Fares are good value for money at around £55 for a 5-day excursion return in second class. The ordinary second-class return works out at around £85. For these services it is compulsory to book in advance—make sure to book well ahead at weekends and during the high summer months. Full details from any British Rail Travel Centre or direct from Hoverspeed, Maybrook House, Dover, Kent, CT17 9QU (tel. 0304–214514).

You can also make the journey to Paris crossing the Channel by one of the conventional ferry services, though this extends the city center to city center journey time to around six hours via the Dover–Calais, and Dover/Folkestone–Boulogne crossings and ten hours via Newhaven–Dieppe. The boat trains for Dover/Folkestone and Newhaven all depart from London (Victoria Station). On all these routes the interchange between rail and ship is easy—although be prepared for crowds and lines in high season. All these routes are really only suitable for daytime crossings.

Finally—as Paris is the romantic capital of the world why not travel there on the world's most romantic train? The *Venice-Simplon-Orient-Express* runs from London to Paris twice a week during the summer. Journey and dine in opulent surroundings on both sides of the Channel—an ideal start to a Parisian adventure. Details from V.S.O.E., Suite 1235, One World Trade Center, New York, NY 10048 (tel. 212–938–6830). In the U.K.: V.S.O.E., Sea Containers House, 20 Upper Ground, London SE1 (tel. 01–928–5837).

Information. For full information on these services contact *British Rail Travel International,* 630 3rd Ave., New York, NY 10017, or Suite 603, 800 S. Hope St., Los Angeles, CA 90017, or 333 North Michigan Ave., Chicago, IL 60601; in Canada—U.K. Building, 409 Granville St., Vancouver V6C 1T2, British Columbia, or 94 Cumberland St., Toronto, Ontario M5R 1A3.

A vital travel aid for train riders is the *Thomas Cook Continental Timetable.* This can be bought in the U.S. by mail from *Forsyth Travel Library,* P.O. Box 2975, 9154 West 57th Street, Shawnee Mission, KS 66201. In the U.K. the timetable can be bought over the counter at any branch of Thomas Cook. One word of advice—be sure to buy an issue which covers the period at which you will be traveling. The summer and winter schedules of the European railway and ferry companies are very different.

Fares. The ordinary adult return fare to Paris works out at around £75. If you are on a very tight budget, traveling overnight will save money, bringing the fare down to around £45 return—but be prepared to be woken up at some unearthly hour! Student fares are also available at around £41 return: contact *Eurotrain,* 52 Grosvenor Gdns., London SW1 (tel. 01–730–6525) or *Transalpino,* 71–5 Buckingham Palace Rd., London SW1 (tel. 01–834–9656).

FROM THE U.K. BY BUS. Paris can be reached by both Hoverspeed's *City Sprint* services and by *International Express.* Hoverspeed operate the fastest service, taking full advantage of the 35-minute Channel crossing using their hovercraft. There are up to four departures daily in the summer and the morning coach arrives mid-afternoon. The coaches run from London (Victoria Coach Station) to Paris (rue Lafayette)—close to the Gare du Nord and Gare de L'Est. The actual traveling time is a little over eight hours, not bad by any standards. The fare is also good news at around £40 return, with a slight reduction for students. For details contact Hoverspeed, Maybrook House, Dover, Kent, CT17 9QU (tel. 0304–214514), or consult the *International Express* brochure which includes the Hoverspeed City Sprint schedules.

International Express offer three other services. Firstly an overnight bus which leaves London (Victoria Coach Station) in the evening and reaches Paris (Porte de la Villette) early the following morning—not the most restful of journeys. Secondly during the summer there are two daytime services. On these services the Channel crossing is by conventional ferry, with a corresponding increase in boarding and crossing time. Details of these *International Express* services (operated by *Eurolines*) are contained in the *International Express* timetable which can be obtained from The Coach Travel Center, 13 Regent St., London SW1Y 4LR (tel. 01–439 9468) or from any National Express travel agent.

Leaving Paris

 VAT REFUNDS. Visitors to France (i.e. normally resident outside the country) may be given the opportunity to save money by being exonerated from part of the value-added tax (*TVA* in French) on certain goods. Discounts obtained in this way range from 13% to 23% (on "luxury" goods such as jewelry or perfumes). You should be aware that offering this discount is not a legal obligation on shopkeepers, so you may not insist on it. You'll find that the easiest places to benefit from the system are the department stores, which have special staff dealing with it, and shops with a large foreign clientele. Small boutiques are emphatically not equipped to deal efficiently with the complicated paperwork involved, and the system is liable to break down.

This is how it works. For a start, the total value of your purchases in a single store must be at least 1,200 frs if you live outside the EEC; if you live in an EEC member state (which of course includes Britain and Ireland), discounts are obtainable only on *single items* costing at least 2,500 frs. Some stores will simply state a price after deduction of the discount. But they'll be taking a risk, because if you don't do your bit by handing on the documentation to the customs, they'll be out of pocket. The great majority will ask you to pay the full amount and the discount will be sent to you in due course. The store will fill out a form in quadruplicate, giving you three copies and keeping one. Make sure that if you live outside the EEC they haven't filled in an EEC form by mistake and vice versa. You must give details of your bank account, or that of friends in France—reimbursements cannot be made to private addresses. If you live outside the EEC you present two of the forms to the customs official on leaving the country, he will probably ask to see the goods in question to make sure that you haven't just been doing a favor to a French friend! Make sure to leave plenty of time for this operation. If you live in an EEC country, the papers are dealt with by the customs official when you reach your own country.

Frankly, you may well think it's not worth the time and trouble, unless you're making really big purchases. And EEC residents in particular should bear in mind that the customs official you present your forms to back home may decide to charge you customs duty on the goods—which will easily cancel out the VAT refund!

 CUSTOMS ON RETURNING HOME. U.S. Residents. You may bring in $400 worth of foreign merchandise as gifts or for personal use without having to pay duty, provided you have been out of the country more than 48 hours and provided you have not claimed a similar exemption within the previous 30 days. Every member of a family is entitled to the same exemption, regardless of age, and the exemptions can be pooled. For the next $1,000 worth of goods a flat 10% rate is assessed.

Included in the $400 allowance for travelers over the age of 21 are one liter of alcohol, 100 non-Cuban cigars and 200 cigarettes. Only one bottle of perfume trademarked in the U.S. may be brought in. However, there is no duty on antiques or art over 100 years old. You may not bring home meats, fruits, plants, soil or other agricultural products.

Gifts valued at under $50 may be mailed to friends or relatives at home, but not more than one per day of receipt to any one addressee. These gifts must not include perfumes costing more than $5, tobacco or liquor.

If you are traveling with such foreign-made articles as cameras, watches or binoculars that were purchased at home or on a previous trip, either carry the receipt or register them with U.S. Customs prior to departure.

Canadian Residents. In addition to personal effects, and over and above the regular exemption of $300 per year, the following may be brought into Canada duty-free: a maximum of 50 cigars, 200 cigarettes, 2 pounds of tobacco and 40 ounces of liquor, provided these are declared in writing to customs on arrival. Canadian Customs regulations are strictly enforced; you are recommended to check what your allowances are and to make sure you have kept receipts for whatever you may have bought abroad. Small gifts can be mailed and should be marked "Unsolicited gift, (nature of gift), value under $40 in Canadian funds." For other details, ask for the Canada Customs brochure, *I Declare.*

British Residents. There are two levels of duty-free allowance for people entering the U.K.: one, for goods bought outside the EEC or for goods bought in a duty free shop within the EEC; two, for goods bought in an EEC country but not in a duty-free shop.

In the first category you may import duty free: 200 cigarettes or 100 cigarillos or 50 cigars or 250 grams of tobacco (*Note:* if you live outside Europe, these allowances are doubled); plus one liter of alcoholic drinks over 22% vol. (38.8% proof) or two liters of alcoholic drinks not over 22% vol. or fortified or sparkling or still wine; plus two liters of still table wine; plus 50 grams of perfume; plus nine fluid ounces of toilet water; plus other goods to the value of £32.

In the second category you may import duty free: 300 cigarettes or 150 cigarillos or 75 cigars or 400 grams of tobacco; plus 1½ liters of alcoholic drinks over 22% vol. (38.8% proof) or three liters of alcoholic drinks not over 22% vol. or fortified or sparkling or still wine; plus five liters of still table wine; plus 75 grams of perfume; plus 13 fluid ounces of toilet water; plus other goods to the value of £250. (*Note:* though it is not classified as an alcoholic drink by EEC countries for Customs' purposes and is thus considered part of the "other goods" allowance, you may not import more than 50 liters of beer).

In addition, *no animals or pets of any kind* may be brought into the U.K. The penalties for doing so are severe and are strictly enforced; there are *no* exceptions.

DUTY FREE. Duty free is not what it once was. You may not be paying tax on your bottle of whiskey or perfume, but you are certainly contributing to somebody's profits. Duty free shops are big business these days and mark ups are often around 100 to 200%. So don't be seduced by the idea that because it's duty free it's a bargain. Very often prices are not much different from your local discount store and in the case of perfume or jewelry they can be even higher.

As a general rule of thumb, duty free stores on the ground offer better value than buying in the air. Also, if you buy duty free goods on a plane, remember that the range is likely to be limited and that if you are paying in a different currency to that of the airline, their rate of exchange often bears only a passing resemblance to the official one.

CAPTURING PARIS

by
JOHN G. MORRIS

John G. Morris has worked all his life with major American newspapers and magazines—Life, The Ladies' Home Journal, The Washington Post, *and* The New York Times *among them. He is now European Correspondent for* The National Geographic, *a Consultant for* The International Herald Tribune, *and lives on that most Parisian of islands, the Ile St.-Louis.*

Some habitués will tell you, "Paris isn't what it used to be." Of course not. I hope to qualify as an habitué, having first come to Paris in 1944, when there was still shooting in the streets; having worked there many times in the intervening years; now, finally hooked, I live there. Paris is the (municipal) love of my life. I have to confess my infidelity to Chicago, New York, Philadelphia, Washington, Los Angeles and London, all cities I have known and loved. While Paris is the most populous city of continental Europe it feels like a small town. I love it.

I love to sit in a café with a *crême* or a *thé citron,* reading the paper to the tinkling musical background of the pinball machine. I can sit there for hours, in the sun or shade, and the waiter will not even fidget. I look up and watch the people around me. Just to my left a couple is making love across the table, elbows firmly planted and hands clasped together, faces virtually invisible. The young man over there is obviously waiting for someone. He alternates coffee and cigarettes. Finally she comes, hands him a little note, and leaves without a word. What has happened between them? . . . The old man on the right orders tea with milk. He unwraps the sugar cube, touches it to his tongue, wraps it again and puts it in his pocket. How long will it last him? . . . A strolling *accordéoniste* comes by, plays just enough not to become a nuisance, passes the hat and quietly goes on . . . followed by a girl selling red roses and, a bit later, by a barechested black man who swallows flaming swords.

It wasn't quite like that in 1944. When I first looked out on the sleepy city from a balcony of the Hotel Scribe, early on a September morning, Paris had just emerged from fifty months of German occupation. The air was heavy with suspense; there was an ominous, audible rumble of war to the North and East. During the night there had been occasional small-arms fire, as the *Résistance* rounded up German soldiers still in hiding—and settled scores with their collaborators.

I had checked into the Scribe, headquarters for Allied war correspondents, in the middle of the night, after hitching rides in jeeps and command cars all the way from Normandy. My mission was to help *Life* magazine re-establish a Paris bureau. I had never been in Paris before, and my French was strictly from high school. How was I to manage, in the vast, unfamiliar and malfunctioning city? *Life* photographer Robert Capa, with whom I had shared both perilous and frivolous moments in Normandy, came to my rescue. At breakfast he said, "I have a French friend who will show you around, a photographer named Henri Cartier-Bresson. He's been living underground in Paris ever since he escaped from a German prison camp. He went to Oxford, so I think you'll understand him." At the door of the Scribe, I was introduced to a slight, blue-eyed young man, shy but friendly. He held a bicycle with one hand, his pants clipped to avoid the gears; with the other he greeted me. Soon we set off, walking the bike, heading for the nearby *New York Times* bureau. It was the beginning of a lasting friendship, and of a resolve that some day I would capture Paris on my own.

First Impressions

Today Paris is a city that really works—well, for the most part. You can drink the water, for example, although wine is more popular. There are certain eccentricities which are hard to love—the irregular lunch-time closing hours of shops and the matter of which holidays are really holidays, for instance. The visitor arriving by air may at first feel he has not left home. The French do not normally look critically at passports. Most travelers with U.S. or British passports go sailing through Immigration, and then, thanks to the rugged luggage carts that all French air terminals provide, though they are not always available, through *Nothing to Declare,* without even a glance at the *douaniers.*

The traditional way to arrive in Paris is, of course, by train. France, blessed with one of the world's great railway systems, makes this an attractive alternative, and far more travelers come by train than plane —for one thing it's far less expensive for a short haul. The principal hazard of rail arrival is thus the sheer numbers of your fellow passengers. A thousand people may pour off the express from Calais, and those in the front cars will hit the taxi lines a full five minutes ahead of those in the rear. However, since a high proportion of travelers immediately head for the métro entrances that abound at every railway station, the taxi lines are normally manageable. One seldom waits more than twenty minutes.

This by no means exhausts the ways one can get to Paris. One can drive—the outer approaches are as modern as the Motorways of Britain, the Interstates of America. One can bike or hitch-hike—an approach recommended only to the young and courageous. One can come by boat. I had one English friend who came annually on his yacht, tying up on the Left Bank just below the Pont de l'Alma. It was madly luxurious to sip a martini on the after deck, with the Tour Eiffel casting a late shadow. And finally, there is the inter-city tour bus, the most painless way of all, but a bit prescribed.

No matter how well planned, a Paris arrival may go awry. There is the story Marlene Dietrich told me, of how she had arrived at Orly on a Sunday night just after the Liberation, making the rounds as an entertainer of the troops. There was no one at Orly to meet her, so she simply boarded an army bus, came into town and checked into the Ritz. The night was young and she decided to go out unescorted, to renew her love affair with the city. In the dimness of the blackout two American soldiers stopped her, mistaking her slacks for the uniform of a Red Cross girl. They asked her how to get to "Rainbow Corner," as the servicemen's club was called. Then they asked her name, and would not believe it when she told them—until she drew them into a lighted doorway. They all had a great laugh; then they took her out on the town.

Toujours la Politesse

You have heard it said that "Paris would be great if it weren't for the Parisians." If a Frenchman says it, it means that he is determined to be provincial. But if it comes from a foreigner, it probably means that he or she has had an unfortunate linguistic encounter. It takes a certain nerve to try out one's French, no matter one's level. A former *New York Times* Paris bureau chief told me he got by only because his French was "audacious." Many foreigners, and I am one, are afraid of being laughed at. The cure for this is to make a *faux pas* so ridiculous that you can tell it on yourself. A young photographer friend of mine, for example, was trying to tell some French friends about his first date with a girl of good family and prim reputation. He thought he was telling them that he had kissed her goodnight—the polite peck. Instead, he was saying that he had bedded her the first night. They were impressed but incredulous.

My own greatest blooper came in our local mom-and-pop produce store. We had noticed that it was possible to order a spit-roasted chicken and one Sunday morning I was dispatched to place such an order. After rehearsing my speech, I pushed my way past the queue of fruit-and-vegetable customers to the rear of the shop and said, "Madame, je voudrais commander un chien rôti" (I should like to order a roast dog). With perfect *politesse* she replied, "Un chien rôti?" Immediately realizing what I had said, I broke up—as did the entire queue of customers. If only I had had the quickness to respond, "Mais oui, madame, vous savez bien que les Américains aiment les hot dogs" (Of course, madame, you know very well that we Americans love hot dogs!).

Paris is the city where every shopkeeper greets you coming and going, where the waiter will not present the bill unless you ask for it, and where the proprietor will shake your hand as you leave the restaurant. It is the city where the bus driver may reopen the door for you if you come on the run, where the taxi driver will probably chase after you if you leave your wallet in his back seat, and where the bellman will not linger for a tip (although he probably won't refuse it). Chivalrous and generous gestures are frequent. There is the saga of the sawn-off legs. We had purchased one of those do-it-yourself kits for a coffee table and then found it too high. My wife carried the legs to a nearby woodworking shop and asked the man to shorten them by ten centimeters. He ran them through the skil-saw. "How much?" she asked. "Madame, just for your smile," was the reply.

Don't take this to mean that Parisians are perfect. There are the usual shady characters who characterize our urbanized world. There are pickpockets, just to make you feel at home. *En garde!* Some are gypsy children, who have developed a special technique. Working in twos and threes, they approach you on the street, hands outstretched. One carries a piece of cardboard, and while you bend over to see what it says, a little hand, under the cardboard, is on its way to your pocket or purse.

Weapons are not often used in Paris crime, but thieves can be ingenious. A friend from Manhattan was the victim of a purely classical ploy. Sensing that his wallet had been lifted while he was standing in awe of Notre Dame, he whirled on the probable thief, a gypsy girl of about twelve. To attest her innocence, she lifted her dress, revealing a totally naked brown body. Our friend was too flustered to pursue the matter further. The crime rate in Paris has risen, but remains far lower than both New York's and London's.

Capital Crisscross

Spoiled by expense accounts, it was years before I learned to take the Paris métro. Now I'm sorry. If there's a better municipal transit system in the world, I don't know of it. The métro is cheap, clean and quiet. Service is frequent. It is normally quite safe. The 13 regular lines and seven high-speed suburban lines crisscross so effectively that there is nary a point in Paris that cannot be reached from any other point in less than an hour; most in ten to twenty minutes.

Before you take the métro you need to look at a map. There's one at most every métro entrance and on every métro platform. Some stations have those electric maps where you press a button for your destination and bingo—your route shows up as a string of lights. Foldout maps of the major streets and landmarks are free, at all hotels, courtesy of the department stores. However, it is wise to purchase an indexed foldout map, which clearly shows every street, avenue, boulevard, square, circle, passage and *impasse* in the city. Thus armed with foreknowledge of your destination, you are prepared to step down to the métro. Don't be afraid of it.

It's harder to read a bus map than a métro map, but bus travel in Paris is delightful, if less efficient. Buses run far less frequently than trains, and the routes are puzzling to the beginner. But, since you see where you're going, even if you don't know where you are, you can jump off for a course correction. If desperate, a good place to abort is at a taxi stand.

If you have the money, and it's not much by the standards of other cities, the luxurious way to get around is by taxi—if you can find one.

In Paris a taxi is—a taxi, and while it may not be as commodious as one of London's or as charmingly decrepit as one of New York's, a taxi can make a trip to almost any address in Paris fairly painless. Provided, that is, you are prepared to pay in francs and to show, not tell, the driver your destination. Parisian taxi drivers are not noted for understanding the English pronunciation of French place names.

Taxis have their eccentricities. For instance they are not supposed to take four passengers. Occasionally, the inducement of an extra *pourboire* will do the trick. "You're talking 'taxi language,' " one driver said to me, accepting. But if there's already a mascot dog in the front seat, forget it. Taxis may be called by radio, and there is a phone—often not answered—at every taxi stand. Public telephone booths, by the way, are now more common than they used to be; you can also make a call from almost any café—ask at the bar.

Driving your own car presents a different set of problems. It's not really terribly difficult if you know your international road signs: the French think they should suffice and do not offer much additional advice. However, a working knowledge of French highway terms is highly recommended. The French take right-of-way as a life-support principle. On a first voyage round the Etoile or place de la Concorde one is well advised to sneak warily around the perimeter. The really exasperating problem for motorists is parking. There are now some underground car parks (marked with a big "P"). Aside from those, one follows the French example, which requires bravado and ingenuity, and occasionally leads to a ticket, or worse, a tow-away or locked wheel. One shrinks to think of the consequences.

Prepare to walk. The rewards are endless. The walk may be a simple trip to the *tabac* to get matches or a lottery ticket. It can be a stroll along the cobbled banks of the Seine, kibitzing on lovers and loafers, sunbathers and barge men. It can be pushing a carriage through the Luxembourg gardens, under the chestnut trees. It can be a promenade on the Champs-Elysées or a zig-zag back and forth to compare prices on both sides of a narrow street. In one block the walker may pass a noisy school yard, a night club, a café or two, an *épicerie*, boutiques specializing in lingerie, dolls and oriental spices; plus a hotel offering rooms by the hour.

A City of Blood

Paris is not France, but France would be unimaginable without Paris. Here past and present co-exist, sometimes comfortably, sometimes uneasily. Children play house in the playground of the Cluny museum, on the spot where Romans took their leisure in baths a hundred meters long.

Called Lutetia by the Romans but renamed for the Parisii, a Celtic tribe, Paris has been a settlement on the Seine for more than two millennia. Blood has flowed here as constantly as the river. Crossing the place de la Concorde, one still shivers at the thought of the 1,344 persons beheaded there by the guillotine, including King Louis XVI and Marie Antoinette.

Tourists flock to Sacré Coeur, at once the ugliest and boldest church in Paris, on the hill named Montmartre for the Christian martyrs, one of whom, St. Denis, is said to have carried his severed head in his hands as he walked north out of the city in the third century. Joan of Arc was wounded in Paris in 1429, but it was another woman, Geneviève, a shepherdess from Nanterre, who became the special Saint of Paris. She rallied the city against Attila the Hun, and now students of the Sorbonne study in a reading room, long as a football field and high enough for a drop kick, in the library of her name.

A department store, La Samaritaine, backs up against the church of St. Germain l'Auxerrois, from whose tower bells rang on the night of August 24, 1572, to signal the pre-arranged massacre of some 3,000 Huguenots. A short walk away, at a Jewish restaurant called Goldenberg's in the heart of the Marais district, a mini-massacre, on August 9, 1982, took the lives of six people at lunch time.

If the French have a knack of putting the past into perspective (they take their time about naming streets for statesmen; artists and scientists have a better chance) they nevertheless have a problem with the turbulent present. In Paris, the tourist may have an opportunity not only to observe history, but to participate in it. Scarcely a month goes by without a *manifestation* (demonstration) of some kind, and sometimes they get out of hand. It's wise not to get caught between protesters and police. The city, too, has its share of terrorist activities—the occasional bomb or an Algerian remembering past wrongs, the normal *va-et-vient* of European life—but which has a lot less effect on the visitor than does violence on the New York subway.

For those of us who lived through World War II, Paris is full of poignancy. Around the corner from where I live on the Ile St. Louis there is a large apartment house. A plaque near the front door says: "A la mémoire des 112 habitants de cette maison dont 40 petits enfants deportés et morts dans les camps allemands en 1942"—"To the memory of 112 residents of this building of whom 40 were little children, deported to and died in German camps in 1942." Last year on April 28, the National Day of the Deportation, a silent little parade formed at the synagogue just across from here in the Marais. With bared heads, muffled drums and tri-colored sashes, the little procession—no doubt including relatives of those 112—filed across to the Ile de la Cité, on whose point, facing up the Seine, is the Memorial to the Deported.

There the Unknown Deportee sleeps in a bed of stone, as the river flows silently by on both sides. It is a moving, and little visited shrine, only a stone's throw from the gardens of Notre Dame.

The Art of Politics—or the Politics of Art

Only London and Rome can even pretend to hold such treasures of the past as does Paris. Think for a moment of the entire city as one big museum. Adolf Hitler, furious with the retreat of his forces in World War II, ordered the museum burned. Fortunately his own commander failed him and Allied forces swept in, supporting the insurrection started by the *Résistance,* to save the city. To sense the grandeur that would have gone, try sitting on a bench above the Seine on the pedestrian Pont des Arts, which offers a kind of gracious scaffolding over the river. Face downstream and set your watch by the gold-handed clock of the Institut Français, on the Left Bank, as the rays of the sun, setting into the muddy green river, gild the towers of the Louvre, on your right. Or look upstream, at the Pont Neuf as it crosses the prow of the Ile de la Cité. Beyond, but out of sight, is the Ile St. Louis, perhaps the world's most perfect village, standing almost exactly as it began, as a real estate development built on pastures of the 17th century.

I first entered the Louvre in 1944, only to find it virtually empty. The foresighted French had evacuated and hidden most of the great masterpieces at the onset of war. All that remained of the *Mona Lisa* was a chalk scrawl to indicate its normal hanging place. Nevertheless, the Grande Galérie of the Louvre was just as staggering a spectacle as it is today. The Louvre is a palace so vast that one can make a fresh discovery on every visit; my latest was the private painting collection of Picasso, with exquisite works by friends Cézanne, Renoir, Matisse and many others.

Paris has a museum for every period and taste. Parisians argue museums as Americans do baseball teams. They tend either to loathe or love the Centre Pompidou, its red and blue insides all exposed like an oil refinery. Nobody quarrels with the Pompidou's permanent collections, but the temporary thematic exhibitions are often disasters. While Pompidou (known also as Beaubourg) attracts bigger crowds, drawn partly by the endless show of street performers in its piazza, the Musée d'Art Moderne has exhibitions of equal importance. Unlike almost any other city, Paris' artistic life is closely tied in to its political realities. The battle royal between Jacques Chirac (in his role as Mayor) and Mitterrand's cultural impresario, Jack Lang, raged up and down the avenues and boulevards and, even after they have moved on to other jobs, the only-too-solid evidences of their struggle are still around —the Buren Pillars at the Palais-Royal among the most controversial.

The exciting new Musée d'Orsay, is dedicated to the art of the period 1848–1914, and now houses the great collection of Impressionists that was formerly in the Jeu de Paume.

Great exhibitions are not limited to museums. The Grand Palais, a marvel of turn-of-the-century iron and glass construction, and its little neighbor of the same vintage, the Petit Palais, occasionally attract queues that stretch far down the Avenue Winston Churchill. As if those are not enough, the city is building another huge complex, a kind of fairground of halls, playgrounds and theaters (one of which is enclosed in a shining sphere) on the site of the former slaughter houses of La Villette, on the city's outskirts.

There are another dozen or so art museums. The Musée Guimet has Oriental art; the Marmottan is a mansion for Monets and others. Museums have been created in the studios of Rodin, Delacroix and Brancusi. And that's by no means all. Paris has major museums of anthropology, natural history, history and science, and smaller ones dealing with everything from advertising and bread to urban transport and wine. The Musée Grévin, the wax-works museum on the boulevard Montmartre and in the Forum des Halles, is perhaps the most amusing of all.

Those are all public places. Being a nosey type, one who loves to poke and peek, respectful audacity takes me far in Paris. The rewards are dependent on one's interests. At the Bourse, the stock exchange, there is a guided tour, but you can try to talk your way into a look at the trading floor. Nearby at the Bibliothèque Nationale, without a reader's card, you can look into the main reading room, or the equally impressive periodical room. Just don't try to push it too far. For lawyers, a place of interest is the Palais de Justice, with courtrooms where black-robed judges and *avocats* hear and plead cases all day long. Just walking the halls there is a spectacle; one can tiptoe into courts in session. For only 62 francs (wine included) one may enjoy recess by having lunch with the lawyers in the Buffet du Palais de Justice. In the waiting rooms of the nearby Préfecture de Police you will find scenes of poverty and desperation reminiscent of Daumier. Notre Dame is just a bit further, and for your first visit try coming in through the north portal instead of through the nave, as most tourists do. You will then immediately confront the most glorious of the three rose windows. Stay for a mass or organ concert. While you may not find a wedding at Notre Dame, you will find marriages proceeding at the *mairies* (city halls) throughout the city, particularly on Saturday mornings. Finally, if you are fascinated by the celebration of life eternal, as are the Catholic French, you can quietly visit Père Lachaise, one of the world's most famous cemeteries, and well worth seeing for its exotic and nostalgic monuments to the *célèbres*.

Eating by Hearsay

Some of our friends come to Paris just to eat. They come laden with research, with starred lists, credit cards, and calculated appetites. They have done their homework well, in one or more of the several useful books that devote themselves to mouth-watering description of Parisian delicacies. Our own approach is more casual. For one thing, it's rather difficult to get a *bad* meal in Paris!

The sheer profusion of places to eat in Paris is a bit staggering. There are, for example, 12,000 places where one can get a cup of tea or coffee—*or* a glass of wine or beer—a convenience that is one of the finer attributes of French civilization. Without disparaging published restaurant recommendations, we tend to browse our way through Paris cuisine. We go sometimes by hearsay, sometimes by looks, often by ambience. The *carte* (*menu* is something else) posted at the door offers further clues, especially as to price. The same rules apply in Paris as elsewhere: one tends to pay for name and fame. Some places seem so cheap that one gets suspicious, but there is often more fun in a bistro than in an elegant two-star.

The French Tourist Office, that most helpful, overworked institution on the Champs Elysées near the Arc de Triomphe, offers a listing of 420 Paris restaurants. Like many of the good things in Paris it is free—and understandable in English. In a line or two it charts ten attributes of each place. The least snobbish of restaurant guides, it gives equal lineage to the most expensive restaurant (Maxim's) and the cheapest (several offer menus of 40 francs or less). Among specialties, you will not only find pig's feet *béarnaise,* but also milkshakes, macrobiotic food, stuffed carp, "60 kinds of crêpe," and "exotic sherbets"—not to mention the conventional gourmet dishes. As for ambience, you can dine in a cellar or in a skyscraper, in a former stable or a former monastery. You may have the elegant surroundings of Louis XV or the Second Empire, the bustle of a railroad station or the calm of a farmhouse. You may look out on the Louvre, on the Tour Eiffel, or on Notre Dame—or you may look up at them as you glide along aboard a Bateau Mouche *au restaurant.* For entertainment with dinner you can have flamenco or carioca, polkas or can-can. For music, it can be violins, accordion or oom-pah-pah band. The listed restaurants represent only a small fraction of what Paris has to offer when it comes to food and drink. In addition there are the thousands of wine bars, bistros and cafés. It's fun to make your own discoveries. At cafés and wine bars, and at most brasseries, no reservations are required. If the table has no table cloth, you can normally just sit down. Your best chance of getting a table, if you have not called ahead, is to go early. Not before 7.30, or you will find the staff eating. Go a little before 8, when the first diners arrive, and you often get a table. Once seated you have no problem. Some restaurants take credit cards, and almost any business establishment in Paris will take a Eurocheck in francs. Don't hurry, and when you leave, you pay for your coat and shake hands with the proprietor.

Relaxations

Next to dining, entertainment is the most appealing industry of Paris. The week begins on Wednesday, with the appearance of *Pariscope* (one of the three weekly bibles for those who go out often). A typical issue will list the 300 films that play the 384 cinemas of Paris and vicinity in an average week. That total includes 98 revivals, but not the films playing in the 14 film festivals (Films of Hitchcock, etc.), nor the 43 films screened free at the film libraries of the subsidized Centre Pompidou and Palais de Chaillot; nor the 23 "special screenings" of various kinds.

So much for cinema. In this same typical spring-time week there are 18 works being performed in the ten publicly supported theaters (Comédie Française, the Opéra, etc.). Another 101 theatrical pieces are being performed on 76 commercial stages, including works by Shakespeare, Strindberg, Brecht, Aristophanes, Chekhov, Sartre, Neil Simon and Sam Shepard—most but not all in French. Another 160 cafés, cabarets, music halls, discos and nightclubs offer programs ranging from political satirists to sophisticated nude shows, New Orleans jazz and the traditional can-can. Churches often offer chamber music. For serious music lovers in this week there were 96 concerts; 13 ballet companies performed.

There is an easy informality about attending the Paris theater. Many of them are small and intimate. One can normally get tickets at the last minute, except for hit shows, and prices are low. Take one night at the Opéra. We thought, early one New Year's Eve, wouldn't it be nice to go to the Opéra? Everyone knows you can only get opera seats months in advance. And on this New Year's Eve, Nureyev was dancing, in his own choreography, *Don Quixote*. We didn't bother to call; we simply went to the box office ten minutes before curtain time. "What do you have?" I asked. "Standing room, no view, twenty francs," was the quick reply. We bought two, and climbed the onyx and marble staircase under the chandeliered dome with ceiling by Chagall. Checking our coats, we rented opera glasses and were ushered to a box right over the stage. For the first act we stood, looking down over the shoulders of those in the first row. At the interval, hoping to do better, we climbed to the Opera's top circle. There we found a series of little pie-shaped loges. One was open and empty—save for one chair. My wife planted herself while I scavenged another. Then, with a quick trip to the bar for a demi of champagne and two glasses, we enjoyed the second and third acts with a full view of the stage. The *soirée* in our little aerie had cost the equivalent of twelve dollars for the evening. "Paris is a moveable feast."

One day one spring Robert Capa invited me to go with him to the races at Longchamp. It seemed like a good idea as it was a lovely day, but what terrified me was the idea of betting. I was sure I would lose all my money. Capa, on the other hand, was an inveterate gambler— one who played poker all night with the "boys"—like Irwin Shaw and Peter Viertel and John Huston. And occasionally won. So off we went. On the way to the track Capa gave me some good tips. He recommended playing the French equivalent of the Daily Double, the *jumelée* (*jumelles* means twins). He assured me that the payoff would be enormous, but I noticed that he bet his own francs quite differently. Needless to say I won, he lost. He never quite forgave me as I gathered the receipts in my arms (it was in the days before devaluation).

Few tourists come to Paris for the sake of sport, but that's almost too bad, for the French themselves indulge quite heavily. It's true that baseball and cricket have not exactly caught on. But the six-day bicycle races that Hemingway described so vividly are now housed in a new Palais Omnisports Bercy that grows grass on its sloping exterior walls, making it resemble a meadow that has exploded. And the annual Tour de France always comes to its breathless finish on the Champs-Elysées. For amateurs there is of course jogging (the Paris marathon can draw 15,000 runners), sailing, kayaking and wind surfing (all of these are now done on the Seine). Roller skaters and skate boarders make the plaza in front of the Palais de Chaillot hazardous for pedestrians. For swimmers there are private and public pools all over Paris (including one that sits like an enormous bathtub in the Seine across from the Place de la Concorde). Best of all, there is sunbathing, often topless.

Children and Dogs

Few cities are as thoughtful as Paris when it comes to the needs of children—and dogs. Dogs are incredibly spoiled; it won't take you long to learn how Parisians interpret dog license. The children of Paris remain relatively unspoiled, despite the immense attention they receive. Television has little to offer them, but they are besieged by live entertainment: in a typical week there were 38 plays for children, including seven with marionettes. A department store offers them books, records, games and crafts while mother makes her rounds. There are circuses throughout the year. Our favorite is a family circus, where father is the clown, mother the animal trainer; the sons and daughters are young jugglers and acrobats. They bow and shake hands as you leave the tent after the grand finale.

Since one never knows what will intrigue, or bore, the very young, Paris takes no chances. Most parks and open spaces have games and gimmicks for children. At the new Parc de la Villette, there's a slide in the shape of a dragon, thirty meters long. Entering at the tail, a child crawls up and down his undulating belly and finally emerges, triumphantly sliding, from his fierce and fiery mouth. In the Luxembourg gardens there are donkey rides. At the central pool in the garden of the Tuileries, with or without child, you can rent a toy sailboat. In the Bois de Boulogne there is a child-size amusement park, complete with merry-go-rounds, a roller coaster, a hall of mirrors, an "enchanted river," go-carts and bumper cars. One can sit in a barnyard cafe and have pizza or ice cream surrounded by sheep and goats and geese. For wild animals, there is the beautifully-kept zoo at Vincennes, with its lions and tigers, seals and elephants, bears and zebras and giraffes—even a panda that is apt to show off when it hears the horn of the zoo's little passenger train. Coke and ice cream are ubiquitous in Paris, and on the major boulevards there are fast food restaurants, where juveniles who scorn *nouvelle cuisine* may have hamburgers and "French fries." There is the Bateau Mouche, almost guaranteed to keep a child happy for an hour, and that tallest Tinker Toy of all, the Eiffel Tower.

The Human Ambience

A woman's Paris, I have discovered, is somewhat different from a man's. Parisian women, no matter their station, all seem to have a certain flair. To them it comes naturally; but emulation is apparently easy for the female visitor. It is only a matter of a day or two before she acquires a certain *chic*. There will be something new about her neckline, perhaps just the addition of a scarf. On the third day you will see her at the cafe, ordering her *menthe à l'eau* or *citron pressé*. By the fifth day she will be *branchée*—connected.

A man, on the other hand, may find little to buy in Paris. The basement hardware department of the BHV department store is a marvel to behold, but who wants to take home a bunch of nuts and bolts, or appliances of the wrong voltage? Increasingly, however, male tourists are learning that clothes from Paris will also look good on Main Street, and clothing stores are adept at translating sizes.

However, the sport of shopping in Paris ultimately brings the sexes together. There are boutiques for every budget. There are the fabulous flea markets, where you can buy almost anything you don't really need.

There are markets for animals, birds, stamps, textiles and flowers (but only three flower markets left). There are lovely old shopping arcades. Artcurial (Avenue Matignon) is a kind of modern art supermarket. There is the world's most concentrated antique market: Le Louvre des Antiquaires, with 240 shops in one palatial building.

Best of all are the food markets, so redolent, so cheap, so lively in their hustle-bustle. There are 20, in all of Paris. Parisians are loyal to their favorite markets. One that almost everyone respects is the rue Mouffetard, which has changed little since the heyday of the '20s. Don't make the mistake of going there when you are starving—you will stagger home under your burdens. One warning: many markets are open only in the mornings, and there are no markets on Sunday afternoon. Even the fleas virtually shut down.

Paris is the home of the exile. It is here that Chopin came to compose, Picasso to paint, Joyce to write *Ulysses.* In Paris, even more than in London and New York, it is possible to live as a citizen of the world. It is almost possible to forget one's race, one's religion, almost possible to believe all men are brothers. Almost. There are plenty of paradoxes in Paris, and one is that despite all the beauty, the world's ugly sores of racism and greed are still apparent. It is perhaps testimony that Paris, a city of human scale, is very human. Burnous and sari, blue jeans and *haute couture* walk side by side. Gallic cynicism and *la vie en rose* go together. Victor Hugo aptly stated the message of Paris:

"Cities are bibles of stone. This city possesses no single dome, roof or pavement which does not convey some message of alliance and of union, and which does not offer some lesson, example or advice. Let the people of all the world come to this prodigious alphabet of monuments, of tombs and of trophies to learn peace and to unlearn the meaning of hatred. Let them be confident. For Paris has proven itself. To have once been Lutèce and to have become Paris—what could be a more magnificent symbol! To have been mud and to have become spirit!"

L'EMPEREUR ... S DE

THE CITY OF LIGHT

From Caesar to de Gaulle

Intersecting northern France in the first century B.C. were two great natural highways. One well-trodden route led from the Rhine south to the far distant Mediterranean. The other was the River Seine, meandering from east to west. They met at the river's most easily forded point—a small, rather swampy island that today is the Ile de la Cité. Being easily defended, the island formed a natural strong bastion. Under its first known inhabitants, a Gallic tribe called the Parisii, it enjoyed relative prosperity as a trading post of no very great importance. But the Parisii felt secure enough to build two bridges connecting it to the banks of the river on the sites of the present day Pont-Neuf and Petit-Pont. The settlement was called Lutetia, meaning marsh. Such were the inauspicious beginnings of Paris.

Despite its position of natural strength, the little community fell to the Romans in 52 B.C. during the Gallic Wars. In his Commentaries, Caesar describes how it was besieged and eventually burned to the ground. But the Roman occupation brought its benefits as a long period of peace followed and the original settlement was rebuilt. At the same time Lutetia spread beyond its island, which was both cramped and damp, being no more than half its present-day size and prone to flooding.

A new Roman settlement grew up on the left bank around the foot of the Montagne Sainte-Geneviève. At this time the right bank was a flat and thoroughly uninviting swamp bordered by hills. In their new town on the left bank the Romans built baths, a theater and an arena. Yet despite its prosperity and position on the great trade routes, the city was still only small and enjoyed no particular significance. What little standing it did have was decreased as the barbarian hordes from the north and east closed in on the Roman Empire during the third century. The tiny settlement suffered badly and was besieged and taken on numerous occasions and burned several times. Gradually the new town on the left bank was abandoned and the beleaguered Parisii withdrew to the security of their island fortress. They hemmed it in with a massive stone wall seven-and-a-half feet thick and set thirty yards back from the river making the settlement even more cramped and confined than before. As the city shrank in size, so it shrank in importance. At the same time its name was changed. A milestone on the Rheims road dating from 307 records the city's name as Paris for the first time.

The Coming of Christianity

From the end of the fifth century to the ninth, following the departure of the Romans and the collapse of their empire, a period of relative stability allowed the city, very slowly, to increase in both size and status. This was principally the result of its increasing importance as a religious center. Christianity had come to Paris in the third century. The city's first bishop was St. Denis, who was martyred there in 272. According to legend the executioner chopped off the good man's head in vain, for the bishop smartly picked it up and, clutching it under his arm, marched himself off to an area outside the city that is now named after him.

It was not for another hundred years, however, that Christianity gained a real footing on the island and the first humble wooden church was built in about 390. By the fifth century the city had been hallowed by the memory of Ste. Geneviève whose prayers had saved the city from Attila and his marauding Huns in 451. Churches and chapels commemorating her sprang up, not on the tiny island itself, where space was too precious, but among the fertile vineyards of the left bank and the marshy reeds of the right. As these religious institutions grew, houses and then communities appeared alongside them until a series of small semi-autonomous interlinked villages almost surrounded the original city on the island.

At the same time the political importance of Paris was increased. The first king to make Paris his capital was Clovis in 508. He had defeated the Visigoths in the south and wanted to bring his seat of authority nearer his new lands. The Frankish kings Clotaire, Chilperic and Caribert also all made Paris their capital.

However, during the reign of Charlemagne (771–814), the city lost much of its new-found political status. The Holy Roman Empire that embraced most of France and present day Germany had its center in Aachen on what is now the Belgian/German border. Paris languished to the west, far removed from the great emperor's ambitious and benevolent court. Worse was to follow for, following his death, the Normans made havoc of the city, besieging it in 885–6. The riverbank settlements were again deserted and the terrorized population poured back into the cramped and teeming city. The third century defenses were rebuilt and strengthened, and the first fortified tower constructed, the Châtelet. Conditions in the early medieval city during times of war can easily be imagined; small, filthy, wet and unhealthy, a maze of unplanned streets and mean dwellings, with the permanent threat of terrible and violent death to haunt the vulnerable population. However, peace was finally made with the Normans in 911 and again the city expanded.

The area around the island—including the land belonging to the religious communities on the river banks—began gradually to be brought under cultivation, though for the most part the surroundings of the city were still either marshes or woods. At Charonne, for example, the early kings bred dogs and hawks for hunting.

Prosperity and Peace

From the beginning of the 11th century the chaos of the Dark Ages slipped away following the accession of the Capetian dynasty to the throne of France. Paris became the center of French political life and has remained so to the present day. The city now began to grow rich on new trading connections and the resulting influx of wealth caused it to expand rapidly. Louis VI, at the beginning of the 12th century, moved the increasingly important mercantile quarter to a new site near the rue St. Denis where until recently the marvellous Halles Centrales, an enormous enclosed food market, stood. The cultivation of the land around the city continued rapidly and the lush and fertile fields on the

left bank in particular kept the city fat and well-fed. At the same time
the Grand Pont, on which the money changers had their shops, was
rechristened the Pont au Change in 1142, reflecting the merchants'
increasing importance to the life of Paris. But it was principally to its
religious and academic institutions that Paris owed its pre-eminence at
this date.

Philippe Auguste reorganized the diversified and expanding city into
one clearly defined and coherent unit during the 30 years spanning
1200. He built a new city wall that settled the limits and extent of the
city—with the added strength of a chain across the river at one end and
the combined fortifications of the Louvre and Tour de Nesle at the
other. More religious orders arrived to found monasteries on reclaimed
fields and a great spate of church building followed. The exquisite
Sainte-Chapelle, the glittering Saint-Germain-l'Auxerrois and the extravagant Saint-Séverin, all of which have survived to the present day,
date from this period. The most famous and splendid building, however, is the great church of Notre Dame. Started in 1136 and completed
a hundred years later, the huge church dominated the tiny island on
which it still broods.

The existence on such a large scale of the Parisian religious communities led directly to the city's central importance as an academic
center. At this period, and for a great many years to come, all educational establishments were organized by the church and were entirely
dependent on it. It was under the auspices of the Chancellor of Notre
Dame that the most celebrated school of the period, the École de Notre
Dame, was administered. Rival schools were started at the same time
on the left bank by the ever increasing numbers of churches and abbeys
to be found there, the most prestigious and advanced being Ste.-Gene-
viève and St.-Victor. However, they were dependent on the Chancellor
of the great church for the *licentia docendi,* the right to teach. It was
in an effort to escape his rigid control that the professors and students
of the rival schools, who had already formed a community called the
"Universitas," broke away from Notre Dame and appealed directly to
the Pope for the right to organize and control their own teaching
community free from outside influence. This right was granted finally
in 1215.

By the end of the century, the University of Paris, as the new institution came to be known, was the most celebrated center of learning in
Christendom, the then known world. Among its professors were St.
Bonaventura, Albertus Magnus and St. Thomas Aquinas. Students
came to the University from all over Europe. Many colleges were built
along the left bank to house them. The most renowned of these was that
founded in 1253 by Robert de Sorbon. Called the Sorbonne, it is today
still one of the world's leading academic institutions. The University

had an important and sometimes profound influence over the life of Paris. During the so-called Great Schism of 1378–1418, the pronouncements of the faculty and rector, as the mouth-piece of Rome and arbiter of all theological and dogmatic matters in Paris, effectively ended the protracted and confusing squabble that had threatened at times to spark off civil war.

While the University developed along the left bank and brought fame to the city, the mercantile and trading quarters prospered on the right. Today this area is still the central business district. Increasingly also from this date, as a result of the presence of the king, Paris became not only the political capital of France but also the fountain head of manners and taste. The presence of royalty had bestowed a peculiar and distinctive luster on the city and its grander citizens became ever more refined and fashionable. Their opulence and sophistication can be judged by the startling and remarkable fact that some of the streets of the Cité were actually paved. This was considered most advanced!

Plague and the English

Unfortunately for the good citizens of Paris, this period of prosperity and civilization did not last long. It was some time before they could think again only of fashion and learning. The city became the pawn in a protracted power struggle between both the warring factions of the French aristocracy and, later, the national struggle of the Hundred Years' War between France and England.

The Black Death in the 1350s swept through Paris causing appalling suffering and loss of life. A series of uprisings tore the social fabric of Paris apart; Étienne Marcel, a prominent city father, tried to use the chaotic national situation to the benefit of the city—but fell foul of his supporters and was murdered in 1358; in 1380 the citizens rose in revolt at crippling taxes, armed with mallets—hence the rising nickname of Maillotin—only to be brutally suppressed; between 1412 and '13, Paris was subjected to the violent rule of Simonet Caboche, a butcher who, with his maurading band of fellow butchers and skinners (Cabochiens) —supporters of the Duke of Burgundy—terrorized the city by their atrocities.

In 1420 England's Henry V, having conquered the French at the Battle of Agincourt, entered Paris, which was in English hands until 1436. There was an attempt to recapture the city in 1429, when Joan of Arc led a glorious and doomed attempt, only to be beaten back by the Duke of Bedford.

The net result of this long period of war, unrest and plague was to reduce the population and prosperity of the city significantly. Poverty became rife and many were forced to turn to crime. Several districts on either side of the Seine became notorious as the dens of robbers and thieves, many of them so infested that it was no longer safe to walk through them at night. This pestilent and disordered period was immortalized in Victor Hugo's novel *Notre-Dame de Paris*.

Renaissance and Massacre

By the 16th century the chaos and despair of the preceding years had largely disappeared and the city once more embarked on a long period of peace and prosperity. Much rebuilding was undertaken and Paris was restored to its pre-eminent place in the arts and sciences. François I in 1528 began the first of many extensions to the almost ruined Louvre, adorning it in a manner befitting the official royal residence. He also had laid down the lines of a new enclosing wall to encircle the once more expanding city and settle its limits, though this was not built until the reign of Louis XIII in the early years of the 17th century. By this stage, however, it had become clear that all attempts to restrict the size of Paris so as to preserve a healthy balance between it and the size of the other principal cities of the realm were doomed. Henri II, for example, forbade the construction of any new buildings outside the new wall, as did his descendants. Undaunted, the new buildings rose anyway.

Paris also became an increasingly aristocratic city. The Faubourg St. Germain became the favored quarter of the nobility and many magnificent mansions were built there. Catherine de Médicis in 1564 began the creation of the Italianate Tuileries Gardens, which soon became the meeting place of the ever more refined and fashionable court.

However, the peaceful expansion of the city was shattered in 1572 by a terrible and ghastly night of murder and plunder by the Parisian mob. This was the infamous St. Bartholomew's Day Massacre. The causes were complex.

France, in common with the rest of Europe, had for some years been reacting violently against the growing tide of Protestantism. The monarchy and Paris were staunchly Catholic, while many noble families, and especially the greater part of the south, had been converted to the new faith. The Huguenots, as the French Protestants were known, formed a disciplined and formidable political and military force, led by a charismatic aristocrat, Admiral de Coligny. In contrast the monarchy was weak. The Queen Mother, Catherine de Médicis, was the scheming power behind a throne which passed too quickly from one sickly son to another.

By 1570 France had endured three civil wars in ten years, and the government in Paris proposed some form of compromise, which included limited religious toleration. This shaky alliance was sealed with a wedding between Catherine's daughter and the young Huguenot leader, Henri of Navarre. All the leading Huguenots, including Coligny, were invited to Paris for the ceremonies. But fanaticism was running rampant, and Catherine, with characteristic cunning and ruthlessness, decided that this was the perfect time to murder Coligny. The plot backfired, leaving the Admiral only wounded, so the unbalanced young king insisted on a general purge, outrunning his mother's tardy efforts at control.

Thus on the sultry summer's night of August 24th, 1572, the Duke of Anjou, supported by several other noble families and a blood-crazy mob, transformed the selective killings into a wholesale massacre of all Huguenots and more or less anybody else they objected to.

The blood-bath shocked and traumatized Paris and continued for many years to influence the capital. It also sparked off further civil strife which lasted intermittently for another ten years or so. Henri of Navarre ascended the throne as Henri IV. To heal the wounds caused by that terrible night he finally accepted Catholicism and entered the besieged capital saying "Paris is worth a mass."

The new elegance prompted by the Renaissance spreading north from Italy was reflected not merely in the manners and cultivation of the aristocracy but in their new buildings too. They lost their medieval flavor and became instead more ordered. For example, the Pont-Neuf, constructed between 1578 and 1604 and the oldest extant bridge in Paris, was the first classical bridge in the city. An effort was made to plan streets on a grid system and to replace the jumbled maze of the medieval city. It was the king's wish that new houses should have their façades made of stone and not, as had been the custom, of plaster and wooden beams.

The rebuilding and expansion of the city continued apace. The Louvre was continuously added to. Marie de Médicis built the Luxembourg Palace (1615-25). Cardinal Richelieu the Palais Royal (1632) and rehoused the Sorbonne in a building that still forms the nucleus of the college today. An imaginative and daring consortium proposed that the two small islands to the east of the Cité be joined together and used for building. And so, between 1627 and 1664, the Ile Saint-Louis was born. In 1631 the suburbs to the west of the town were incorporated within its limits and a new line of fortifications built around them. However, this new wall did not enclose the new districts that had grown up to the north and south. The childless wife of Louis XIII, Anne of Austria, vowed to create a great church if she was blessed with a son. In 1645 the seven-year-old Louis XIV laid the foundation stone of the magnificent Val de Grâce in recognition of his mother's vow; the church was not consecrated until he was 72.

The Sun King

During the reign of Louis XIV, Paris continued to develop and become progressively more sumptuous and opulent, reflecting the power and grandeur of the Roi Soleil. As Louis was the embodiment of the Divine Right of Kings, so his capital became the most prestigious and elegant in Europe. The Louvre was completed by a magnificent colonnade in 1674, the Tuileries Palace was altered and superbly redecorated and its gardens extended beyond the boundaries of the city by the long tree-planted avenue of the Champs-Elysées. The place des Victoires and the place Vendôme were constructed, both significantly containing statues of the triumphant young king. A new stone bridge over the Seine, the Pont Royal, was built and new stone *quais* built alongside it. And when there was no moon, the streets were illuminated by candles.

Yet, during this period, turmoil and political unrest were ever present facts of life in the French capital. The beginning of Louis's reign had been disrupted by the events of the Fronde in 1649 which had obliged the court to leave Paris for a spell. These disturbances continued for some years and eventually led to Louis assuming absolute power. They also indirectly led to Louis removing his court from Paris to the Palace of Versailles just outside the city. His intention was to put as much tactful distance as possible between the more ambitious and scheming members of the nobility and the potentially destructive Parisian mob. This, however, had no limiting effect on the growth of Paris.

Paris was not only a city of wealth and elegance, there were also the have-nots, a starving multitude, the teeming underworld of Paris. These were humble folk and the ordinary workers who lived in the Faubourg Saint-Denis and the Faubourg Saint-Marcel where the narrow curving streets and noisome alleys of the Middle Ages still survived. Here was to be found the infamous Cour des Miracles, the Courtyard of Miracles, where blind beggars suddenly found they could see, and the lame suddenly walked. These "miracles," repeated to order if necessary, gained the area such a bad name that the Cour des Miracles was eventually destroyed in 1667 by Louis XIV's chief of police, La Reynie. Still, Paris could be proud of its triumphal arches, its *quais* along the Seine, the hospital of the Invalides, and some beautiful squares.

During the 18th century, Paris enjoyed eight unbroken decades of peace, encouraging further its continued development and expansion. The Faubourg Saint-Honoré, like the Faubourg Saint-Germain before it, became an aristocratic quarter. Great boulevards were laid out with large and lavish mansions strung out along them. Small cafés and theaters added to the animation of the city. Villas were built by financiers and nobles on the outskirts. At the same time a new wall was constructed around the city. This had no real military purpose but served to demonstrate the remarkable and rapid expansion of the city. It also helped to introduce an element of unity and cohesion to the vast and sprawling city.

The Terror

The Revolution put a sudden and violent end to the prosperous expansion of the elegant city. The storming of the Bastille prison, a potent symbol of oppression, in July 1789 by a starving and enraged mob was the first act in the confused and ugly events that plunged the city into a long orgy of bloodletting and terror. Yet once the immediate unruly excitement of the early days of the Revolution died down, the influence and significance of Paris, as well as its appearance, increased rather than otherwise. Revolutionary architects took over the city's planning. Their first priority was to clean up the slums. Paris was dirty, unhealthy and epidemic-ridden. It had no mains water. (Even today, many people believe that it is better to drink only wine or bottled mineral water—a belief that stems from pre-Revolutionary days— though faucet (tap) water is in fact perfectly safe). The new builders were not simply concerned with sanitation, however. They built the rue de Rivoli, the square around the Panthéon and the street that leads to it, the rue Soufflot. They also built many streets around the Luxembourg Gardens and in the vicinity of the Chaussée d'Antin.

With their aristocratic patrons dead or in hiding, the luxury trades died out. Who had money now for fine furniture or jewelry? Industry on the other hand began to flourish, weaving and paper making, for example. And the Army of the revolution naturally needed weapons of all kinds. Indeed, as early as 1798 the manufacturers of France organized their first exhibitions.

Seat of Empire

The accession of Napoleon continued these developments. As befits a general, Napoleon regarded it as his first duty to regulate the practical administration of the city. The astonishing effectiveness of his administrative arrangements is demonstrated by the fact that they remained in force until 1967. Two prefects gave Paris her orders: the County Prefect of the Seine and the Prefect of Police. The Municipal Council was nominated in Napoleonic times and only later did it become an elected body. It was also under Napoleon that the dwellings of Paris were numbered house by house and not, as before, by arrondissement. In

1804 the famous cemetery and place of pilgrimage, Père Lachaise, was opened. Around the same time huge new market places were created and the wine trade acquired vast new cellars in the capital. By the last years of the First Empire, Paris had 700,000 inhabitants and the 1,094 paved streets were illuminated by 10,500 lamps.

But the Napoleonic era provided Paris with more than newly designed markets, wine cellars, pavements and lamps. As the self-appointed Julius Caesar of the modern age, Napoleon also built the Arc de Triomphe, the column in the place Vendôme, oversaw the completion of the Madeleine and the start of the Stock Exchange. And, during his Russian campaign, he signed a decree authorizing the foundation of the Comédie-Française.

The defeat of Napoleon and the restoration of the monarchy by the victorious allied powers meant that much of the work of the Revolution had been in vain. The return of a vengeful and aggrieved nobility helped to create a similar climate to that which had existed before 1789. This fermented away through various changes of government, each as ineffective and impotent as its predecessor. The atmosphere of discontent was aided by the growth of the population and the city and the effects of industrialization, which for the most part made people's lives more rather than less miserable and squalid. The principal achievements during this period were the continued building around the outskirts and the introduction of gas lighting in the streets. Railways also appeared, the first running from Le Pecq near Saint-Germain in 1837. Omnibuses were introduced in 1828 and in 1840 a further wall was constructed beyond that built before the Revolution, though the old wall still defined the limits of the town.

Despite improvements of this kind the populace at large, and the idealists in particular, still resented the powerful and repressive governments and the lack of social change. In 1848 the people rose again, toppled the irresolute government and formed the Second Republic.

The Monumental City

It didn't last very long, however, nor did it achieve anything very notable. It was succeded in 1852 by one of the country's more eccentric rulers, the ambitious and secretive Napoleon III. His plans were great, his successes few except in one significant respect. He wanted to glorify himself, as despots do, by leaving some monument after his death, something permanent and solid. With a stroke of characteristic daring, he chose to rebuild Paris—and he very nearly succeeded.

Despite its many fine monuments and splendid buildings, both private and public, Paris in the middle of the 19th century still had many of the characteristics of a medieval town, and much of the building of the previous ages had been unplanned or bore little relationship to areas or buildings around it. Despite the work of the Revolution, there were still many dark, narrow and pokey areas which were as unhealthy as they were unsightly. Napoleon decided that he would make it in all respects a modern city.

He appointed as his lieutenant the controversial Alsatian Baron Haussmann, a ruthless and canny civil servant and Prefect of the Seine Department since 1853. Together they cut through the tangle of small buildings on the left bank and laid out the boulevards that are found there today. Enormous straight vistas were created, tree-lined and elegant with sumptuous houses lining them. They constructed streets leading to the main rail terminals, which were by then the real gates to the city, providing easier and faster access to them. The Halles Centrales, alas no more, were built, again with the necessary roads to provide access. The great crossroads of the place de la République was created. The medieval houses on the Ile de la Cité were torn down and replaced by somber and lavish public buildings. The Louvre was extended. An immense system of sewers was built, new bridges were constructed, public parks created, squares similar to those in London were laid out and a new water system set up. Napoleon transformed Paris.

However, despite his many magnificent achievements, the Emperor had many critics of his great works. In their choice of architects, Napoleon III and Haussmann were not very fortunate. Only Charles Garnier, who designed the spectacularly inventive Opéra, can claim to have been an architect of real imagination and ability. Many of the new buildings were pompous and dull. To some extent, Napoleon brought this on himself. The type of building he wanted had to be monumental, formal and grandiose and turgidly neo-Classical to reflect his own omnipotent magnificence. This tended naturally to produce buildings that had a municipalized and committee-like quality to them. Similarly, the hundreds of identical houses that line the long, endlessly straight boulevards invite criticisms of dull uniformity.

A justifiable accusation against Haussmann was that he was concerned only with the more fashionable areas and the needs of the wealthy who lived in them. Today, in the last quarter of the 20th century, the eastern arrondissements are still fairly overcrowded and unhealthy, though a massive slum clearance and redevelopment scheme is gradually putting an end to this problem. It was Haussmann who decreed that Paris should expand westwards and the movement continues to this day.

It is also true that Napoleon and Haussmann, in building long, straight boulevards, had more than the unification or rationalization of the city in mind. It was much easier to move troops and police down the big new roads than down the narrow, twisting ones they replaced—and, in case of insurrection, the wide vistas would give cannon a clear field of fire. It is also significant that at various strategic points in the city new barracks were built surrounded by immensely strong, mob-proof walls. The threat of revolution hung over France in general, and Paris in particular, throughout the 19th century and the high-handed methods of Napoleon were always likely to spark off discontent and revolt.

Nonetheless, despite the undertones that continued throughout Napoleon's rule, the years of the Second Empire saw a period of pomp, easy living and unceasing entertainment. This was "La Belle Epoque." More and more palaces appeared on the Champs-Elysées. There seemed to be parades every few days: the opening of a new road to be celebrated, a procession led by the Emperor himself accompanied by his entourage and a guard of honor, a foreign dignitary to be received, a glorious victory to be cheered.

But this period of pomp was shortlived. In 1870 war came again to France. Napoleon's bungling and over-ambitious scheming finally proved his undoing when, through a series of calamitous errors, he took on the might of Bismarck and Imperial Germany. France's weak and disorganized armies were overrun and Paris besieged. The city suffered terribly. During the final weeks of the war, in December 1870, the city was starving. Even Castor and Pollux, the two elephants in the Botanical Gardens, were killed and eaten. Each week at least five thousand people died of hunger. Defeat was acknowledged on March 1, 1871. Prussian troops marched triumphantly down the Champs-Elysées and German imperial rule was proclaimed in the Hall of Mirrors at Versailles.

Before this happened, however, in September 1870, when it became clear that France was losing the war, the people rebelled yet again and drove the emperor from his throne. When the ceasefire with the Prussians was signed, the starving people of Paris, so long denied political power, snatched it for themselves and showed their strength on an unprecedented scale. On March 18, 1871, after weeks of disturbances and riots, the Paris Commune was born. However, this new rule of the Proletariat lasted only two months. The new President of the Third Republic, the feared and disliked Thiers, called in the Prussians—France's "ancient, natural enemy"—to defeat a foe he considered even more dangerous. The Commune was overthrown amid great popular dismay. Paris itself presented a sad spectacle. The column in the place Vendôme had been toppled and many public buildings, such as the Hôtel de Ville, parts of the Louvre and the pavilion of the Tuileries built by Napoleon III were left damaged or in ruins.

In 1879 the government returned to the city from Versailles. Plans for making good the damage and for new public works were hampered by the city's immensely large debts. Nonetheless the great white stone mass of the Sacré-Coeur appeared on the summit of Montmartre. It was paid for by public subscription as an act of contrition for the "sins" of the Commune.

A series of world exhibitions provided funds to finance further new building in the city. The Eiffel Tower, which has become the symbol of Paris, was built for the exhibition of 1889 in a storm of controversy and outrage. The exhibition of 1900 bequeathed the Petit Palais and the Grand Palais, which housed the various displays; also the Pont-Alexandre III.

The Twentieth Century

Vast riches were now being amassed in the capital of a country that ruled a far-flung colonial empire of 100 million souls. On the right bank banks and business houses appeared like mushrooms. Cafés and luxury restaurants lined the boulevards—and, at the turn of the century, the famous restaurant Maxim's opened its doors. At that period the jewelers of the rue de la Paix supplied gems and regalia to every royal house in Europe, while the fashion houses of the area adorned the aristocratic and wealthy the world over. Painters settled in Montmartre and Montparnasse. And, aided and abetted by the Moulin-Rouge and the Folies-Bergère, Paris led the world in glittering, spectacular and sometimes rather "naughty" entertainment.

In politics a new word was coined: *revanchisme.* France longed to avenge herself for her defeat in 1870 by imperial Germany at Sedan. She wanted to regain possession of Alsace-Lorraine. Thus World War I was foreshadowed. When the mobilization notices appeared on the streets of the city in the early days of August 1914 Paris seemed overjoyed. But not the workers. Since the fall of the Commune labor was better organized, trade unions had been formed and a Socialist party had become a power in the land. On the eve of war, Jean Jaurès, founder of the Socialist newspaper *L'Humanité,* tried with all his strength and influence to turn the tide of events and organize the Left against the coming catastrophe. But the bullet of a "patriot's" gun put an end to his plans.

On August 30, 1914 the first German plane flew over Paris and dropped the first bombs. By September 2 the Germans had advanced to within a few miles of the capital and the government fled to Bordeaux. The famous Battle of the Marne was fought between September 5 and 10, when General Galliéni, leading reinforcements carried in a fleet of now legendary taxis, beat back Kaiser Wilhelm's invaders. The capital was again in danger in March 1918 when an enormous German gun nicknamed "Big Bertha" began to shell the city, shattering streets, houses and churches. Two hundred and five Parisians died during the five days of the bombardment.

During World War I, France lost 1,390,000 men. Her industry and commerce were ravaged. But by her own efforts, and with the help of her allies, the United States and Britain, France emerged from the holocaust a victor. The peace signed at Versailles was favorable: France regained Alsace and Lorraine, and was awarded a sizable portion of the German colonies. The anniversary of the Armistice, November 11—in spite of the immense sacrifice in blood—became an occasion for great rejoicing. France had won a great victory, and had the booty to show for it. Today November 11 is still celebrated with somber military pomp.

The period between the two world wars was one of illusions and a false sense of security. But always crises threatened at home and abroad. In 1931 a Colonial Exhibit provided Paris with a new zoo at Vincennes and a new Colonial Museum, now the Musée des Arts Africains et Océaniens. The Paris Exhibition of 1937 gave her the Palais de Chaillot, which sits on the other side of the Seine from the Eiffel Tower.

Houses for the people to live in were rather more of a problem. The city fathers had realized this when victory came in 1918, but rampant inflation robbed them of the courage to build new homes for the victors. Only after 1926, when an attempt was made to restore confidence in the franc, was home-building started, though on a small scale. Economic crisis on a world scale, from which France could not be immune, was imminent. Fascism reared its ugly head. French "rightists" attempted a *putsch* on February 6, 1934, which was thwarted by the workers. In spite of this in September 1938 the President, a member of the Radical Party, signed the Munich Agreement, hoping for "peace in our time." The concessions made to Nazi Germany gained nothing but a little time and by September of the following year France was at war.

Apart from the phoney war and the blackout, France seemed scarcely aware that a state of hostilities existed until the first air raids began in May 1940, paving the way for the invading Nazi war-machine. After a week of aerial bombardment the city was in a state of panic. The roads to the south and west were crammed with refugees. Again the government fled to Bordeaux. On June 14 Paris was declared an open city and the Germans entered unopposed.

Most citizens endured the Occupation in helpless resignation, though small groups of members of the Resistance waged a bloody underground struggle against the invaders. For most, especially on days of national remembrance, silent hostility was the only weapon. In

August 1944 the Allied armies were at long last approaching Paris, and then the citizens threw themselves with fierce determination into the struggle for freedom. On the morning of August 19 the French tricolor was again hoisted over the Hôtel de Ville, in which the National Advisory Committee of the Resistance and the Paris Liberation Organization now sat. For seven days the entire city became a battlefield. In front of the Police Prefecture, on the place Saint-Michel, in the Batignolles area, in Ménilmontant, on the place de la République, in the Quartier Latin—everywhere there was the sound of gun fire as the people of Paris took to the barricades once again.

On August 25 General Leclerc's army entered the city to accept capitulation from the German commandant, von Choltitz. The following day General de Gaulle himself marched down the Champs-Elysées to the cheers and tears of countless thousands of citizens. The liberation of Paris had cost the lives of 1,482 of her sons. There were 2,887 German dead.

Postwar Paris

But the tribulations of war were far from over. By May in the following year, 1945, Paris was starving. The bread ration was pitifully small, cheese and meat had practically vanished. Restaurant "meals," in a city renowned for its gastronomic delights, were a grim joke. There were no private cars on the road. There was no gasoline or petrol, so no taxis, which were replaced by bicycle rickshaws. There was virtually no work either, and the army of jobless was swollen by the million returning prisoners of war, plus the 800,000 slave laborers and 600,000 political deportees returning from the Nazi concentration camps. The price index in Paris rose from 307 in December 1944 to 1,354 in December 1947. Inflation seemed unstoppable.

On January 20, 1946, General de Gaulle resigned. When the Socialists took office in 1947, Communists were barred from participating in the Government. A long series of strikes followed, as these were seemingly the only means of forcing the Government and employers to deal with the catastrophic economic situation. In November 1947 and again in August 1953 general strikes paralyzed the whole country, and Paris in particular.

During the fifties colonial wars brought sorrow to France, then fighting her last battles in Indo-China. The capital was rocked by scandals. High-ranking officers, politicians and clever businessmen were involved in currency manipulations in Indo-China. There were leakages of secret information about the state of the French Army on the Far Eastern battlefield, which reached the Vietnamese leaders via unknown negotiators, and the French Right talked of treason. . . . At last, in July, 1954, the war in Indo-China was over, only to be followed almost immediately by a new colonial trial of strength. On November 1, 1954, came news of the uprising in Algeria.

The war in Algeria divided French society from top to bottom. As the numbers of people advocating a policy of "Algeria for the Algerians" grew, the violence of those who believed that Algeria was and should remain a part of metropolitan France increased. In Algiers itself French settlers and colonial officers planned to take the government into their own hands. In France civil war seemed imminent. The middle classes grew terrified. Then once again the man who had represented France in the years of peril and lost hopes, and who during his years of retirement in the village of Colombey-les-Deux-Eglises had seldom visited the capital, was called back to bring peace to France. General de Gaulle resumed power.

Even some members of the Left supported the now aging General. On June 1, 1958, he was elected Prime Minister, and at the end of the same year he became President of the Republic, vested with extraordinary powers. But the war in Algeria went on—until 1962 when de Gaulle ended the cruel conflict by granting the country independence. He restored French self-confidence, as well as France's voice in world affairs (albeit by an assertive nationalism that angered some of her allies). During the war bombs exploded in the streets of Paris. At times police and Algerian workers opened fire on each other. In May and June 1968 large-scale strikes again paralyzed the life of the capital, and the students rose against the archaic educational system, the General and the forces he seemed to represent.

The Once and Future City

Paris underwent radical physical as well as political changes in the '60s and '70s. Under the imaginative direction of André Malraux, de Gaulle's Minister for Culture, the city started a series of programs in which the dirty, eroded buildings that enshrined her long history were cleaned and restored. As the years passed neighborhoods were regenerated; awkward survivals, such as Les Halles, were relocated and the original sites turned to modern uses; the nightmare of traffic congestion was partly resolved by the building of ringroads and by driving expressways slap through the center of the city, but mostly hidden from sight on the very edge of the Seine. All this was done with a keen eye on preserving the past and yet trying to prepare for an unknown future.

Attempts were made, and are still progressing, to shift major sections of the business community of Paris out to the edges of the city. La Défense, on the northwestern edge of town, beyond Neuilly, is a superb example of modern architecture and planning. Conceived in 1958 and still being built, the massive complex contains apartment blocks, the largest shopping center in Europe, offices and much else besides. It is excitingly designed but mercifully out of competition with the historic areas of the rest of the city.

The mixture of renovated period buildings and avant-garde ones works most of the time in Paris, mainly because the concentration has been mostly on the side of preservation. It is a city where whole areas have hardly changed in decades and, where change has occurred, it has mostly been imbued with the spirit of the place. There are notable exceptions—the backside of the Beaubourg among them.

Politically it has been a case of *plus ça change, plus c'est la même chose.* De Gaulle's policies were broadly continued by his successor, Georges Pompidou, and subsequently by Valéry Giscard d'Estaing. But Giscard proved a disappointing President. He came to power as a liberal reformist, then veered towards a somewhat cynical autocracy. By the end of his mandate, in 1981, the French were also growing bored with 23 years of much the same Right-of-center rule and were hankering for change. Yet the normal alteration of power that is healthy in a democracy was hazardous for France. The only alternative on offer was a Left with a large Communist element. Several times the electorate had already baulked at so radical a change.

However, in May 1981 they finally took the risk. They voted in as President the veteran Socialist leader François Mitterrand, and in June they gave his party a huge majority in the National Assembly. For five years Mitterrand suffered ever declining popularity, which reached a nadir in 1986 when he found himself, as a result of a bitterly-fought election, having to work in tandem with his bitter political foe, Jacques Chirac, leader of the opposing Gaullist party—a French dressing of oil and vinegar! This mismatched team of President and Prime Minister is called by the whimsical name of *cohabitation,* and the result of the union is not in sight at press time, but whatever it proves to be, a whole new colorful chapter is being written to French political life and the history of Paris.

SHOPPING IN PARIS

Savoir Flair

We're ready to bet that you'll find shopping in Paris one of the highlights of your trip. Even if you can't afford to buy much, window shopping is a great treat in this city where the art of designing window displays often seems to have reached dizzying heights of perfection. And nowadays you'll find a huge range of different types of stores bulging with goodies, from mammoth department stores to tiny, narrow little shops selling the latest fashion accessories or household goods or charming handmade gift items. Specialist retailing has long been a feature of the Paris scene and you'll find many cubbyhole-sized places devoted to a single item—candles, say, or umbrellas, or snuff boxes. You shouldn't forget the colorful open-air markets either. Their main role is to sell beautifully fresh food at prices lower than in regular stores, but you'll also find stalls selling clothes, bags and purses, shoes, household goods, maybe even books and toys.

Paris is of course a thoroughly cosmopolitan city, so you can find Indian jewelry, British cashmeres, just about everything made in Hong Kong, Taiwan and so on. But you can find them back home too, so we've concentrated in this chapter on the sort of typically French goods you're likely to want to take back with you as souvenirs of your trip or to give as presents to friends and family.

Shops are open from roughly 9 or 9.30 A.M. to 6.30 or 7 P.M. Fashion boutiques and antique shops may not open until 10 and may shut for lunch, especially in the summer when some staff are on vacation. Small food shops open earlier (8 or 8.30) and don't close until around 7.30 or 8 P.M., but they have a long lunch break, usually from 12.30 or 1 to 3.30 or 4. Department stores stay open all day, from around 9.30 to 6.30. Many small shops close for at least a month in the summer, when most of their regular customers are away from Paris, but a surprising number of shops are open on Sunday mornings, and small food shops are generally open in the morning on public holidays. However, Monday is a bad day for food shopping, as many food shops are closed in the morning. Many other shops that are open all day on Saturday may well close for at least part of Monday.

Discounts, Credit Cards, and Orientation

If you're resident outside France you will probably want to benefit from tourist discounts whenever possible. But you should be warned that easily the best places to do so are the department stores and the fashion and perfume boutiques that are used to dealing with foreign customers. Other shops may do their best to be helpful, but they probably won't be equipped to deal efficiently with the paperwork involved and you may never get your discount. (For details of how discounts work, see our *Facts at your Fingertips* section.)

Many shops catering to foreign tourists will accept currency other than French francs. But you'll undoubtedly get a lower rate than in the banks or the official exchange offices. So you must weigh up this factor against the convenience of paying in dollars or pounds and knowing where you stand. Credit cards are gradually becoming more common in France, but we advise you not to count on being able to use yours except in the most tourist-oriented places. Those most likely to be accepted are American Express and Visa, with Diner's Card coming in third; many hotels now take MasterCard too.

Having goods sent direct to your home is always somewhat chancy and many stores are reluctant to do so after some unhappy experiences in the past where the goods got "lost" en route. The best-known firm with a well-organized discount and shipping system is *Michel Swiss,* 16 rue de la Paix, 2e, which sells excellent scarves, perfumes, ties and gifts of all kinds. Otherwise our advice would be to have goods sent only if you're traveling on round Europe and it would be a real inconvenience to carry them with you, or if you're likely to have to pay excess baggage charges when you board your plane. If you do have them sent, be prepared for them to take many weeks, even by air.

Paris is a small city, as capitals go, so you don't need to organize your shopping trips into clearly defined districts—moving from one to another isn't a long business. But it will help you to know that the major department stores are in the Opéra area or near the Hôtel de Ville on the Right Bank, while the Left Bank, especially St.-Germain-des-Prés, is a paradise for lovers of small, specialist shops.

As in most cities, some streets or districts specialize in one type of article. For instance in the rue de Paradis, 10e, you'll find the best choice of china and cut glass, with such great names as *Baccarat* (at no. 30) and *Daum* (at no. 41). However *Lalique* is near the Madeleine in the rue Royale. Most of the city's antique dealers are congregated in St.-Germain-des-Prés—try the rue Bonaparte, the rue Jacob, the rue des Sts.-Pères and the rue du Bac—or in or near the rue du fbg.-St.-Honoré, 8e. Shoe shops are much in evidence in the blvd. St.-Michel, along with student bookshops. Art galleries are to be found again in St.-Germain-des-Prés, particularly in the rue de Seine and the surrounding streets. Fashion boutiques are mainly found near the Madeleine or, for more avant-garde styles, in St.-Germain-des-Prés and round Les Halles. The rue de Rivoli has the lion's share of the city's souvenir shops and is also the place to go for books in English. The newly renovated Marais district has some interesting little craft boutiques, though they tend to come and go rather frequently, so rather than suggesting specific shops, we advise you to watch out for likely places as you visit the district and its marvelous old mansions.

Department Stores

These are the best places for getting the feel of French goods without feeling under any obligation to buy. *Au Printemps,* 64 blvd. Haussmann, 9e, claims to be the "most Parisian of the big stores." It is certainly one of the most upmarket, along with the long-famous *Galeries Lafayette,* next door at no. 40. These two huge stores have everything, including restaurants, hairdressers and multilingual hostesses. The *Galeries Lafayette* are especially tourist concious, and have a number of attractive programs for foreign shoppers—including a tourist discount scheme, free booklets on Paris, a complimentary fashion show every Wednesday at 10.30 (reserve tel. 48–74–02–30), plus multilingual hostesses. Not far from here is the smaller and very select

Trois-Quartiers, 17 blvd. de la Madeleine, 1er, which generally caters to a slightly older age group than the other two.

Two popular stores catering more to ordinary Parisians than to foreign tourists are close together in the Hôtel de Ville area: *La Samaritaine,* 19 rue de la Monnaie, 1er, with a roof terrace offering stunning views over the Seine, and the *Bazar de l'Hôtel de Ville,* 55 rue de le Verrerie, 4e (main entrances in the rue de Rivoli, just opposite the Hôtel de Ville), which is excellent for household articles.

The only department store on the Left Bank is *Au Bon Marché,* 38 rue de Sèvres, 7e, with a well-known antiques section and a faithful following among local residents.

You can't miss the budget chain stores *Monoprix* and *Prisunic,* which are found all over town. They're particularly good for stylish, budget fashion accessories, children's clothes and colorful stationery that makes good presents.

The various *Drugstores* are a typical feature of modern Paris. They stay open to 1.30 A.M. every day of the week and are always packed with people buying newspapers and magazines from all over the world (they're your best bet for U.S. and British papers), books, stationery, records and cassettes, gifts of all kinds, even takeaway food—at a price. Some have a pharmacy counter and all have restaurants that are handy for quick meals. You'll find them at the Arc de Triomphe end of the Champs-Elysées, at the Rond-Point des Champs-Elysées, in the blvd. St.-Germain (diagonally opposite the church of St.-Germain-des-Prés) and in Neuilly (pl. du Marché).

Shopping Arcades

One particularly pleasant feature of Paris is the number of opportunities it offers for window-shopping in covered passageways or arcades (called *galeries* or *passages*), many of them dating from the nineteenth century and splendidly restored to show off to full advantage their arching glass roofs and their many highly decorative trimmings—marble floors, brass lamps, metal or stucco curlicues, even an elaborate staircase sometimes.

Two of the most attractive are the *Galerie Véro-Dodat,* 19 rue Jean-Jacques Rousseau, 1er, with magnificent painted ceilings and slender copper pillars, and the *Galerie Vivienne,* 4 pl. des Petits-Champs, 3e, near the Bourse and the Bibliothèque Nationale, which has some particularly interesting shops and a good tearoom. Other examples, all in the same central area of the Right Bank, are the *Passage des Pavillons,* 6 rue de Beaujolais, 1er; the *Passage des Princes,* 97 rue de Richelieu, 2e; and the *Passage des Panoramas,* 2e, the granddaddy of them all—it was opened to the public as long as 1800. You can usually window-shop until around 9 at night, when the ornamental iron gates at either end are closed.

The nineteenth-century tradition has been revived in recent times with the building of several *galeries* off the Champs-Elysées (all on the north side). The *Galerie du Claridge, Galeries Elysées 26, Galerie du Lido* and *Galerie du Rond-Point* all have chic boutiques plus restaurants and snackbars and are ideal places for wet-weather shopping. The stylish glass and concrete *Forum des Halles* is yet another example of the Paris tradition of shopping malls, with its dozens of boutiques arranged on several levels and interspersed with restaurants, cafés and furniture stores.

The ground floor of the *Tour Montparnasse* is for those who like doing all their shopping under one roof—it has dozens of fashion and other boutiques, plus a branch of the famous Galeries Lafayette department store. The ground and lower ground floors of the *Palais des Congrès* at the Porte Maillot, 17e, offer a good choice of fashion boutiques, antique shops, beauty products, stationery, even a post office. You also find temporary stalls selling craft items from all over France.

Markets—Food, Flowers, Birds and Fleas

Paris's open-air food markets are an unending delight, whether you're shopping for a picnic lunch, looking for goodies to take home, or out spotting picturesque material for your photo album. They're also a good place to admire and learn from the perfectionist skills of French food shoppers, both male and female. You'll find too that prices are a lot lower than in regular food shops. The colorful pyramids of fruit and vegetables are particularly appealing, but best not pick up the items you wish to buy, or you may well be treated to some equally colorful language from the stallholder! The shining displays of mouthwateringly fresh fish are another sure-fire attraction for camera freaks and will help you get your eye in before venturing into one of the city's many fish restaurants to sample some French specialties. If you're collecting the ingredients for a tasty picnic, you'll soon find yourself drooling over the astounding range of different varieties of cheese on offer.

Over the Christmas and New Year period the stallholders really go to town, vying with one another to produce the most tempting displays of seasonal specialties—fruit and nuts, every conceivable type of charcuterie, with *foie gras* and pâtés fashioned to look like miniature ducks, and terrines decorated with seasonal trimmings.

Every district has at least one open-air food market, which may be held daily or just once or twice a week. Saturday and Sunday are usually good days for market lovers, Monday the least likely. You may prefer to head for the best-known, which can incidentally easily be combined with sightseeing: the centuries-old rue Mouffetard, 5e, in the heart of the Latin Quarter; the rue de Buci and the rue de Seine, 6e, bang in the middle of St.-Germain-des-Prés; the rue Clerc, 7e, near the Invalides and the Eiffel Tower; the rue Lepic, 18e, in Montmartre; and the pl. du Marché in Neuilly (just by the Les Sablons métro stop), a good bet if you feel like a Sunday stroll in the Bois de Boulogne (though it's also open Wednesday and Friday).

Many food markets are open in the morning only, from around 8 or 8.30 to 12.30 or 1, and the early part of the morning is the time to see them at their picturesque best.

The famous flower market on the Ile de la Cité near Notre Dame—another feast for lovers of local color—is the place to buy top-quality cut flowers or house plants at reasonable prices for your French hosts. Other good flower markets are held beside the Madeleine church, 8e, and in the pl. des Ternes, 17e. All these flower markets are open all day, from around 8 A.M. to 7 P.M., every day of the week except Monday. You will also find at least one flower stall in the open-air food markets.

On Sundays a bird market takes the place of part of the flower market on the Ile de la Cité, and you may also like to wander along the Quai de la Mégisserie on the Right Bank (north side) of the river Seine, which specializes in birds and animals.

Philatelists should head for the well-known stamp market held on Thursday, Saturday, Sunday and public holidays on the av. Marigny and the avenue Gabriel just off the southern half of the Champs-Elysées (around 10 A.M. to dusk). You'll enjoy browsing through the many old postcards on sale here—a view of Paris or one of your favorite parts of France as it looked decades ago makes a good souvenir of your visit.

You're sure to have heard of Paris's unbeatable *marché aux puces* (flea market), which celebrated its centenary in 1985. It started life in the area round the Porte de Saint-Ouen, 17e, and Porte de Clignancourt, 18e, on the northern edge of Paris in 1885 and now covers a staggering 6½ kilometers (4 miles). Its hundreds of stalls and little shops are open all day on weekends and on Mondays and you can have great fun browsing round them, though you must get there early if you're determined to pick up a genuine bargain. Various other flea markets are held on the southern and eastern edge of Paris, but they're much smaller and have a depressingly large amount of real tat, so are best avoided, except by obsessive bargain hunters.

If you're in Paris in March or September don't miss the centuries-old *Foire au Jambon et à la Brocante* (Ham and Bric-à-Brac Fair), also sometimes known as the *Foire à la Ferraille* (Scrap Metal Fair). It's held on the Ile de Châtou just to the west of Paris and is easily reached on the RER (express métro). Here you'll find a colorful mixture of bric-à-brac, including some genuine antiques at reasonable prices, and displays of every type of charcuterie you've ever seen and lots more you never even dreamed of, including vast whole hams. Open-air mini-restaurants, with benches and trestle tables, serving mostly charcuterie of course, with generous helpings of conviviality, add greatly to the fun of it all.

Souvenirs

To find a good selection of souvenir shops you should head for the Tuileries end of the rue de Rivoli, 1er (between the rue Cambon and the Palais Royal). Here you'll spot headscarves with pictures of the Eiffel Tower, the Sacré-Coeur, the Arc de Triomphe, the Louvre or the Beaubourg/Pompidou Center—or maybe all five at once. Some stores sell handkerchiefs printed with outline drawings of the same buildings, and all have miniature Eiffel Towers, either by themselves, in various sizes, or adorning everything under the sun—ashtrays, keyrings, charm bracelets, earrings, pendants, you name it. Miniature busts of Napoleon, ranging from inexpensive models to quite elaborate ones set on plinths and selling for hefty sums, are another popular souvenir of Paris. You'll also find such items for sale from stalls or barrows near the city's major landmarks, especially the Eiffel Tower, and in some newsagents.

Illustrated books on France in general or Paris in particular make a good memory-jogger to take home. For books in English the rue de Rivoli is again your best bet, with two well-known English-language bookshops, *Galignani* and *W.H. Smith,* at nos. 224 and 248 respectively, and *Brentano's* at 37 av. de l'Opéra close by. Several of the French bookshops in the Palais Royal area also have books in English on France, particularly on French art. You might like to see what's on offer in the growing number of museum bookshops, which generally have a good selection in both French and English. Try for instance those in the Musée des Arts Décoratifs, the Louvre, the Musée d'Orsay, the Pompidou/Beaubourg Center and the Musée Rodin. The big student bookshops on the boulevard Saint-Michel, 5e, often have bargains in the way of books on French art and artists at considerably reduced prices, generally to be found on trestle tables outside.

A good place for choosing from a wide stock of books in French and English on all the arts in France—movies, theater, music and dance as well as painting, sculpture and the applied arts, is *La Hune,* 170 blvd. St.-Germain, 7e, which is conveniently open till midnight Monday-Friday (till 7.30 on Saturday). Postcards of works of art will also be found here.

If like many foreign visitors to Paris you've fallen under the spell of French cuisine, you'll probably like the idea of taking home a cookbook, either for yourself or to give friends as a gift. You'll find a good range in English in the big English-language bookshops in the rue de Rivoli, but you may also like to call in at Paris's specialist food and wine bookshop, *Le Verre et l'Assiette,* 1 rue du Val-de-Grâce, 5e, when you're visiting the Luxembourg/Observatoire area.

Perfumes

What could be more French than an elegant bottle of one of the world's most famous perfumes? But buying scents is a complicated business these days, if you want to get the best price possible. It seems that everybody's offering some sort of discount, and if you are prepared for the hard sell that goes with this sort of buying, and can keep your head among the bewildering variety of prices available, you may well be able to buy French perfumes at only about a third of what you'd have to pay at home. But this assumes that you'll have benefited from the tourist discount too, so you should bear in mind first that you probably won't get some of the discount till you get back home, and second that you have to make a large purchase in one store for the discount to operate (see *Facts at Your Fingertips*).

If you already know what you want, that's fine. Head for one of the stores specializing in upmarket discount sales, such as *Liz* at 194 rue de Rivoli, 1er; Galerie Elysées 26 at 26 av. des Champs-Elysées, 8e; and 112 rue du fbg. St.-Honoré, 8e; or the old-established *Michel Swiss,* 16 rue de la Paix, 2e. *Paris Look,* 13 av. de l'Opéra, 1er, advertises 25% off the major names; and *Patchouli,* at 3 and 50 rue du Cherche-Midi, 6e, which is also a beauty salon, offers 20% off. Two reliable family-run discount businesses are *Catherine,* 6 rue de Castiglione, 1er, and *Maré-chal,* 232 rue de Rivoli, 1er. If what you know you want happens to be a *Guerlain,* you must head for one of their own exclusive boutiques, at 2 pl. Vendôme, 1er; 29 rue de Sèvres, 6e; 68 av. des Champs-Elysées, 8e; or 93 rue de Passy, 16e.

If your main aim is to be able to sniff at a wide variety of perfumes at your leisure, aim either for the major department stores near the Opéra, *Galeries Lafayette* and *Au Printemps,* which will be able to give you 20% discounts when you pay for many well-known makes, or for the splendid *Sephora,* at 50 rue de Passy, 16e, and in the Forum des Halles, which claims to be the world's largest perfumery store (and may well be right) as well as offering some good prices on both perfumes and beauty products.

Jewelry

The famous names are conveniently grouped together in or around the place Vendôme near the Tuileries. Here you'll find *Boucheron, Chaumet* and *Van Cleef & Arpels,* while the great *Cartier* is just around the corner at 13 rue de la Paix and the stylish *Jean Dinh Van* at no. 7 on the same street. *Fred,* in the nearby rue Royale, has been attracting visitors to Paris for generations and also has a branch in the Galerie du Claridge off the Champs-Elysées. *La Boutique du Crillon* in the Hôtel Crillon in the place de la Concorde has a good selection of pieces at the top end of the market and is conveniently open till 8 P.M. every day of the week.

For fine silver pieces in a much lower price bracket, we recommend *Fleurmay,* 204 rue de Rivoli, 1er. Another good place for elegant modern pieces at affordable prices is *Fabrice,* with two little stores in the rue Bonaparte, 6e (at nos 33 and 54). The department stores have a good selection to suit all tastes and pocketbooks and all over Paris you'll find neighborhood shops with some pretty pieces. At First Communion time in the early summer they have some lovely pieces designed as presents for small girls—the silver and turquoise bracelets and necklaces are particularly appealing.

If you long for some fun bits and pieces in the latest styles, head for *Agatha,* which can now be found in St.-Germain-des-Prés (97 rue de Rennes), on the Champs-Elysées (Galerie des Champs at no. 84) and in the Forum. Good for fashion-conscious youngsters.

Fashion

Not surprisingly, considering that Paris is generally thought of as the fashion capital of the world, many visitors soon find themselves longing to take home a stylish outfit for themselves, or as a gift for their fashion-conscious friends and relations. If you can afford *haute couture* —and it really is very pricey these days—you should sally forth to the avenue Montaigne, 8e, where you'll find such hardy perennials as *Christian Dior, Guy Laroche, Nina Ricci* and *Emanuel Ungaro,* or to the rue du fbg. St.-Honoré, 8e, for *Louis Féraud, Lanvin,* and *Torrente.* Most of the other big names are in streets adjoining one of these two: *Balmain, Courrèges* and *Ted Lapidus* in the rue François-1er; *Givenchy* in the av. George-V; *Yves Saint-Laurent* in the av. Marceau; *Chloé* in the av. Franklin-Roosevelt; *Chanel* nearby in the rue Cambon.

St.-Germain-des-Prés is the place for more avant-garde styles, with couture designers *Sonia Rykiel* (6 rue de Grenelle) and *Chantal Thomass* (5 rue du Vieux-Colombier) and long-famous boutiques such as *Dorothée Bis* (33 rue de Sèvres), *Anastasia* (18 rue de l'Ancienne-Comédie), *Gudule* (72 rue St.-André-des-Arts) and *Tiffany* (12 rue de Sèvres). All of these specialize in ready-to-wear. You'll also find a wealth of attractive and up-to-the-minute fashions in the huge number of boutiques in and around the blvd. St.-Germain. *La Gaminerie* (137 blvd. St.-Germain) is an old favorite, with good accessories too.

The place des Victoires near the newly renovated Les Halles district has become one of *the* centers of *avant-garde* fashion. Come here for the great *Kenzo* and for a good selection in *Victoire.* In and around Les Halles itself *Agnès B* in the rue du Jour is a favorite with lovers of sophisticated yet wearable outfits, while the punningly named *Halles Capone,* 12 rue Turbigo, 1er, is very "in" for well-cut jeans. In the *Forum* multistory shopping mall you can browse through a wealth of fashion boutiques.

If you prefer to compare the latest creations of many different designers, best go to the chic department stores *Galeries Lafayette* and *Le Printemps,* with their floors of "shops-within-shops." The nearby rue Tronchet is another center of Paris fashion, with the ever-classic *Cacharel, Erès* for sleek and sophisticated swimwear and beach outfits, and the long-popular *Madd.*

Accessories

The rue Tronchet is also a good place for accessories. *La Bagagerie* at no. 22 is a reliable store for beautiful bags and purses to go with your new outfit, while *Carel* at no. 4 has really fabulous shoes, as does *Renast* at no. 33. *Hélion,* at no. 22 specializes in sleek gloves. The city's most famous sellers of leather goods are all in this part of Paris, with the great *Hermès* a short walk away in the fbg. St.-Honoré, at no. 24, and two major specialists at no. 265 and 271 rue St.-Honoré, *Sellerie de la Cour* and *Sellerie de France. Lancel,* 8 place de l'Opéra is another good bet.

On the Left Bank, *La Bagagerie* has another store in the rue de Rennes, and several good shoe shops are to be found nearby: *Carel* and *Tilbury* in the rue du Four, *Cassandre, Céline* and *Charles Jourdan* all in the rue de Rennes, *François Villon* at 58 rue Bonaparte and trendy *Maud Frizon* at 83 rue des Sts.-Pères.

Most of the city's fashion boutiques sell some accessories carefully selected to go with their outfits and you should also consider examining the huge range of bags and purses, silk headscarves and fashionable umbrellas in the department stores. Some of the open-air markets have bargains in shoes and bags too. And talking of bargains, you may like to know about the *Club des 10,* 58 rue du fbg. St.-Honoré, 8e, which offers 30–40% off designs by some of the best-known couture and ready-to-wear names.

Fabulous Fabrics

Rather than going for a Paris outfit you may prefer to buy a length of fabric and style it yourself for a great deal less than you'll have to pay in the city's boutiques or department stores. The best-known place is the huge *Marché Saint-Pierre,* 2 rue Charles-Nodier, 18e, at the foot of the Sacré-Coeur hill in Montmartre, which has a range to suit all pocketbooks, including some designed by the top couturiers a year or so ago. For beautiful silks you should head for *Le Jardin de la Soie* near the Madeleine (16 rue Duphot, 1er) or on the Champs-Elysées (12–14 rond-point des Champs-Elysées, 8e).

Edible Goodies

A favorite choice for presents to take home from a visit to this highly food-conscious country is a sample of its delectable food or drink. Pretty boxes of French regional specialties can be found in many places in Paris, from the little corner grocery or bakery to the gastronomic temples, such as those two *very* superior grocers, *Fauchon* at 26 pl. de la Madeleine, 8e, or *Hédiard,* also in the pl. de la Madeleine, at no. 21, and at 126 rue du Bac, 7e, 106 blvd. de Courcelles, 17e, and in the Forum des Halles. For last-minute shoppers a good selection can also be had at Orly and Roissy/Charles-de-Gaulle airports.

Those with a sweet tooth will surely be tempted by the *fruits confits* (candied fruit) of southern France or by local specialties such as *calissons d'Aix* or *bergamotes de Nancy* and many other types of sweets or candies. Delicious nougat from Montmélimar comes in all shapes and sizes and colors. Beautifully arranged boxes of wrapped hard candy flavored with every fruit imaginable are a delight to the eye as well as the palate, while perhaps nicest of all, and very typically French, are the delightful yet inexpensive little boxes or round and oval tins of *réglisse* (licorice), whose presentation hasn't changed for centuries. *Aux Douceurs de France,* 70 blvd. de Strasbourg, 10e, specializes in candies from all over France, but you'll find many of them in other food shops.

Dried herbs make good (and conveniently lightweight) presents, particularly if they're sold in sachets made from colorful Provençal fabrics. Many food markets have a stall selling little cellophane bags of herbs and spices at lower prices than in regular stores.

Tins or cans of foie gras or truffles, if you can afford them, will delight a gourmet's heart. Snails and preserved wild mushrooms in cans or glass jars are other delicacies you won't find so easily back home.

And if you're careful to select ones that aren't too ripe, France's amazing range of literally hundreds of cheeses will surely tempt you into taking at least one back home with you. The city's best-known cheese store (may well be the world's best too) is *Androuët,* 41 rue d'Amsterdam, 8e.

As for wine, corner groceries or the *Nicolas* chain of wine shops will suit your picnic needs and will provide bottles to take home if you prefer not to use the duty-free shops at the airports. But if you want something really special, don't miss *Vins Rares et de Collection,* 3 rue Laugier, 17e, which has a large selection of France's most famous wines in rare vintages, many of them very old. The young Swedish manager, Peter Thustrup, will offer you free tastings in his cellar and we doubt if you'll be able to resist the temptation to buy at least one bottle, with prices mostly very reasonable (cheapest is around 20 francs), though if you really must have a Château Lafite-Rothschild it will set you back a cool 9,000 francs!

Gorgeous Gifts

Many of the items we've mentioned in this chapter would make good presents to take home, but for those who want to find a more unusual gift we've picked out a few places that have something really special on offer.

For instance *Isabelle Valogne,* 53 av. de la Bourdonnais, 7e, specializes in charming scent bottles, both antique and modern, and also has some nice art déco brooches. *La Rose des Vents,* 65 rue de Seine, 6e, is a pretty little shop with a good range of "natural products"—pots pourris, wonderfully scented soaps, dried flowers, natural beauty products, scented candles and the like. *Monsieur Renard,* 6 rue de l'Echaudé, 6e, is full of antique dolls and automata. *Le Monde en Marche,* 34 rue Dauphine, 6e, is a good place for presents for small children, with many wooden toys and puppets. *Françoise Thibault,* 1 rue Jacob, 6e, and 1 rue Bourbon-le-Château, 6e, is an old favorite for attractive gifts, with some delightful handpainted boxes and picture frames. *Léon,* 220 rue de Rivoli, 1er, has been going for over a hundred years and is a must for magical little porcelain boxes decorated with flowers, exquisite thimbles and paperweights, and reproductions of Sèvres porcelain.

If you prefer to take home an antique object, try the *Louvre des Antiquaires* emporium in the pl. du Palais-Royal, 1er, the *Village Suisse,* 54 av. de la Motte-Piquet, 15e, the *Cour des Saints-Pères,* off the street of the same name, 7e, or the *Jardins Saint-Paul,* 4e, again off the street of the same name, which also has some craft stalls and workshops.

And for art-lovers a print makes a good buy. The best area here is the rue de Seine, 6e, and the surrounding streets, including the book-stalls along by the river, which sometimes have some good prints. On the Right Bank the happiest hunting ground is the avenue Matignon, 8e, but prices are high here. The *Chalcographic Department in the Louvre,* with literally thousands of prints from old plates, is another must if you've set your heart on a print.

PRACTICAL INFORMATION FOR PARIS

SECURITY WARNING. Paris is being plagued by a wave of violence and crime that is unfortunately affecting tourists as well as residents. The police warn that even such famous tourist areas as the Champs-Elysées are infested with thugs after 10 at night—literally thousands of incidents of mugging, bag-snatching, and violent thefts from cars are reported to them each month. Other danger spots to avoid late at night are the Esplanade des Invalides, the Halles/Beaubourg area, the place and boulevard St.-Michel and surrounding streets and the rue du faubourg Montmartre.

Security in the métro has improved, but pickpocketing is still rife, as it is in any large city. Best wear your purse slung across you, as most Frenchwomen do, rather than over one shoulder, where it is easy prey to bag-snatchers on foot or on mopeds. And beware of small groups of children—most of them Gipsies and too young to prosecute—who, police say, are the worst offenders.

GETTING TO TOWN FROM THE AIRPORTS. You have various methods of traveling from Paris's two airports to the city center. If you have heavy bags, you'd best get a taxi or the special airport buses, but be sure to allow plenty of time during rush hours (especially Friday evenings) as the roads to the airports get traffic-clogged. The other alternatives are train/express, métro and ordinary city buses.

By Bus. Buses leave from both termini at Roissy/Charles-de-Gaulle airport every 12 minutes between 5.45 A.M. and 11 P.M. for the air terminal at the Porte Maillot on the western edge of Paris. From here you can travel on by métro or taxi. Fare is around 40 frs and journey time outside rush hours is 30–45 minutes. From Orly-Ouest and Orly-Sud airports buses leave every 12 minutes during the day, less often in the evening, for the Les Invalides city terminal in the 7th *arrondissement* south of the River Seine. Fare is around 30 frs and journey time around 35–40 minutes, longer during rush hours. Special buses also operate between the two airports (around 70 frs), taking at least 1¼ hrs.

By Train. Free shuttle buses leave from Gate 30 (arrivals floor) at Terminal 1, and Gates A5 and B6 at Terminal 2 at Roissy/CDG airport for the rail station called Roissy-Aéroport CDG, from where you can take the *Roissy-Rail* service into Paris's Gare du Nord mainline station, which enables you to get off at any station on line B of the RER (express métro) network. This line is slotted into the ordinary métro system, so connections are easy, and by 1988 it should also have direct connections with RER line C. Trains operate at 7–15 minute intervals, depending on the time of day.

Fares. 24 frs to the Gare du Nord, 26.50 frs through to any métro or inner-circle RER station. This service is fast and efficient, but it involves a fair amount of walking, as does *Orly-Rail,* the sister service from Orly airport. Here trains leave at 15-minute intervals (30-minute in the evening) from Gate F (arrivals floor) at Orly-Ouest and Gate H at Orly-Sud and take you to Pont-de-Rungis-Aéroport d'Orly station. From here the C line of the RER takes you into the Gare d'Austerlitz, the Gare des Invalides and many other stops, with connections to métro lines from most stations.

Fares. To Paris–Austerlitz, 17 frs; to any métro or inner-circle RER station, 20 frs.

By City Bus. The regular 351 bus will take you from Roissy rail station (take the shuttle bus there from the airport) to the Nation or Vincennes métro stops. No. 350 goes from Roissy to the Gare de l'Est and Gare du Nord rail stations. From Orly regular buses 215 and 183A will take you to Denfert-Rochereau and Porte de Choisy respectively, both in southern Paris.

By Taxi. A taxi from Roissy/CDG airport to a spot in central Paris will cost 150–200 frs including tip; from Orly a little less.

By Helicopter. *Héli-France* (tel. 45–57–53–67) offers the fastest means of getting from one airport to another.

TOURIST INFORMATION. The main Paris Tourist Office is at 127 av. des Champs-Elysées, 75008 Paris (tel. 47–23–61–72). Open 9 A.M. to 9 P.M. Mon.–Sat. in summer, 9 A.M. to 8 P.M. Sun. and public holidays; in winter, 9–8 Mon. to Sat., 9–6 Sun. and public hols. This office is crammed with information on Paris and can also supply brochures for other parts of the country if you're traveling on. The multilingual hostesses can make hotel reservations for a small charge (not more than 5 days in advance) and in the same building you'll find the main office of the SNCF (French Rail) tourist office. Be prepared for long queues at weekends and all week in summer.

There is a special recorded-message telephone information service for details of the week's events—concerts, ballet, exhibits, parades, son-et-lumière, special events of all kinds; called *Sélection Losisirs,* it offers a version in English, reached by dialing 47–20–88–98 (though you may need to listen to it twice round).

There is also a tourist information office in the *Mairie* or City Hall in Paris (just by Hôtel-de-Ville métro stop). And the City of Paris puts up posters all over the city giving details of one-off events.

There are branch offices at Austerlitz Est, Lyon and Nord rail stations and at the Eiffel Tower, but these may be closed on Sun. and public holidays.

Information on what's on in Paris during your stay is best gleaned from the weekly *L'Officiel des Spectacles* or the slightly more expensive *Pariscope,* both available from all newsstands and drugstores and full of information. Both appear on Weds., the day the movie programs change. Your hotel will probably have a copy of the free weekly *Paris-Sélection,* which is also obtainable from some travel agencies and from tourist offices.

The national dailies *Le Figaro* and *Le Monde* give full details of movies, theaters, opera and ballet, exhibits and other events. Other useful sources are the *International Herald Tribune,* published daily in Paris, and the English-language fortnightly *Passion.*

Over 50 of Paris's top hotels have installed an electronic information system known as *Cititel,* which will provide answers to a huge range of questions about cultural events in Paris and the whole of the Ile de France region, as well as hotel room availability, airline and rail timetables and so on.

 USEFUL ADDRESSES. Embassies and Consulates. *U.S. Embassy,* 2 av. Gabriel, 8e (tel. 42–96–12–02); *U.S. Consulate,* rue St.-Florentin, 1er (tel. 42–60–14–88). *British Embassy,* 35 rue du fbg. St. Honoré, 8e (tel. 42–66–91–42); *British Consulate,* 2 Cité du Retiro (3rd Floor), 8e (tel. 42–66–91 –42). *Australian Embassy,* 4 rue Jean Rey, 15e (tel. 45–75–62–00). *Canadian Embassy,* 35 av. Montaigne, 8e (tel. 42–25–99–55). *New Zealand Embassy,* 9 rue Léonard-de-Vinci, 16e (tel. 45–00–24–11).

Medical Emergencies. Hospitals with English-speaking staff: *American Hospital,* 63 blvd. Victor-Hugo, Neuilly (tel. 47–47–53–00); *British Hospital,* 48 rue de Villiers, Levallois-Perret (tel. 47–58–13–12). Pharmacies or chemists open long hours: *Dhéry,* galerie des Champs, 84 av. des Champs-Elysées, 8e (tel. 45–62–02–41), open non-stop; *Drugstore,* on the corner of blvd. St.-Germain and the rue de Rennes, 6e has a pharmacy counter open daily to 2 A.M.; *Pharmacie des Arts,* 106 blvd. Montparnasse, 6e is open to midnight Mon.–Sat. and 8 P.M. to midnight on Sun.

In an attempt to prevent drug addicts taking up doctors' and pharmacists' time at night, the police will generally have to stamp any prescription you need to have made up outside normal opening hours before giving you the name of a local pharmacist who can help you. Contact the nearest *Commissariat de Police.*

Emergency Telephone Numbers. *Ambulances,* 43–78–26–26; *Medical,* 47–07 –77–77; *Dentists* (8 P.M. to 8 A.M. weekdays, all day weekends and public holidays), 43–37–51–00; *Vets* (8 P.M. to 8 A.M. Sun. and public holidays only), 48–32–93–30. Automatic call boxes are to be found at main crossroads for use in emergencies requiring police help *(Police-Secours)* or medical help *(Services Médicaux).*

An *SOS Service* for English-speakers is offered after 7 P.M. if you call 47–23–80–80. They'll do their best to help you, whatever your problem. The U.S. Embassy (42–96–12–02) has a Welfare Service and the American Aid Society (open mornings only). The British Embassy (42–66–91–42) will do their best to help too. But if your problem is that your wallet, passport or other papers have been stolen, you *must* first go to the nearest police station *(commissariat de police)* and get them to sign and stamp a form giving details of the theft.

$P£ **CHANGING MONEY.** At press time fewer and fewer banks were offering exchange facilities for foreign visitors. Those few that were, inevitably became jam-packed with tourists desperate to change money. Ordinary banks are generally open 9.30–4.30, but there are no regular hours and you'll find some open later (to around 5.15) and others closing for at least an hour at lunchtime. In the summer, with staff on holiday, many close their exchange counter between around 12 and 2, even if the rest of the bank is open. *Important:* all banks close at 11.30 or noon the day before a public holiday.

There are exchange offices in major tourist areas like the Opéra, Champs-Elysées and St.-Germain which open longer hours than the banks, and at the main rail stations: *Gare d'Austerlitz,* 7.30 A.M.–8 P.M.; *Gare de l'Est,* 7.30 A.M.–8 P.M. daily; *Gare de Lyon,* 6 A.M.–11 P.M. daily; *Gare du Nord,* 6.30 A.M.–10 P.M. *Gare St.-Lazare,* 7.30 A.M.–8 P.M. However, these opening hours may change without warning, so allow plenty of time, as you may have to stand in line a long while, particularly at the height of the summer tourist season and on weekends.

The *Société Générale* bank has branches at Orly and Roissy/CDG airports open 6.30 A.M.–11.30 P.M.

The following banks are open longer than standard hours:

CIC at the Gare de Lyon, 7 A.M.–11 P.M. daily.

CCF, 103 av. des Champs-Elysées, 8e, 9 A.M.–8 P.M. Mon. to Sat.

UBP, 154 av. des Champs-Elysées, 8e, open weekends, 10.30–1 and 2–6.

American Express has an exchange counter at 11 rue Scribe, 9e, that is open 9–5 Mon. to Sat.

You may find it helpful to know the addresses of the following U.S., Canadian and British banks, but they are open only standard hours, or even shorter hours:

Bank of America, 43 av. de la Grande-Armée, 16e (mornings only).

Banque de l'Union Occidentale française et canadienne, 47 av. George-V, 8e.

Barclay's, 33 rue du 4-Septembre, 2e; 157 blvd. Saint-Germain, 6e; 6 rond-point des Champs-Elysées, 8e; 108 rue St.-Lazare, 8e; 24 av. Kléber, 16e.

Lloyd's Bank International, 43 blvd. des Capucines, 1er.

Morgan-Guaranty Trust Co, 14 pl. Vendôme, 1er.

Royal Bank of Canada, 3 rue Scribe, 9e.

Major hotels, many stores and some restaurants will accept travelers' checks, but you should be warned that the rate they use will not be as favorable as that offered by banks and official exchange offices. Always check first.

Credit Cards. See under *Taking Money Abroad* in the *Facts at Your Fingertips* section. You might also like to know the telephone numbers to call in Paris if you lose your credit cards while there. They are:

American Express 47–08–31–21;

Diners Club 47–23–78–05;

MasterCard 43–23–42–49 in the week, 43–23–46–46 at weekends; *Visa* 42–77–11–90.

CLOSING DAYS. Some small stores and many food shops are closed on Mon. The same applies to the majority of hairdressers and barbers. Many museums close Mon. or Tues. (see separate section). Newsstands are usually closed evenings, though at main rail stations and on major streets they'll stay open till around 10 P.M.; most are closed Sun afternoons. The Drugstores, selling a wide range of goods as well as French and foreign newspapers and magazines, are open till around 1.30 A.M.

Theaters are usually closed one day a week (often Mon.) but have performances on Sun. afternoons. Many restaurants close one or two days a week (see our listings).

Small food shops and tobacconists usually open Sun. morning and you'll have no difficulty in finding material for a picnic lunch in any part of Paris.

Public holidays vary a great deal. Buy the current edition of one of the What's On publications to see which museums, theaters and exhibits are open. Restaurants closing on Sun. will usually shut on all public holidays. Department stores are often now open on at least some public holidays.

TELEPHONES. Public telephones in Paris are fairly reliable. They can be found in post offices, in many cafés and on some streets, generally attached to bus stops. The majority of public telephones now operate only with coins (50 centimes, 1 fr and 5 frs), enabling you to make calls both to France and abroad. You put the coin or coins in first, to obtain the dialing tone, and any unused coins are returned when you replace the receiver; a flashing light warns you that you must insert more coins. Full instructions for international dialing are posted up in such pay stations. The older type of telephone (often called a Taxiphone) requires *jetons* (slugs or tokens), which are bought from a café counter. You start by putting in the slug, then dial your number and press the button on the front of the phone when your party answers. You can't make international calls from these phones, and sometimes not even calls outside Paris. *Jetons* usually cost 1 fr or 1.20 frs, but may be even more. The newest system operates with a credit card, the *Télécarte,* which you can buy in tobacconists, post offices and many newsstands. Each card has a certain number of units, generally 20 or 100, and is debited automatically.

Telephone calls in France are expensive. The basic unit at our presstime was 74 centimes and international calls mount up quickly. If you want to call home, best dial direct and ask to be called back at your hotel; some post offices also have phones that can be called from elsewhere. Person-to-person *(préavis)* calls for a stated time must be made through the operator, who will undoubtedly encourage you to dial direct instead! *PCV* (collect/reverse charge) calls no longer exist within France; check locally to see if this applies to international calls. Hotel switchboards can put in long-distance calls, but are notorious in

Europe for their high mark-ups, anything up to 300%, so be warned. For calls put through by post office operators you'll likely have to stand in line for a long time.

A number of changes were implemented in the French telephone system at the end of 1985. All Paris numbers are now eight-figure numbers. If you have been given a seven-figure number, or find one in an old list, merely add a 4 in front of it. This also applies to the inner suburbs, such as Boulogne, or Neuilly, or Saint-Mandé. To dial from another Paris or inner-suburb number, dial the number with no prefix. To dial from a number outside Paris, dial 16, wait for a second tone, then dial 1 and the eight-figure number.

Provincial numbers and Paris outer-suburb numbers are now also eight-figures. They are formed from the old number (six or seven figures) plus the former area code (one or two figures). To obtain a provincial number from Paris or the inner suburbs, dial 16, wait for the second tone, then dial the eight digits. To phone from anywhere *outside* Paris and the inner suburbs to anywhere else *except* Paris and the inner suburbs (even to a number within the same town or area) merely dial the eight-figure number—do *not* use the 16 prefix.

The number to dial for the international network is 19. This will give you a second tone, after which you must dial the country code, followed by the area code and then your party's number. The code for the U.S. is 1, for the U.K. 44.

Call charges inside France have a complicated colour coding. The point to remember is that calls are cheaper after 6.30 P.M. Mon.–Fri., Sat. P.M. and Sun. and public holidays all day; they are now cheaper still at certain times of day (ask for a leaflet at post offices). Calls to the U.S. and Canada are cheaper between 10 P.M. and 10 A.M. French time, and all day on Sun. and French public holidays. Calls to the U.K. are cheaper 9.30 P.M. to 8 A.M., and again on Sun. and French public holidays.

 MAIL. Stamps can be bought either at post offices or at the cigarette counter in any café displaying the red TABAC sign outside. Paris post offices are open 8 A.M.–7 P.M. Mon. to Fri., 8–12 Sat.; on Sun., the main post office in each *arrondissement* is open 8–12. Paris has one post office that is open round the clock, at 52 rue du Louvre, 1er—be prepared to stand in line for some time in the tourist season. The post office at 71 av. des Champs-Elysées, 8e is open longer hours than usual: 8 A.M.–11.30 P.M. Mon. to Sat., 10–12 and 2–8 P.M. Sun. *Telegrams* and *cables* can be sent by telephone at any time of the day or night; call 42–33–21–11 for telegrams sent in English. They can also be sent at night from the rue du Louvre post office or the telegram office at 8 pl. de la Bourse, 2e.

At our presstime the following postal rates were operating, but we advise you to check locally, as rises occur frequently: *Letters* weighing up to 20g (¾ oz) cost 2.20 frs within France and to all EEC countries except Britain, Ireland and Denmark, for which the rate is 2.50 frs, and 3.10 frs to all other countries by surface mail. *Postcards* cost 1.80 frs to France, all EEC countries, Canada (surface mail) and Switzerland, no matter how much you write. *Airmail* to the

U.S. is 4.05 for 5g, plus 70 centimes per 5g extra. Aerograms to all destinations cost 4.00. Airmail paper is a good investment, as postage mounts up quickly, but note that mail to the U.K. goes airmail anyway.

TIPPING. Tipping is a common custom in France, as in most of Europe, and many people providing you with a service will expect a tip. However, a service charge is automatically added to your bill in hotels, restaurants and cafés and there is no need to leave anything on top of that unless you wish to demonstrate that you have been particularly pleased with the service offered. In practice many people leave a small amount in the saucer with the bill in restaurants and cafés—often merely some of the small change returned to them—and if you stay more than two or three days in a hotel it is customary to leave something for the chambermaid (say a round figure approximating to 10 frs per day). Incidentally, you can check whether or not the service charge is included in prices posted in hotel rooms or on menus by looking for the words *prix nets* or *service compris* (service included). If they're not there, bear in mind that the bill you receive will have 12 or 15 percent added.

In expensive hotels you'll probably use the services of a baggage porter (bell boy) and the hotel porter or *concierge,* and possibly the telephonist. All of them will expect a tip. Reckon on around 10 frs per item of baggage for the baggage porter, but the other tips will depend on how much you've used their services—instinct must be your guide here. In moderate and inexpensive hotels you'll be lucky to find anyone to carry your baggage and the only person you'll come across regularly is the receptionist, who need not be tipped unless you ask for a special service.

In hotels providing room service, give 5 frs to the waiter, but this does not apply to breakfast served in your room. If the chambermaid does some pressing or laundering for you, give her 5 frs on top of the charge made.

In restaurant and nightclub cloakrooms with an attendant give 5 frs, but there is no need to proffer anything if the waiter merely helps you in to your coat. Give washroom attendants 5 frs. Washrooms at rail stations normally have a fixed charge (generally around 5 frs), which you'll see posted up. The same applies to theater cloakrooms.

Anyone showing you to your seat, in theaters, opera houses or movies, and at sports events such as tennis tournaments, should be given a tip of not less than 5 frs.—except in some state or municipal theaters where tipping is not allowed.

If you're lucky enough to find a rail porter (they're a dying breed in France) you'll notice a metal tag pinned to his overalls stating the fixed charge per item of baggage, which will range from 6–10 frs depending on the station. If he's been particularly helpful, add 2–5 frs extra.

Give 10–15 percent to taxi drivers and to hairdressers (though the service charge is included in many salons now—if in doubt, ask). Museum guides should be given 5–10 frs if you've taken a full guided tour; it is also standard practice to tip couriers if you've taken an excursion, and the driver too if he's been helpful—the amount will depend on the length of your tour, the number of people you're traveling with and so on.

ELECTRICITY. Paris has officially finished the change-over to 220 volts (50 cycle), though if you're staying in a private home make sure that your hosts aren't still on 110 volts. Apparatus marked 220/240 volts will operate without problems in Paris, but not as efficiently as back home. A series of adapters to fit the wide range of lamp sockets and wall sockets in France will prove a godsend. Hotels with modern bathrooms will have special sockets for razors only, as will overnight trains. Best have an ordinary razor to hand in case of emergencies, though.

CONVENIENT CONVENIENCES. Visitors to France will soon discover that plumbing is not the nation's strong point. Even private homes seem to be remarkably short of toilets and many cafés and some restaurants (including some fashionable and expensive ones) still have toilets of the hole-in-the-ground variety. Sad to say, really clean and properly ventilated toilets are the exception rather than the rule and those in museums, métro stations and underground garages are best avoided. Those in rail stations generally have an attendant (and a fixed fee, around 2 frs) and are slightly better, and those at gas stations on motorways are usually reasonably clean. It is normal practice to have at least a coffee or a drink before using the toilet in cafés. The good news is that a self-cleaning coin-operated public lavatory called a *Sanisette* (now copied in London, incidentally) has blossomed in the streets of Paris. Distinctly more hygienic than most alternatives, but make sure not to let children use them alone, as there have been some nasty accidents.

Getting Around

ORIENTATION. If you're staying more than a day or so, the first essential step is to buy a booklet called the *Plan de Paris par arrondissement,* which contains good maps of each district or *arrondissement* and lists places of interest, post offices, churches etc. with map references; it also has public transport maps. It is on sale at newsstands, in most bookstores, stationers and drugstores. But you must bear in mind that street names are listed alphabetically under the *first* part of the name. Thus avenue Franklin-Roosevelt and rue du Général Leclerc will be found under F and G respectively (*not* R or L as you might expect).

Paris is a small city, as capitals go, so you may well find you can walk to many places. Our district maps will help you pinpoint places of interest (see *Exploring Paris* section). Otherwise you can travel by public transportation—bus or subway—or by taxi, or of course you may have your own car.

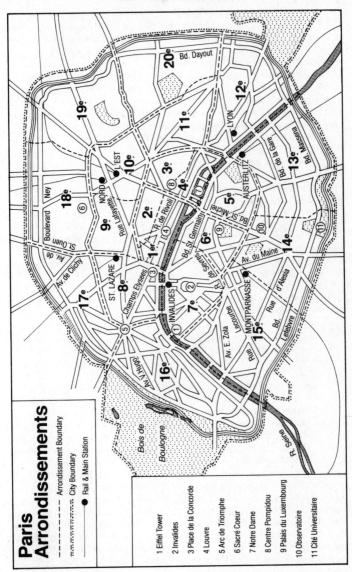

Paris Arrondissements

- – – – Arrondissement Boundary
- ····· City Boundary
- ● Rail & Main Station

1 Eiffel Tower
2 Invalides
3 Place de la Concorde
4 Louvre
5 Arc de Triomphe
6 Sacré Coeur
7 Notre Dame
8 Centre Pompidou
9 Palais du Luxembourg
10 Observatoire
11 Cité Universitaire

THE ARRONDISSEMENTS. One thing you'll soon be aware of in Paris is that the city is divided into twenty districts (called *arrondissements*), each with its own *mairie* or town hall. You won't have any difficulty remembering them, because they're simply called 'the first', 'the second' and so on. (Apart from the first, which is *le premier,* you just add the letters *ième* on to the number—*deuxième, troisième* etc.) You'll find that people are always talking in terms of these districts, and will say: "I live in the seventh," or "There are lots of new restaurants in the tenth these days.' If you're studying a list of museums or suchlike, don't be puzzled because it doesn't seem to be in any apparent sequence, alphabetical or otherwise—it'll be arranged in the order of the *arrondissements,* though this won't be mentioned. We give here a simple plan of the way the *arrondissements* are arranged; but if you want to have more details buy the pocket-sized and very useful *Plan de Paris par Arrondissement,* with each district given its own map (or occasionally two maps for the large ones). With this you'll soon get the feel of the capital's geography.

To help you get to grips with the system, we have pinpointed below the features of each district that you might like to bear in mind. As you'll see from the map, the numbering starts in the heart of Paris, then spirals round like a swiss roll or a snail shell, finishing up with the *vingtième* in the far east. To the west lie two suburbs that are normally thought of as part of Paris proper, Boulogne-Billancourt and Neuilly-sur-Seine.

The **first** includes the Louvre and the Palais-Royal, the Tuileries Garden and the elegant Place Vendôme, the Ritz and the Comédie Française; it crosses the Seine by the Pont-Neuf and contains half of the Ile de la Cité, with the Sainte-Chapelle. This is tourist country *par excellence,* and even the area round the former Les Halles food market, once rather working-class, is now distinctly chic. Many of the capital's Superdeluxe hotels are here, close to the expensive shops in the rue de Rivoli area; but you'll also find a number of Inexpensive hotels in the side streets.

The **second** lies north of the first and can be divided roughly into two halves: the Opéra area, the avenue de l'Opéra and the exclusive rue de la Paix, with its jewelers' shops, plus the major banks, the stock exchange *(Bourse)* and the famous Bibliothèque Nationale; this area has quite a few expensive hotels and is also full of theaters and movie houses; the other half, to the east, is much less exclusive and has many reasonably priced hotels for those who like browsing in the expensive areas but want to keep hotel costs to a minimum.

The **third** is a good hunting ground for those who love exploring old Paris—it includes part of the renovated Marais district, with the National Archives and the excellent Musée Carnavalet, but there are few hotels here suitable for foreign tourists. The **fourth** covers the rest of the Marais, with the beautiful place des Vosges, but it also includes the Beaubourg/Pompidou Center in an area that is becoming trendier every day, with attractive little restaurants and boutiques, and the Hôtel de Ville with its popular department stores (La Samaritaine and the Bazar de l'Hôtel de Ville), plus the other half of the Ile de la Cité, including

Notre-Dame and the whole of the delightful Ile St-Louis, a wonderful place to stay if you can get into one of its peaceful hotels.

The first four *arrondissements* are north of the Seine (or on the Right Bank, as the Parisians say), but when we come to the **fifth** we have to cross over to the Left (i.e. south) Bank and the Latin Quarter. Here we are in student territory, with the Sorbonne and the Panthéon, the lively boulevard St-Michel and, further away, the Jardin des Plantes; there are many Inexpensive hotels in the streets around the Sorbonne, and you'll never go short of food in a district that is crammed with restaurants, ranging from intimate candlelit places to bustling student-jammed cafeterias, and including the busy rue Mouffetard/place de la Contrescarpe area, which is a center of youthful nightlife. We would advise women traveling alone not to stay around the place Saint-Michel.

The **sixth** is still the Latin Quarter, but is rather more elegant; resolutely artistic and intellectual, it has the lion's share of the capital's bookshops, smart little antique shops, 'in' nightclubs and literary cafés. Plenty of hotels here, to suit every pocketbook. The **seventh** is generally thought of as a residential area (and a very exclusive one), but it also contains the great majority of the ministries and government buildings, as well as the Eiffel Tower and the Invalides, with Napoleon's tomb; here, too, is the new Musée d'Orsay, devoted to 19th- and early-20th-century art. Hotels in this part of Paris are usually quiet and discreet.

The **eighth** is neither quiet nor discreet, but it is very chic and very expensive on the whole—not surprising when you realize that the Lido and the Crazy Horse are here, not to mention half the capital's luxury hotels, and of course the Champs-Elysées, that mecca of wealth. But this is a large area and it also includes the place de la Concorde and the place de la Madeleine, the luxury shops on the faubourg St.-Honoré, the American and British embassies—and the presidential palace. To the north lie the residential area around the delightful Parc Monceau—a good area for quiet hotels and distinguished restaurants—and the less elegant streets round the St-Lazare station, with quite a few well-run hotels in the medium price range.

The **ninth** is a smaller district west of the eighth and north of the second. It's the area for serious shoppers (the smart department stores are here), theater and opera lovers (it has the Opéra and the major commercial theaters too), and for business; pleasure is more in evidence in the north, where brash Pigalle lies. The **tenth** is due east of the ninth and is known to most tourists as the place where they start or end their travels—at the Gare du Nord or the Gare de l'Est rail stations. The eleventh, twelfth and thirteenth are off the usual tourist map: the **eleventh** is very much the people's Paris, a densely populated area radiating out from the place de la République; thanks to the Gare de Lyon, the **twelfth** has several good hotels, mostly used by businessmen or people spending the night before taking a train south; the **thirteenth** is a large district in the southeast, with huge tower blocks, some little provincial-type houses, and Austerlitz rail station.

The **fourteenth** is intellectual and student country—Montparnasse and the Cité Universitaire—but also has the gigantic Tour Montparnasse, the deluxe

Méridien Montparnasse and the still-smart Coupole. There are many fashionable little restaurants here. The **fifteenth** is a mixture, with narrow little streets
full of small shops but also huge new apartment blocks overlooking the Seine,
and some of the capital's modern luxury hotels, while the **sixteenth** is still, as
it always has been, a fashionable residential area; it includes the Bois de Boulogne, the village-like Auteuil district and the aristocratic avenue Foch. There
are some comfortable hotels, with good old-fashioned service.

The **seventeenth,** too, has this type of hotel, usually in the quiet and dignified
residential avenues, but it also has vast modern hotels grouped around the
international congress center at the Porte Maillot. The Sacré-Coeur is the major
landmark in the **eighteenth,** which covers the Montmartre district (more sex
shops than can-can these days). Finally the **nineteenth** and the **twentieth,** in the
northeast and east, are working-class districts with no tourist hotels, though
there are some good meat restaurants near the old slaughterhouses in the
nineteenth.

As for the two inner suburbs, **Boulogne** has smart residential streets inhabited by wealthy middle-class families, as well as more modest small shopkeepers,
while aristocratic **Neuilly** is increasingly becoming a major business area, with
many advertising agencies and the headquarters of several multinational companies, but it still has attractive village-like corners and leafy residential avenues.

 BY MÉTRO. Paris's subway or underground system,
known as the métro (an abbreviation for Métropolitain),
is one of the world's best, providing a fast and efficient
service. Trains run at 90-second intervals during the day
and still pretty frequently at night, with first services starting at termini at
around 5.30 A.M., last services reaching termini at around 1.15 A.M. What's more,
it's really easy to find your way around. Our map on pp. 78-9 will help you get
your bearings, but there's a large clear map at the entrance to every station, and
inside many of them you'll find a handy push-button map enabling you to find
out at a glance the quickest way to get to your destination: your route lights up
when you press the knob opposite your station. Some stations now have machines producing cards telling you the quickest way to get to specific places—
museums, historic buildings and so on.

Stops are close together and the system is shallow, with few time-consuming
journeys up and down escalators. There is only one ticket, which may be bought
singly or in blocks (*carnets*) of ten. At certain times of day you may use
second-class tickets in first class. Check locally, as times tend to vary. You may
make as many connections (*correspondances*) as you like on a single ticket.
Tickets can be bought from the ticket window in stations, at some rail stations
and from the tobacconists counter in TABAC cafés; there are also a few slot
machines in the street nowadays. You put your ticket into the machine at the
entrance to platforms to enable you to reach the platform. Keep it, as inspectors
sometimes come through the train, but you won't otherwise need to show it on
alighting.

Each métro line has a number, but is normally known by the names of the stations at either end. Thus line no. 1, which goes from east to west through the middle of Paris, is known as Vincennes–Neuilly, because it goes from the Château de Vincennes to the Pont de Neuilly. That's what you should ask for if you're stuck, and that's also what you should look for when making a connection—the names are clearly visible on the orange illuminated signs on platforms in junction stations. So when you study the métro map, always look for the last station on the line you're planning to take

By Express Métro (RER). Paris now has an express métro system called the *Réseau Express Régional* or *RER*. Fast, modern trains take commuters and others out to the suburbs and to nearby towns such as Saint-Germain-en-Laye or Versailles. But the RER is also very convenient for inner-city traveling, as it is now fully slotted in to the ordinary métro system and you can use métro tickets for all journeys that do not go beyond city limits. For instance a journey from the Place Charles-de-Gaulle/Etoile to the Gare de Lyon on line A is a real time-saver. There are three lines, labeled A, B and C, and routes are clearly marked on métro maps.

For journeys outside city limits you must purchase your ticket from one of the ticket-vending machines inside stations, pressing buttons to indicate your destination, single or return, and so on. All tickets must be fed into machines to get you on to the right platform, as in the métro, but *keep your ticket handy*, as you will need to feed it back into another machine to enable you to leave the system, or to change from the métro to the RER or vice-versa. When you reach the end of your journey the machine lights up with the word *Passez* and swallows up your ticket; if you're continuing, you'll see the words *Reprenez votre ticket* ("Take your ticket back") and you should do just that. It may sound complicated, but you'll soon get the hang of it.

 BY BUS. Paris has a good daytime bus network but only a few lines run in the evenings and many do not run on Sundays or public holidays. Ask at métro stops for route maps, with running times clearly indicated. As Paris has a number of bus lanes, the buses are fairly speedy except during rush hours, but naturally not as quick as the métro. But they're a good way of seeing the city, and as each has a map of the route inside, with each stop marked, you needn't worry about missing your stop. Ring the bell to ask the driver to stop if the red sign *Arrêt demandé* ("Stop requested") isn't already lit up.

Second-class métro tickets are used on the buses. *Carnets* cannot be bought on the buses, so you'll have to buy single tickets if you're not already equipped. For short journeys a single ticket is enough, for longer ones you'll need two, or even four in the case of the circular PC (Petite Ceinture) line running right round the city. Clear route maps at all bus stops indicate how many tickets you'll need.

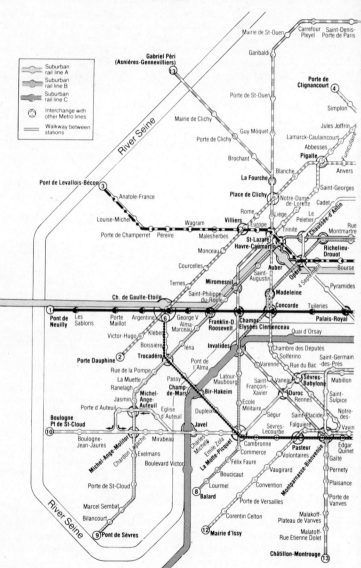

Suburban rail line A
Suburban rail line B
Suburban rail line C
Interchange with other Metro lines
Walkway between stations

River Seine

Gabriel Péri
(Asnières-Gennevilliers) ⑬

Mairie de St-Ouen   Carrefour   Saint-Denis-
                     Pleyel   Porte de Paris

Garibaldi

Porte de Clignancourt ④

Porte de St-Ouen   Simplon

Mairie de Clichy   Guy Môquet   Jules Joffrin
                                      Lamarck-Caulaincourt
Porte de Clichy   Abbesses
                        Brochant   Pigalle   Funiculaire
Pont de Levallois-Bécon ③   Blanche   Anvers
           Anatole-France   La Fourche
                                                     Saint-Georges
  Louise-Michel   Place de Clichy   Notre-Dame-
                         Rome   de-Lorette   Cadet
Porte de Champerret Péreire Wagram Villiers Liège Le   Rue
                         Malesherbes Europe Trinité Peletier Montmartre
                Monceau   St-Lazare   Richelieu-
                           Havre-Caumartin   Drouot
         Courcelles   Saint-   Auber   Bourse
                               Augustin Opéra
      Ternes   Miromesnil   4 Septembre Pyramides
                  Saint-Philippe- Madeleine
   Ch. de Gaulle-Etoile du-Roule Concorde Tuileries
① Pont de Les   Porte   Argentine ⑥ George V Franklin-D. Champs- Palais-Royal
  Neuilly Sablons Maillot   Alma- Roosevelt Elysées Clemenceau
                                     Marceau
           Victor-Hugo Kléber   Quai d'Orsay
② Porte Dauphine Boissière Iéna   Invalides Chambre des Députés Saint-Germain
                  Trocadéro   Varenne Rue du Bac -des-Prés
      Rue de la Pompe Pont de   Latour- Saint- Vaneau Sèvres- Mabillon
      La Muette   l'Alma   Maubourg François-   Babylone
      Ranelagh Passy   Xavier Duroc Rennes Saint-
Michel- Jasmin Champ- Bir-Hakeim Ecole   Rennes   Sulpice
Ange-   de-Mars   Militaire Ségur Saint-Placide Notre-
Auteuil Eglise   Duplex   Sèvres- Falguière des-
  Porte d'Auteuil d'Auteuil Javel   Lecourbe   Vavin
⑩ Boulogne   Edgar
  Pt de St-Cloud Boulogne- Mirabeau Charles Cambronne Pasteur Quinet
  Michel-Ange-Molitor Jean-Jaurès Michels Emile Zola Volontaires Gaîté
            Chardon Lagache Exelmans   La Motte-Picquet Montparnasse-Bienvenüe Pernety
                  Boulevard Victor Commerce   Vaugirard Plaisance
      Porte de St-Cloud   Félix Faure   Porte de
                      ⑧ Boucicaut Convention   Vanves
      Marcel Sembat   Lourmel   Malakoff-
                   ⑧ Balard Porte de Versailles Plateau de Vanves
      Bilancourt   Corentin Celton Malakoff-
                                                     Rue Etienne Dolet
⑨ Pont de Sèvres
River Seine   ⑫ Mairie d'Issy   Châtillon-Montrouge ⑬

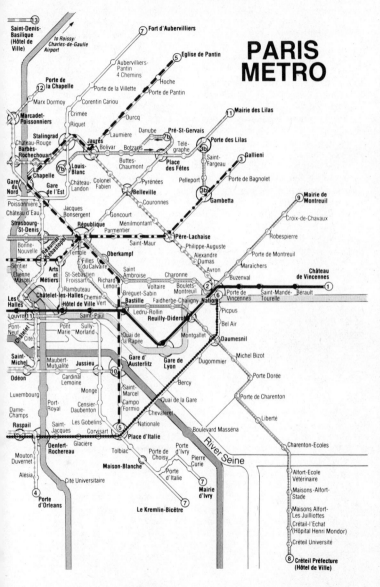

PARIS METRO

TICKET BARGAINS. The Paris Public Transportation System (RATP) offers a number of season tickets, but the only one likely to be of use to tourists is the *carte orange* or *monthly orange pass,* which is valid for all journeys on the métro, within city limits on the RER and on the buses. The pass can be obtained at métro or rail stations—take along a passport-sized photo—free of charge, and you then buy a monthly coupon, which looks like a métro ticket, but is orange in colour instead of yellow. You must copy the number of your pass on to the coupon, or you may get fined. More expensive coupons are available for those regularly traveling outside city limits. If you're planning to do a lot of traveling you may well find that a *carte orange* is worth it even for a visit lasting only a couple of weeks. And it's much more convenient than having to keep buying tickets.

In the métro, slot your coupon into the machine as usual. But on the buses, show the whole pass to the driver when you enter: *do not slot the coupon into the machine as that will cancel it for good.*

Another bargain is the *Paris Sesame* pass, which is valid for 2, 4 or 7 consecutive days, entitling you to unlimited travel on the métro and RER (first class) and on all RATP bus lines in the city, plus a few outside. Again you slot it into the machines in the métro or RER, but must simply show it to the driver in buses. You may buy the pass before leaving home at French National Tourist Offices. When in Paris, go either to one of the RATP's tourist offices, at 53bis quai des Grands-Augustins, 6e or 20 pl. de la Madeleine, 1er (on the right when you're facing the Madeleine church); or to one of over 50 métro or RER stations (lists posted up on métro platforms); or to one of the main rail stations; or to Roissy/CDG airport (terminal 1, gate 28) or Orly airport (both Ouest and Sud); at the Banque Nationale de Paris at 2 blvd. des Italiens, 2e or place Clichy, 18e; or the Crédit Commercial de France, 115 av. des Champs-Elysées, 8e. Take your passport for identification.

BY TAXI. Taxis are often a problem in Paris, as at many times there aren't enough of them to meet the demand. A taxi with its sign lighted is free, but many drivers are reluctant to stop in the street. Better make for a taxi rank *(tête de ligne)* with the blue-and-white TAXI sign. Cruising taxis may not be hailed within 20 meters of a rank. If your hotel porter is willing to call a taxi for you, take advantage of this—it'll be well worth the tip he'll expect. Taxis picking you up at rail stations or airports are entitled to make an extra charge of 4 frs or thereabouts. Baggage charges are also made. You should note that few drivers are willing to take more than three passengers at a time, so a party of four will need to pay for two taxis. Fares are based on mileage and are divided into three zones: inner-city; inner suburbs; and outer suburbs (with lower rates here if you keep the taxi for the return journey). Daytime (6.30 A.M. to 9 P.M.) rates at our presstime were 2.39 frs, 3.72 frs and 5 frs per kilometer respectively. Nightime rates were 3.72 frs, 5 frs and 5 frs respectively. Waiting time was charged at 65 frs per hour. It is customary to tip the driver around 10–15 per cent on top of the fare. These prices may be increased by early '88.

Saloon cars without meters outside rail stations, nightclubs and hotels are not registered taxicabs, may not be insured and can charge you anything you let them get away with. If you still decide to take one, make sure to agree the price before you step inside.

In 1985 a new venture was started: taxi scooters to beat traffic jams. They have been a success, though few are available as yet.

 BY CAR. Bringing your own car requires only proof of third-party insurance. You may use your home driving license for a period of one year. For information, contact your travel agency or automobile association: *Royal Automobile Club,* 8 pl. Vendôme, 75001 Paris; *Automobile Club de France,* 6 pl. de la Concorde, 75008 Paris.

Self-drive Cars.

Rates will vary considerably depending upon the car you choose and the length of hire. You can usually choose between unlimited mileage and a charge per kilometer. Full-insurance cover is usually extra. Your own driver's license is adequate except for long trips or international trips.

Among the internationally-known car hire firms are: *Avis,* 99 av. Charles-de-Gaulle, Neuilly-sur-Seine, Galeries Elysées-Rond-Point, 47 av. Franklin-Roosevelt, 8e, or 5 rue Bixio, 7e (central reservations tel. 46–09–92–12); *Hertz,* central reservations on 47–88–51–51, main office is at 27 rue St.-Ferdinand, 17e (45–74–97–39); and *Europcar,* central reservations on 30–43–82–82, main office at 145 av. Malakoff, 16e (45–00–08–06). All three also have service at the airports. Other firms include: *Mattei,* 205 rue de Bercy (43–46–11–50); *Citer,* 25 rue de Constantinople, 8e (tel. 45–22–17–38).

Chauffeur-driven Cars.

You can hire a car with a driver on either a time or a trip basis. You will see them lined up, displaying cards announcing their availability, in various centers frequented by tourists. Agree on the price beforehand. Most of these drivers speak English. *Chauffeurs-Assas Service,* 132 rue d'Assas, 6e (tel. 43–26–71–98) is a well-known firm.

Road and Traffic Conditions.

For those who have never driven in Paris, their first taste of the hurly-burly of the city's streets and drivers is something they are not liable to forget quickly. Parisian drivers are not noted for their scrupulous adherence to the finer points of the highway code or for gentle consideration toward their fellow road users. Their attitude might at best be considered cavalier, at worst brutal, bordering on the sadistic. They are particularly unforgiving of anyone displaying the slightest sign of weakness and have no hesitation in making full use of their horns. The difficulties are compounded by the virtual lack of all marks on the roads, the narrowness of many of them, poor surfaces and the vast number of snarling, congealing cars. Nonetheless, if you think you can survive in this maelstrom, here are some points to bear in mind.

The French drive on the right; no problem for American visitors but British drivers may find it takes them a little while to acclimatize. Normally this takes no longer than 30 minutes or so. Paris itself though is not the best place to start. Ideally somewhere a little less frenetic should be sought. The rule-of-thumb as far as traffic regulations go is: priority for traffic from the right, except on traffic circles. Similarly, when a small road crosses a main one, traffic from the right does not have priority; but it is always signalled by one of the international traffic signs (indicating STOP or GIVE WAY) with which you should be familiar. You might purchase a French *Code de la Route* from a garage when you arrive. Yellow car lights, though not obligatory, are a good idea. It is mandatory to wear seat belts in front seats for cars first registered after 1 April 1970 (which will include all rented cars). There are severe penalties for failure to do so. Flashing warning lights or a red warning triangle are also compulsory. Children under 10 may not sit in the front passenger seat.

The breathalyser (referred to in France as the *alcootest*) is a relatively recent feature in French motoring and is much feared. Heavy on-the-spot fines are common, and you can even go to prison for a first offense in extreme cases, so keep off the drink if you're driving.

Speed limit inside Paris is 60 km/hr (around 35 miles/hr).

Parking. Parking meters are now to be found in most central Parisian streets. Instead of individual meters some streets each have several meters issuing tickets to be placed on the inside of your car windshield.

Rates are about 8–12 frs per hour. It is wise to have a supply of 1 fr and 50 centime pieces on hand—the meterwomen in their periwinkle blue suits have been known to stick a ticket on your windshield between the time you park and dash to the nearest café for some change. In most places meters do not operate on Sundays or before 9 A.M. and after 7 P.M. In some streets (and usually in Paris suburbs) you do not need to pay on Saturdays either, or between 12 and 2. Outside rail stations parking time is severely limited (usually half an hour). In many areas parking is free in August: read the posted signs.

Although street parking at night is free, it is usually very hard to find space in any central area, especially in the entertainment districts on the Left Bank. It may be necessary to park in one of the many underground garages, where rates are from around 8 frs an hour. Better still—take a taxi!

Motor Fuel. Gasoline (petrol), or *essence,* costs about 5.30 frs per liter for the best grade, around 4.85 frs for the regular. Most British cars demand premium grade.

Where to Stay

Paris has a very large number of hotels, ranging from the Superdeluxe to modest spots with few modern comforts suitable only for youngsters on a tight budget. However, the eternal popularity of Paris makes it difficult to find hotel accommodations. Also, at certain times of the year (mainly spring, and September through mid-November) a long list of trade fairs, congresses, seminars and the like is held in Paris, filling the hotels to bursting. When you realize that a number of special, time-hallowed events, especially the biannual couture and ready-to-wear fashion shows and the biennial Motor Show, jampack the city's accommodations even further, you'll see why we urge you to reserve well ahead of time, particularly if you prefer to stay in small hotels. French National Tourist Offices abroad now issue a helpful calendar indicating which periods are likely to be heavily booked in the year in question. Best ask for this calendar and plan accordingly.

When deciding where to stay, you may well base your choice on what you want to do during your visit. It's therefore important to get the geography of the place into your head. We give an explanation (and plan) of the way Paris is divided into *arrondissements* on pp. 73-6.

Grades and Prices. The official French system grades hotels with stars, the category depending partly on price, but also on amenities—such as TV, or direct dialing from your room. The top grade here is L****, i.e. four-star deluxe, followed by four-star, three-star, two-star, and one-star. However, we think it more helpful to grade according to price, so we have arranged our lists by *arrondissement* and in Superdeluxe (S), Luxury (L), Expensive (E), Moderate (M) and Inexpensive (I) order.

At the (S) end of the listings, prices range from around 1,700 frs per night for a double with bathroom, to a steep 2,750 frs. (L) rates are 1,000–1,700 frs per night for a double room, (E) 600–1,000 frs, (M) 350–600 frs, and (I) 170–350 frs. We must emphasize that prices vary enormously not only within each category but also within the same hotel, and our price ranges are only approximations. One establishment, for instance, may have a couple of really special rooms costing more than the average rooms, and/or some that have fewer facilities than most of their rooms and are priced at a lower rate. Our gradings are based on the *average* price of a room; where there are major discrepancies we have indicated. But we do urge you to check very carefully before making your reservation, so that you know exactly what you will be paying—especially as prices change frequently.

In France, you pay for the room, not per person. It is increasingly common, however, for hotels to make a small extra charge (usually around 40–60 frs) if a double room is used by three people. Single rooms are becoming rare, the majority of new or renovated hotels having mostly twin-bedded rooms. In older hotels, single rooms are liable to be poky, and on a top floor.

Credit Cards. We have given information on credit card acceptance as follows—AE, American Express; DC, Diners Club; MC, MasterCard; V, Visa. These are constantly changing, so be sure to check.

About Hotels. Standards in Paris hotels vary widely. In Superdeluxe hotels you'll find service, amenities and furnishings that compare with anywhere in the world at this price range. In our last guide we said we had been noticing problems, with some hotels tempted by a constant stream of reservation requests into allowing some rooms and public areas to get distinctly shabby, causing disappointment to some of our readers. Happily, many hotels have now undertaken the extensive modernization and redecoration needed, but this has inevitably led to higher prices. Some previously 'Inexpensive' hotels are 'Expensive' this year. It's good to know that Paris has recently acquired some new groups, such as the Timhôtels, dating from the mid-eighties, which offer modern amenities and bright, attractive rooms at reasonable prices. The large modern hotels grouped round the Palais des Congrès and air terminal at the Porte Maillot naturally offer good modern facilities, but they rarely have the pleasant service and welcoming feel that is found in the longer-established places. As for the picturesque little spots on the Left Bank, it's as well to be aware that they're likely to be a bit run down as regards wiring and plumbing—but this will probably be compensated for by a friendly personal welcome. Those with modern bathrooms are liable to be small, not to say cramped—as likely as not carved out of what was once a fair-sized room.

You should also be aware that in French *salle de bain* (bathroom) does not necessarily mean it contains a bathtub. It may just have a wall shower. If you've a fondness for soaking away in plenty of hot water, specify that you want a *baignoire* (bathtub), not just a *douche* (shower).

Noise can be a problem in crowded Paris. An increasing number of hotels have double glazing, and air-conditioning is becoming more common too (we specify this in our lists). So in humid summer temperatures you may have to choose between insomnia through suffocation or noise! Much better specify a room away from the street when you make your reservation and insist on getting it when you arrive. Most buildings in Paris are built round a courtyard, so ask for a room *sur cour* (on the courtyard) rather than *sur rue* (on the street).

Another cause of insomnia can be lack of a pillow! The French favour a long bolster called a *traversin,* which is often hard and lumpy and takes quite a bit of getting used to. Take our tip and check as soon as you get to your room whether it has pillows on the bed or, more likely, in a cupboard. If not, ask for them immediately (the term is *oreillers*)—don't wait till late at night when the linen closet will be locked up and the receptionist won't have the key.

In most hotels these days you'll find someone at reception who speaks at least a little English, but don't expect chambermaids and other staff to, except in the more expensive places.

In Inexpensive hotels the price of breakfast may be included. In other categories it will probably be an extra—check the price posted up by law in the room to see if it specifies an extra charge for your *petit déjeuner.* In small, family-type hotels you can normally have breakfast in your room for no extra charge—this is a pleasant French habit that we recommend you make the most of. But this applies only to 'Continental breakfasts' of tea, coffee or chocolate accompanied by rolls or croissants, plus butter and jam or honey—all in small quantities.

Some of the newer small hotels have a breakfast room, but may still give you the option of having breakfast in your room. In Expensive hotels with a full room service you'll likely have to pay for the service, not to mention giving the waiter a tip (see our *Tipping* section). If you want extras, such as eggs or fruit juice, be prepared to pay heavily for the privilege—better still, take your breakfast in a neighborhood café with the locals!

Only a small number of Paris hotels have restaurants, and most of them are in the Superdeluxe, Luxury or Expensive category. Our lists specify if there is a restaurant. On the whole, we advise you to eat away from your hotel, unless we give particular praise to its restaurant. One of the delights of Paris is trying out some of its thousands of restaurants, and our lists give plenty of ideas to suit all tastes and pocketbooks.

First arrondissement

Intercontinental-Paris (S), 3 rue de Castiglione (tel. 42–60–37–80). 460 rooms and suites. Top floor rooms redecorated, some have jacuzzis. Wonderfully comfortable, and with excellent service. Offers an assortment of pleasant restaurants, cafeterias and grill-rooms, with openair dining summer lunchtimes. Well-placed near the Tuileries Gardens. Air-conditioned. AE, DC, MC, V.

Meurice (S), 228 rue de Rivoli (tel. 42–60–38–60). 161 rooms. Halfway between the *Ritz* and the *Crillon,* this was once known as the hotel of kings, because so many of them had stopped here; kings are scarcer now, but the hotel is still one of the top-notchers. With a grill and small bar. Air-conditioned. AE, DC, MC, V.

Ritz (S), 15 pl. Vendôme (tel. 42–60–38–30). 164 rooms and suites. Situated midway between the Opéra and the Tuileries Gardens, the *Ritz* underwent a facelift in the early 1980s after being bought by the same Egyptian family who now own London's Harrods. It has lost none of its old-world charm, however; the restaurant is good, with delicious *haute cuisine* and fabulous wines. The rooms have been redecorated from top to toe; some of the suites are named after famous guests, such as Coco Chanel, Marcel Proust, and King Edward VII of England. Two small but renowned bars, a pretty courtyard garden, and secretarial service available. Air-conditioned. Now has pool too. AE, DC, MC, V.

Castille (L), 37 rue Cambon (tel. 42–61–55–20). 76 rooms, all with excellent bathrooms. The Castille's 1925 decor has been renovated, and the hotel now has some well-equipped duplexes. It is in a convenient location just across from the Ritz, and between La Madeleine and the Tuileries gardens; there's a bar, and a good restaurant, *Relais de Castille.* AE, DC, MC, V.

Jolly Hôtel Lotti (L), 7 rue de Castiglione (tel. 42–60–37–34). 130 rooms and suites. A famous name for a hotel that is now completely renovated; rooms at the front can be noisy. Restaurant and bar. AE, DC, MC, V.

Louvre-Concorde (L), pl. André-Malraux (tel. 42–61–56–01). 223 rooms, 213 with bath. Just by the Comédie-Française and the Palais-Royal. Restaurant and bar. AE, DC, MC, V.

Duminy-Vendôme (E), 3 rue du Mont-Thabor (tel. 42–60–32–80). 79 rooms, all with bath or shower. Recently renovated and expanded. Small garden. AE, DC, V.

Mayfair (E), 3 rue Rouget-de-l'Isle (tel. 42–60–38–14). 53 rooms, all with bath or shower. On a quiet side street off the rue de Rivoli. AE, DC, MC, V.

Normandy (E), 7 rue de l'Echelle (tel. 42–60–30–21). 120 rooms, all with bath. Comfortable. Restaurant and wood-paneled bar. AE, DC, MC, V.

Novotel Paris Les Halles (E), pl. Marguerite-de-Navarre (tel. 42–21–31–31). 285 rooms, all with bath or shower. In the heart of the renovated Les Halles district. Air-conditioned. Restaurant (light meals available 6 A.M.–midnight), bar. AE, DC, MC, V.

Régina (E), 2 pl. des Pyramides (tel. 42–60–31–10). 130 rooms, all with bath. Facing Tuileries. Restaurant and bar. AE, DC, MC, V.

Continent (M), 30 rue du Mont-Thabor (tel. 42–60–75–32). 28 rooms, 25 with bath or shower. Just behind the rue de Rivoli. AE, V.

Londres Stockholm (M), 13 rue St.-Roch (tel. 42–60–15–62). 28 rooms, 26 with bath or shower. Conveniently placed near the Palais-Royal.

Violet (M), 7 rue Jean-Lantier (tel. 42–33–45–38). 30 rooms, all with bath or shower. Attractive rooms. Close to the pl. du Châtelet. AE, DC, MC, V.

Timhôtel Le Louvre (M), 4 rue Croix-des-Petits-Champs (tel. 42–60–34–86). 56 rooms all with bath or shower. Member of good new chain. AE, DC, MC, V.

Family (I), 35 rue Cambon (tel. 42–61–54–84). 25 rooms, 22 with bath or shower. Friendly—has long-established clientele. A few (M) rooms.

Palais (I), 2 quai de la Mégisserie (tel. 42–36–98–25). 19 rooms, a few with bath or shower. Close to the Seine and opposite the Sainte-Chapelle on the Ile de la Cité. Adequate.

Second arrondissement

Westminster (S), 13 rue de la Paix (tel. 42–61–57–46). 102 rooms, all with bath or shower. Completely renovated. Restaurant, bar. Air-conditioned. AE, DC, MC, V.

Edouard-VII (L), 39 av. de l'Opéra (tel. 42–61–56–90). 100 rooms, all but 7 with bath or shower. Close to the Opéra. Has a good restaurant, the *Delmonico*. AE, DC, V.

Opéra d'Antin l'Horset (E), 18 rue d'Antin (tel. 47–42–13–01). 60 rooms, 52 with shower. A member of the well-run Horset chain, well-placed for the Opéra and the big department stores. AE, DC, MC, V.

Choiseul-Opéra (M), 1 rue Daunou (tel. 42–61–70–41). 43 rooms, all with bath or shower. On the same street, near the Opéra, as the celebrated Harry's Bar, AE, DC, MC.

Cusset (M), 95 rue de Richelieu (tel. 42–97–48–90). 115 rooms, 100 with bath or shower. In the Bourse area. Bar. MC, V.

Gaillon-Opéra (M), 9 rue Gaillon (tel. 47–42–47–74). 26 rooms, all with bath or shower. Well situated close to Opéra. Bar. AE, DC, MC, V.

Third arrondissement

Pavillon de la Reine (L), 28 pl. des Vosges (tel. 42–77–96–40). 49 rooms, all with bath or shower. On the famous square; newly opened, with a peaceful garden. AE, DC, MC, V.

Marais (M), 2bis rue Commines (tel. 48–87–78–27). 38 rooms, all with bath or shower. Rooms small but comfortable; some communicating rooms for parents with children AE, V.

Fourth arrondissement

Deux-Iles (E), 59 rue St.-Louis-en-l'Ile (tel. 43–26–13–35). 17 rooms, all with bath or shower. Attractive small hotel in a 17th-century house on the Ile St.-Louis, with bar and sitting-room in the old cellars.

Lutèce (E), 65 rue St.-Louis-en-l'Ile (tel. 43–26–23–52). 23 rooms, all with bath or shower. Small, peaceful and delightful hotel on the Ile St.-Louis. Some rooms are duplexes.

Bretonnerie (M), 22 rue Ste.-Croix-de-la-Bretonnerie (tel. 48–87–77–63). 30 rooms, all with bath or shower. 17th-century building near the Hôtel de Ville, Pompidou Center, and the Marais. Some rooms with antiques. Bar. MC.

Place des Vosges (M), 12 rue Birague (tel. 42–72–60–46). 16 rooms, all with bath or shower. Small and pleasant; just by the pl. des Vosges. AE, DC, MC, V.

Saint-Louis (M), 75 rue St.-Louis-en-l'Ile (tel. 46–34–04–80). 21 rooms, 17 with bath or shower. Attractive rooms on five floors—the top story has a marvelous view—with good modern bathrooms. Good value (some (I) singles).

Vieux Marais (M), 8 rue du Platre (tel. 42–78–47–22). 30 rooms. Charming hotel, with small but very clean rooms. No restaurant. MC.

Célestins (I), 1 rue Charles-V (tel. 48–87–87–04). 15 small but pretty rooms all with shower. On a quiet street in the south of the Marais, near the Seine.

Fifth arrondissement

Colbert (E), 7 rue de l'Hôtel Colbert (tel. 43–25–85–65). 40 rooms, all with bath or shower. By the river, just opposite Notre-Dame, an 18th-century building with attractive, smallish rooms. AE, V.

Collège de France (M), 7 rue Thénard (tel. 43–26–78–36). 29 rooms, all with bath or shower. Deep in the Latin Quarter. Some rooms have oak beams. AE.

Avenir (I), 52 rue Gay-Lussac (tel. 43–54–76–60). 44 rooms, only 7 with bath or shower. A modest budget hotel with very low prices. On six floors, though no elevator.

Esmeralda (I), 4 rue St.-Julien-le-Pauvre (tel. 43–54–19–20). 19 rooms, 16 with bath or shower. 17th-century building, with smallish rooms, but pleasantly furnished. Just by the pretty square Viviani opposite Notre-Dame.

Museum (I), 9 rue Buffon (tel. 43–31–51–90). 24 rooms. Just behind the Jardin des Plantes and near the Austerlitz station. Simple but clean. V.

Sorbonne (I), 6 rue Victor-Cousin (tel. 43–54–58–08). 37 rooms, all with bath or shower. Some (M) rooms. AE, DC, MC.

Sixth arrondissement

L'Hôtel Guy-Louis-Duboucheron (S), 13 rue des Beaux-Arts (tel. 43–25–27–22). 27 rooms, all with bath. Attractive, and very "in." Furnished with antiques, including Mistinguett's mirror-lined bed. (You can also sleep in the room where Oscar Wilde died!) Restaurant, bar. Air-conditioned. AE.

Lutétia-Concorde (L), 45 blvd. Raspail (tel. 45–44–38–10). 293 rooms, all with bath or shower. Near Bon Marché department store, with a pleasant atmosphere and good, old-fashioned service. Renovated from top to toe in the mid-1980s under the eagle eye of famous fashion-designer Sonia Rykiel, whose designs are fabulously art deco, and supremely elegant. Restaurant and bar. Some rooms at (S) rates. Air-conditioned. AE, DC, MC, V.

Relais Christine (L), 3 rue Christine (tel. 43–26–71–80). 51 rooms, all with bath. 16th-century cloisters converted into a delightful hotel in St.-Germain-des-Prés. Good service. Bar. AE, DC, MC, V.

L'Abbaye Saint-Germain (E), 10 rue Cassette (tel. 45–44–38–11). 45 rooms, all with bath or shower. Quiet and attractive hotel in former monastery.

Angleterre (E), 44 rue Jacob (tel. 42–60–34–72). 30 rooms, all with bath or shower. Once the home of the British Ambassador, and Hemingway used to live here too. Excellent service, traditional. Highly recommended. AE, DC, V.

Littré (E), 9 rue Littré (tel. 45–44–38–68). 96 rooms, all with bath or shower. Popular with the wealthier publishers. Restaurant. AE, MC, V.

Madison (E), 143 blvd. St.-Germain (tel. 43–29–72–50). 55 rooms, all with bath or shower. In a tiny square facing the church. The front rooms have a delightful view but are rather noisy. Extensively modernized and redecorated in 1986. Bar. AE, V.

Odéon (E), 3 rue de l'Odéon (tel. 43–25–90–67). 34 rooms, all with bath. Apparently this mansion once belonged to Madame de Pompadour. Bar. AE, V.

Le Sainte Beuve (E), 9 rue Sainte-Beuve (tel. 45–48–20–07). 23 rooms, all with bath. Newcomer on the scene. Fine bathrooms; excellent breakfasts, plus 24-hour room service. Best rooms on the top floor; some apartments available. Delightful bar. AE, MC, V.

Avenir (M), 65 rue Madame (tel. 45–48–84–54). 35 rooms, all with bath or shower. Quiet, well-run hotel. Has been extensively modernized. AE, MC, V.

Bréa (M), 14 rue Bréa (tel. 43–54–76–21). 21 rooms, all with bath or shower. An old favorite, now renovated. AE, V.

Marronniers (M), 21 rue Jacob (tel. 43–25–30–60). 37 rooms, all with bath or shower. Quiet, with a delightful courtyard garden. Light lunches served in bar or garden.

Pas-de-Calais (M), 59 rue des Sts.-Pères (tel. 45–48–78–74). 41 rooms, all with bath or shower. Has been here since the early-19th century and remains popular. Built around a tiny courtyard, but try to get a room away from the street.

Saints-Pères (M), 65 rue des Sts.-Pères (tel. 45–44–50–00). 37 rooms, all with bath or shower. An old favorite. A few (E) suites.

Seine (M), 52 rue de Seine (tel. 46–34–22–80). 30 rooms, all with bath or shower. Well-placed, in the heart of Saint-Germain-des-Prés. AE, DC, V.

Académies (I), 15 rue de la Grande-Chaumière (tel. 43–26–66–44). 21 rooms, 17 with bath.

Principautés-Unies (I), 42 rue de Vaugirard (tel. 46–34–11–80). 29 rooms, 25 with bath or shower. Some suites with mini-kitchen. A few (M) rooms. Closed Aug.

Saint-André-des-Arts (I), 66 rue St.-André-des-Arts (tel. 43–26–96–16). 32 rooms, 28 with bath or shower. Close to pl. St.-Michel, on pedestrians-only street. Modest but very conveniently sited.

Studio (I), 4 rue du Vieux Colombier (tel. 45–48–31–81). 34 well-renovated rooms with bath. In the heart of Saint-Germain-des-Prés.

Vieux Paris (I), 9 rue Gît-le-Coeur (tel. 43–54–41–66). 21 rooms, 14 with bath or shower. On a picturesque street close to the Seine and pl. St.-Michel. A very old building, with lots of charm—though a bit run down. Friendly service. Has a few (M) doubles.

Seventh arrondissement

Pont-Royal (L), 7 rue Montalembert (tel. 45–44–38–27). 75 rooms, all with bath or shower. Near the new Orsay Museum. Some of the rooms rather cramped for this category, but pleasant atmosphere. Attractive bar; restaurant. Air-conditioned. AE, DC, MC, V.

Sofitel-Bourbon (L), 32 rue St.-Dominique (tel. 45–55–91–80). 112 rooms, all with bath. Near Les Invalides, modern, well-run. Good restaurant; bar. Air-conditioned. AE, DC, MC, V.

Bourgogne et Montana (E), 3 rue de Bourgogne (tel. 45–51–20–22). 35 rooms, all with bath. Just by the National Assembly. Restaurant and bar. AE, MC, V.

Cayré (E), 4 blvd. Raspail (tel. 45–44–38–88). 130 rooms, all with bath or shower. Quiet; popular with writers. AE, DC, MC, V.

Jardins d'Eiffel (E), 8 rue Amélie (tel. 47–05–46–21). 44 rooms, all with bath. Newly opened, close to Les Invalides. Well equipped and comfortable rooms. Private parking. Some (M) rooms.

Montalembert (E), 3 rue Montalembert (tel. 45–48–68–11). 61 rooms, 60 with bath. Next door to Pont Royal, but considerably less expensive. MC.

Résidence Elysées-Maubourg (E), 35 blvd. de Latour-Maubourg (tel. 45–56–10–78). 30 rooms, all with bath or shower. Close to Les Invalides and the Eiffel Tower. Small and comfortable. Bar. AE, DC, MC, V.

Saxe-Résidence (E), 9 villa de Saxe (tel. 47–83–98–28). 52 rooms, all with bath or shower. In a quiet cul-de-sac near the Ecole Militaire. AE, V.

Université (E), 22 rue de l'Université (tel. 42–61–09–39). 28 rooms, all with bath or shower. In a small, converted mansion; attractive decor. Some (M) singles.

Bellechasse (M), 8 rue de Bellechasse (tel. 45–51–52–36). 32 rooms, all with bath or shower. On a quiet street close to the Seine and the Orsay Museum. Small, modern rooms, a few with old beams. AE, DC, MC, V.

Bourdonnais (M), 111 av. de la Bourdonnais (tel. 47–05–45–42). 60 rooms, all with bath or shower. Restaurant (closed weekends and August) and quiet, cheerful bar. DC, V.

Pavillon (M), 54 rue St.-Dominique (tel. 45–51–42–87). 19 rooms, 17 with bath or shower. Set back from the street, near Les Invalides and the Eiffel Tower. Has some (I) rooms. V.

Saint-Germain (M), 88 rue du Bac (tel. 45–48–62–92). 29 rooms, all with bath or shower. Well managed, close to Saint-Germain-des-Prés. AE.

Suède (M), 31 rue Vaneau (tel. 47–05–00–08). 41 rooms, 37 with bath or shower. With pretty inner courtyard. Bar. AE.

Solferino (M), 91 rue de Lille (tel. 47–05–85–54). 34 rooms, all with bath or shower. Attractive decor. Closed over Christmas holidays.

Varenne (M), 44 rue de Bourgogne (tel. 45–51–45–55). 24 rooms, all with bath or shower. A converted mansion, peaceful and friendly, with a quiet little patio. Good value. AE.

Verneuil St.-Germain (M), 8 rue de Verneuil (tel. 42–60–24–16). 26 rooms, all with bath or shower. Pleasant atmosphere on a quiet street; small, very attractive rooms, with beams and stylish wallpaper or fabrics. AE, MC, V.

Empereur (I), 2 rue Chevert (tel. 45–55–88–02). 40 rooms, 23 with bath or shower. Close, as its name suggests, to Napoleon's tomb in Les Invalides. Bar.

Palais Bourbon (I), 49 rue de Bourgogne (tel. 47–05–29–26). 34 rooms, 26 with bath or shower. Close to Rodin Museum. Small rooms. Bar.

Eighth arrondissement

Bristol (S), 112 fbg. St.-Honoré (tel. 42–66–91–45). 200 rooms and suites. One of the most elegant hotels in Paris and also one of the most expensive, close to the British Embassy and a stone's throw from the Elysée Palace. Both rooms and suites are luxurious. Chic clientele includes many diplomats. Pool and good restaurant. Air-conditioned. AE, DC, MC, V.

Crillon (S), 10 pl. de la Concorde (tel. 42–65–24–24). 189 rooms. Grandiose site, with views across to the National Assembly building on the far side of the Seine. Was completely refurbished in the early 1980s. Popular with wealthy Americans (and has been since the time of Benjamin Franklin and Thomas Jefferson, when they visited it as a private palace). Has one of the best hotel restaurants in Paris, *Les Ambassadeurs*. Air-conditioned. AE, DC, MC, V.

George V (S), 31 av. George V (tel. 47–23–54–00). 292 rooms. Off the Champs-Elysées, this fashionable hotel is often used by rich Arab businessmen. Reception halls and some rooms furnished with antiques. Its bar is almost a club for visiting U.S. impresarios, starlets, businessmen, and the press. The restaurant is the setting for modern art displays. Air-conditioned. AE, DC, MC, V.

Lancaster (S), 7 rue de Berri (tel. 43–59–90–43). 67 rooms, all with bath. Quiet, a bit overpriced. Charmingly furnished suites overlook a courtyard. Restaurant and bar. Air-conditioned. AE, DC, MC, V.

Plaza-Athénée (S), 25 av. Montaigne (tel. 47–23–78–33). 218 soundproofed rooms and suites. Set just far enough off the Champs-Elysées to escape the noise and the glitter, but covenient for theaters and haute couture shops. Its *Régence* restaurant is where you'll see some of the prettiest girls in town at lunch, while the *Relais-Plaza* is a chic spot for an expensive after-theater supper; and the smart snackbar is the place if you just want a single main dish. On winter evenings the downstairs bar becomes an intimate disco. Air-conditioned. Great Sunday brunch. AE, DC, MC, V.

Prince de Galles (S), 33 av. de George V (tel. 47–23–55–11). 171 rooms. Friendly, attractive place under same management as the *Meurice* (First Arrondissement). Restaurant. Air-conditioned. AE, DC, MC, V.

Royal Monceau (S), 37 av. Hoche (tel. 45–61–98–00). 220 rooms, all with bath. Set not far from the Etoile and near the chic Parc Monceau. Good restaurant serves Paris's most popular brunch Sundays; also bar and pool. Air-conditioned. AE, DC, MC, V.

Balzac (L), 6 rue Balzac (tel. 45–61–97–22). 70 rooms, all with bath or shower. Used to be the old-established *Celtic* but has now been luxuriously renovated and renamed. Air-conditioned. Deluxe restaurant, bar. AE, DC, MC, V.

Castiglione (L), 40 rue du fbg. St.-Honoré (tel. 42–65–07–50). 105 rooms, all with bath. Single rooms are small. Restaurant. AE, DC, MC.

Napoléon (L), 40 av. de Friedland (tel. 47–66–02–02). 140 rooms, 100 with bath. The sort of charm you don't get in most of the newer hotels. Some less-expensive rooms. Elegant restaurant and pleasant bar. AE, DC, MC, V.

Pullman-Windsor (L), 14 rue Beaujon (tel. 45–63–04–04). 135 rooms, with bath or shower. Close to the Etoile, quiet, and rather elegant. Has a good restaurant (but closed weekends, August and Christmas). Air-conditioned. AE, DC, V.

San Régis (L), 12 rue Jean-Goujon (tel. 43–59–41–90). 32 rooms, all with bath or shower. Quite close to the Champs-Elysées and grands couturiers but comparatively quiet. Restaurant. DC, V.

La Trémoïlle (L), 14 rue de la Trémoïlle (tel. 47–23–34–20). 112 rooms, all with bath or shower. Run by the same management as the *Plaza-Athénée* (see above). Close to the Champs-Elysées and the couture houses, and popular with top models and their escorts. Good service, all modern facilities, and period furnishings. Restaurant and bar. Air-conditioned. AE, DC, MC, V.

Warwick (L), 5 rue de Berri (tel. 45–63–14–11). 147 rooms, all with bath or shower. Paris's latest Luxury hotel. A stone's throw from the Champs-Elysées. Good restaurant—*La Couronne*—and a bar. Air-conditioned. AE, DC, MC, V.

Bedford (E), 17 rue de l'Arcade (tel. 42–66–22–32). 147 rooms, all with bath. Near the Madeleine. Restaurant (closed Aug., Sat. and Sun.) and bar. MC, V.

Powers (E), 52 rue François Ier (tel. 47–23–91–05). 56 rooms, all with bath or shower. Close to the Champs-Elysées, has a very pleasant atmosphere. Bar. AE, V.

Résidence Lord Byron (E), 5 rue Chateaubriand (tel. 43–59–89–98). 30 rooms, all with bath or shower. Pleasant small hotel close to the Etoile.

Roblin (E), 6 rue Chauveau-Lagarde (tel. 42–65–57–00). 70 rooms, 62 with bath or shower. Well-placed near the Madeleine and good for serious shoppers —fbg. St.-Honoré and the big department stores are in walking distance. Restaurant and bar. AE, DC, MC, V.

Royal (E), 33 av. de Friedland (tel. 43–59–08–14). 57 rooms, all with bath or shower. Friendly service. Restaurant and bar. AE, DC, MC, V.

Royal-Malesherbes (E), 24 blvd. Malesherbes (tel. 42–65–53–30). 102 rooms, all with bath. Restaurant and bar. AE, DC, MC, V.

Vernet (E), 25 rue Vernet (tel. 47–23–43–10). 63 rooms, all with bath or shower. Very close to the Etoile and the Champs-Elysées. Restaurant and bar. AE, DC, MC, V.

Alison (M), 21 rue de Surène (tel. 42–65–54–00). 35 rooms, all with bath. Very modern rooms with comfortable lobby. Just off La Madeleine. AE, DC, MC, V.

Angleterre-Champs-Elysées (M), 91 rue La Boëtie (tel. 43–59–35–45). 40 rooms, all with bath. AE, DC, V.

Arcade (M), 7–9 rue de l'Arcade (tel. 42–65–43–85). 47 rooms, all with bath or shower. On a narrow street close to the Madeleine. Well-run.

Arromanches (M), 6 rue Chateaubriand (tel. 45–63–74–24). 27 rooms, all with bath or shower. Another pleasant, small hotel close to the Champs-Elysées. AE, DC, MC, V.

Bradford (M), 10 rue St.-Philippe-du-Roule (tel. 43–59–24–20). 48 rooms, 44 with bath or shower. Good service and mostly large, comfortable rooms.

Brescia (M), 16 rue d'Edimbourg (tel. 45–22–14–31). 38 rooms. Completely renovated, comfortable, with patio, in quiet street. AE, DC, MC, V.

Chambiges (M), 8 rue Chambiges (tel. 47–23–80–49). 30 rooms, 25 with bath or shower. Very pleasant little hotel, close to the Seine and the av. Montaigne. A few doubles are in the (E) price range.

Flèche d'Or (M), 29 rue d'Amsterdam (tel. 48–74–06–86). 65 rooms, 60 with bath or shower. Near St. Lazare station. AE, DC, MC, V.

Madeleine-Plaza (M), 33 pl. de la Madeleine (tel. 42–65–20–63). 53 rooms, 48 with bath or shower. Just by the Madeleine church. AE, V.

Mayflower (M), 3 rue Chateaubriand (tel. 45–62–57–46). 24 rooms, all with bath or shower. Small and cozy, close to the Etoile. V.

Queen Mary (M), 9 rue Greffulhe (tel. 42–66–40–50). 36 rooms, all with bath or shower. On a side street close to the big stores.

Washington (M), 43 rue Washington (tel. 45–61–10–76). 23 rooms, all with bath or shower.

Bellevue (I), 46 rue Pasquier (tel. 43–87–50–68). 48 rooms, 16 with bath or shower. Near St. Lazare station. Modest.

Champs-Elysées (I), 2 rue d'Artois (tel. 43–59–11–42). 40 rooms, 19 with bath or shower. Modest, but well sited.

Wilson (I), 10 rue de Stockholm (tel. 45–22–10–85). 37 rooms, only 8 with bath or shower. Modest, but convenient for St. Lazare station.

Ninth arrondissement

Ambassador-Concorde (L), 16 blvd. Haussmann (tel. 42–46–92–63). 300 rooms, all with bath. Rather impersonal and commercial atmosphere, but convenient for the major department stores and the Opéra. Restaurant and bar. Air-conditioned. AE, DC, MC, V.

Grand (L), 2 rue Scribe (tel. 42–68–12–13). 588 rooms, all with bath or shower. Close to the Opéra; large but well-run, with old-fashioned personal service. Restaurant and bar. AE, DC, MC, V.

Commodore (E), 12 blvd. Haussmann (tel. 42–46–72–82). 160 rooms, all with bath. Has two restaurants, one a convenient bar-cum-grill room. AE, DC, MC, V.

Royal Médoc (E), 14 rue Geoffroy-Marie (tel. 47–70–37–33). 40 rooms, all with bath. Very comfortable; close to the Opéra and the Grands Boulevards.

Bergère-Mapotel (M), 34 rue Bergère (tel. 47–70–34–34). 135 rooms, all with bath or shower. Quiet, appears slightly off the beaten track, but it is in fact near the Opéra and the Bourse. Good service. AE, DC, V.

Blanche Fontaine (M), 34 rue Fontaine (tel. 45–26–72–32). 49 rooms, all with bath or shower. Near Pigalle area. AE, V.

Central Monty (M), 5 rue de Montyon (tel. 47–70–26–10). 66 rooms, all but 1 with bath or shower. Near the *grands boulevards* and the Bourse. Bar. AE, DC, MC, V.

Excelsior-Opéra (M), 5 rue Lafayette (tel. 48–74–99–30). 53 rooms, all with bath or shower. Almost next door to Galeries Lafayette. AE, DC, MC, V.

Hollandais (M), 16 rue Lamartine (tel. 45–26–86–13). 46 rooms, 35 with bath or shower. Small, quiet and friendly.

Impérial (M), 45 rue de la Victoire (tel. 48–74–10–47). 37 rooms, 29 with bath or shower. Small hotel not far from the big stores; some (I) singles.

London Palace (M), 32 blvd. des Italiens (tel. 48–24–54–64). 49 rooms, 47 with bath or shower. This well-run hotel is unusual in having reduced rates in July and August. MC, V.

Moulin Rouge (M), 39 rue La Fontaine (tel. 42–81–93–25). 50 rooms, all with bath or shower. New; excellent rooms and breakfast. Close to Pigalle. AE, DC, V.

Diamond (I), 73 rue de Dunkerque (tel. 42–81–15–00). 48 rooms, 33 with bath or shower. Close to the Gare du Nord.

Peyris (I), 10 rue du Conservatoire (tel. 47–70–50–83). 50 rooms, all with bath or shower. On a side street close to the *grands boulevards*. Restaurant and bar. V.

Tenth arrondissement

Pavillon-l'Horset (E), 38 rue de l'Echiquier (tel. 42–46–92–75). 91 rooms, all with bath or shower. A bit out of the way, but good if you're a china fiend—the rue de Paradis, where all the finest china and porcelain showrooms are, is close by. AE, DC, MC, V.

Frantor-Paris Est (M), Cour d'honneur, Gare de l'Est (tel. 42–41–00–33). 33 rooms, all with bath or shower. Right by the Gare de l'Est. Restaurant and bar. MC, V.

Modern'Est (M), 91 blvd. de Strasbourg (tel. 46–07–24–72). 30 rooms, 29 with bath. Right opposite the Gare de l'Est.

Europe (I), 98 blvd. Magenta (tel. 46–07–25–82). 36 rooms, 26 with bath or shower. Convenient for both the Gare du Nord and the Gare de l'Est. Bar. MC, V.

Londres et Anvers (I), 133 blvd. Magenta (tel. 42–85–28–26). 43 rooms, 13 with bath or shower. Near the Gare du Nord and the Gare de l'Est. AE, DC, V.

Eleventh arrondissement

Holiday Inn (L), 10 pl. de la République (tel. 43–55–44–34). 333 rooms, all with bath or shower. Completely modernized reincarnation of what was once a grand and traditional hotel. Very comfortable, though not very central. '20s-style restaurant; bar. Air-conditioned. AE, DC, MC, V

Twelfth arrondissement

Claret (M), 44 blvd. de Bercy (tel. 46–28–41–31). 52 rooms, all with bath or shower. Charming hotel close to the newly opened Palais de Bercy. AE, DC, MC, V.

Modern Hôtel Lyon (M), 3 rue Parrot (tel. 43–43–41–52). 53 rooms, all with bath or shower. Quiet, but close to the Gare de Lyon. Popular with businessmen. Bar. AE, MC, V.

Paris-Lyon Palace (M), 11 rue de Lyon (tel. 43–07–29–49). 128 rooms, all with bath or shower. Also near the Gare de Lyon. Restaurant. AE, DC, MC, V.

Terminus Lyon (M), 19 blvd. Diderot (tel. 43–43–24–03). 61 rooms, 60 with bath or shower. Again, close to the station. Bar. AE, MC, en

Thirteenth arrondissement

Equinoxe (M), 40 rue Le Brun (tel. 43–37–56–56). 49 rooms, all with bath or shower. Very comfortable rooms though a little noisy. Near Les Gobelins. AE, DC, MC, V.

Gobelins (I), 57 blvd. St.-Marcel (tel. 43–31–79–89). 45 rooms, all with bath or shower. Close to Austerlitz station, yet not far from the Latin Quarter. Bar.

Timhôtel Italie (I), 22 rue Barrault (tel. 45–80–67–67). 73 rooms, 68 with bath or shower. One of a group of new, well-run hotels with contemporary furnishings and pleasant service. Restaurant and bar. AE, DC, MC, V.

Timhôtel Tolbiac (I), 35 rue de Tolbiac (tel. 45–83–74–94). 54 rooms, all with bath. Another member of the new group. A little out of the way, but good for Austerlitz station and Orly airport. AE, DC, MC, V.

Fourteenth arrondissement

Meridien Montparnasse (L), 19 rue Commandant-Mouchotte (tel. 43–20–15 –51). 950 rooms, all with bath. Large, rather impersonal hotel near the Tour Montparnasse, now part of the Air France chain. Wonderful view from the top floors. Free bus service between Porte Maillot air terminal and hotel. Restaurants, bars, shops. Air-conditioned. AE, DC, MC, V.

PLM-Saint-Jacques (L), 17 blvd. St.-Jacques (tel. 45–89–89–80). 797 rooms, all with bath. Not on the usual tourist track, but convenient for Orly airport (airport bus actually stops here). A variety of restaurants and bars to suit all tastes and purposes. Air-conditioned. AE, DC, MC, V.

Aiglon (M), 232 blvd. Raspail (tel. 43–20–82–42). 50 rooms, all with bath. Close to the Coupole and all the Montparnasse restaurants and cinemas, yet quiet. AE, V.

Lenox (M), 15 rue Delambre (tel. 43–35–34–50). 52 rooms, all with bath. New hotel in Montparnasse; well equipped rooms; light dinners served at bar until 2 A.M. AE, DC, V.

Orléans Palace (M), 185 blvd. Brune (tel. 45–39–68–50). 92 rooms, all with bath or shower. Near the Cité Universitaire. AE, DC, MC, V.

Parc Montsouris (M), 4 rue du Parc (tel. 45–89–09–72). 35 rooms, all with bath or shower. Near the pretty Parc Montsouris and the Cité Universitaire. V.

Royal (M), 212 blvd. Raspail (tel. 43–20–69–20). At top end of price category. MC, V.

Delambre (I), 35 rue Delambre (tel. 43–20–66–31). 36 rooms, 34 with bath or shower. Close to the Tour Montparnasse.

Idéal (I), 108 blvd. Jourdan (tel. 45–40–45–16). 69 rooms, 67 with bath or shower. Close to the Cité Universitaire. AE, V.

Fifteenth arrondissement

Hilton (L), 18 av. de Suffren (tel. 42–73–92–00). 479 rooms, all with bath and balcony, and some at (S) rates. Two restaurants (the rooftop one closed August), coffee shop, boutiques, hairdresser, bank. Air-conditioned. AE, DC, MC, V.

Nikko (L), 61 quai de Grenelle (tel. 45–75–62–62). 777 rooms, all with bath. Ultra-modern hotel owned by Japan Airlines, overlooking the Seine to the west of the Eiffel Tower. Mixture of Japanese and French décor. Japanese and French restaurants, pool; sauna, shops—the lot. Air-conditioned. AE, DC, MC, V.

Sofitel-Paris (L), 8–12 rue Louis-Armand (tel. 45–54–95–00). 635 rooms, all with bath. Near the Exhibit Center at the Porte de Versailles, and a bit out of the way unless you're motorized or have come for one of the fairs. Restaurants (good chef), conference rooms, pool, nursery, gym, sauna. Air-conditioned. AE, DC, MC, V.

Holiday Inn (E), 69 blvd. Victor (tel. 45–33–74–63). 90 rooms, all with bath. Close to the Exhibit Center at the Porte de Versailles. Restaurant and bar. Airconditioned. AE, DC, MC, V.

Grenelle (M), 140 blvd. de Grenelle (tel. 45–75–26–54). 28 rooms, all with bath or shower. This new hotel has pleasant, modern rooms and rather elegant decor and furnishings. AE, MC, V.

Lecourbe (M), 28 rue Lecourbe (tel. 47–34–49–06). Well-renovated rooms, plus attractive courtyard-garden. Bar. AE, DC, MC, V.

La Tour Suffren (M), 20 rue Jean-Rey (tel. 45–78–61–08). 407 rooms, all with bath. Just by the Eiffel Tower. Restaurant, bar, garden. Air-conditioned. AE, DC, MC, V.

Timhôtel Montparnasse (I), 22 rue de l'Arrivée (tel. 45–48–96–92). 33 rooms, 31 with bath or shower. Just by Montparnasse station. Another member of the new group of well-run, attractive, small hotels, with contemporary furnishings, good modern bathrooms, and pleasant service. And remember: you get the 11th night that you stay at a Timhôtel in any one year for free. AE, DC, MC, V.

Sixteenth arrondissement

Raphaël (L), 17 av. Kléber (tel. 45–02–16–00). 87 rooms, all with bath. Close to the Etoile and exclusive. Well-decorated with period furniture. Comfortable and very quiet; all rooms have balcony. Restaurant and bar. AE, DC, MC, V.

Résidence du Bois (L), 16 rue Chalgrin (tel. 45–00–50–59). 20 rooms, all with bath. Close to the Etoile. Quiet and attractive, with some rooms overlooking a peaceful garden. Must reserve well ahead. Belongs to the *Relais et Châteaux* group.

Alexander (E), 102 av. Victor-Hugo (tel. 45–53–64–65). 62 rooms, all with bath or shower. In the heart of the chic Victor Hugo district. Bar.

Kléber (E), 7 rue de Belloy (tel. 47–23–80–22). 22 rooms, all with bath. Halfway between the Etoile and the Trocadéro. Very well-run. AE, DC, MC.

Majestic (E), 29 rue Dumont-d'Urville (tel. 45–00–83–70). 30 rooms and suites, all with bath. Attractive rooms, especially on top floor. Near the charming pl. des Etats-Unis. AE, DC, MC, V.

Résidence Foch (E), 10 rue Marbeau (tel. 45–00–46–50). 25 rooms, all with bath. In the chic Foch district. AE, DC, MC, V.

Victor-Hugo (E), 19 rue Copernic (tel. 45–53–76–01). 76 rooms, all with bath or shower. Close to the Etoile, with spacious rooms. Bar. Air-conditioned. AE, DC, MC, V.

Longchamp (M), 68 rue de Longchamp (tel. 47–27–13–48). 23 rooms, all with bath. Recently renovated. Well situated between Trocadéro and Etoile.

Mont-Blanc (M), 51 rue Lauriston (tel. 45–53–04–70). 46 rooms, all with bath or shower. Top end of price range. Bar. AE, DC, MC, V.

Queen's (M), 4 rue Bastien-Lepage (tel. 42–88–89–85). 22 rooms, all with bath or shower. Redecorated and now with all modern amenities, but still reasonable prices.

Régina de Passy (M), 6 rue de la Tour (tel. 45–24–43–64). 62 rooms, 57 with bath or shower. In Passy, near the Trocadéro. AE, DC, V.

Sévigné (M), 6 rue de Belloy (tel. 47–20–88–90). 30 rooms, all with bath or shower. Same management as the *Kléber* (see above), and same good service. Close to the Etoile. Has a few (E) rooms. AE, DC, MC.

Poussin (I), 52 rue Poussin (tel. 46–51–30–46). 28 rooms, all with bath or shower. Close to the Auteuil racecourse. A few doubles are up in the (M) range.

Ranelagh (I), 56 rue de l'Assomption (tel. 42–88–31–63). 29 rooms, only 9 with bath. A rarity in this chic part of Paris—a modest spot for budget travelers.

Seventeenth arrondissement

Concorde-Lafayette (L), 3 pl. du Général-Koenig (tel. 47–58–12–84). 990 rooms, all with bath. Deluxe rooms on top floor with VIP service. In a vast complex with conference rooms, secretaries, restaurants for all tastes and most pocketbooks. Smart and expensive shopping arcade, nightclub, movies. Very convenient for Roissy/Charles-de-Gaulle air terminal, but rather impersonal, and service can be indifferent. Air-conditioned. AE, DC, MC, V.

Méridien (L), 81 blvd. Gouvion-St.-Cyr (tel. 47–58–12–30). 1,027 rooms, all with bath. Efficient, huge, American-style hotel, with four restaurants (including excellent *Clos Longchamp*); Sunday brunch; bar with jazz after 10 P.M., boutiques. Again, convenient for Roissy air terminal, though some readers have complained of poor service. Air-conditioned. AE, DC, MC, V.

Etoile (E), 3 rue de l'Etoile (tel. 43–80–36–94). 25 rooms, all with bath or shower. AE, DC, MC, V.

Regent's Garden (E), 6 rue Pierre-Demours (tel. 45–74–07–30). 41 rooms, all with bath. In a 19th-century mansion near the Etoile, with a pretty garden. Has been extensively modernized. Excellent service. AE, DC, MC, V.

Splendid Etoile (E), 1 bis av. Carnot (tel. 43–80–14–56). 57 rooms and suites, all with bath. Pleasant furnishings, some rooms in the (L) price category. Close to the Etoile. Restaurant and bar. Large and beautiful garden. AE, DC, MC, V.

Agena (M), 13 rue de l'Ecluse (tel. 42–93–41–48). 28 rooms, all renovated, with bath. Just off pl. Clichy. Welcoming.

Banville (M), 166 blvd. Berthier (tel. 42–67–70–16). 40 rooms, all with bath. A little far out, but quiet and friendly. Attractive wallpaper and furnishings (different in each room). V.

Etoile (M), 3 rue de l'Etoile (tel. 43-80-36-94). 25 rooms, all with bath or shower. Modern rooms; bar, library corner. Close to Etoile. AE, DC, MC, V.

Mercure (M), 27 av. des Ternes (tel. 47–66–49–18). 56 rooms, all with bath or shower. Second inner-city hotel owned by this well-known medium-priced chain. Bar. Air-conditioned. AE, DC, MC, V.

Médéric (I), 4 rue Médéric (tel. 47–63–69–13). 29 rooms, all with bath or shower. Close to the Parc Monceau. V.

Eighteenth arrondissement

Mercure Paris Montmartre (E), 3 rue Caulaincourt (tel. 42–94–17–17). 308 rooms, all with bath. The first venture into the capital by this well-known chain. Air-conditioned. AE, DC, MC, V.

Terrass' (E), 12–14 rue Joseph-de-Maistre (tel. 46–06–72–85). 108 rooms, all with bath. Close to Montmartre cemetery and delightful—surprisingly quiet for this rackety area of Paris. Restaurant and bar. AE, DC, MC, V.

Regyn's Montmartre (M), 18 pl. des Abbesses (tel. 42–54–45–21). 22 rooms, all with bath or shower. Small, attractive, modern amenities. Very convenient for visiting the heart of Montmartre. AE, DC, V.

Timhôtel Montmartre (I), 11 pl. Emile-Goudeau (tel. 42–55–74–79). 61 rooms, 50 with bath. Another welcome find high up on an atmospheric square where Picasso used to live. Good value. AE, DC, MC, V.

Nineteenth arondissement

Le Laumière (I), 4 rue Petit (tel. 42–06–10–77). 54 rooms, all with bath or shower. Good value and charming; close to Les Buttes-Chaumong park.

Neuilly

Club Méditerranée (L), 58 blvd. Victor-Hugo (tel. 47–58–11–00). 330 rooms, all with bath. Run rather differently from an ordinary hotel, in the typically friendly Club Med style, with a lot of do-it-yourself gadgets. Pleasant atmosphere, excellent buffet, though a bit overpriced. Large garden. Air-conditioned. AE, DC, V.

Jardin de Neuilly (E), 5 rue Paul-Déroulède (tel. 46–24–94–84). 30 rooms, all with bath or shower. Attractive small hotel near the Bois. Tiny courtyard garden. Top end of price range. AE, V.

Maillot (I), 46 rue de Sablonville (tel. 46–24–23–45). 30 rooms, 23 with shower. Small, friendly hotel close to the air terminal at the Porte Maillot. Very reasonable for this expensive area. Breakfast at any time.

Suburbs and Airports

With old Paris bursting out of city limits, there has been a frenzy of building in nearby suburbs, now well-connected to Paris by good transportation facilities. If central accommodations are scarce, and particularly if you have a car, the suburban hotels might be a good bet. However, they can be impersonal, not to say cold, and they tend to be geared more to business visitors than to tourists.

All the hotels listed here have restaurants.

Bagnolet

Novotel Paris-Bagnolet (E), 1 av. Republique (tel. 43–60–02–10). 611 rooms, all with bath. Two restaurants, bar, pool. Air-conditioned. AE, DC, MC, V.

Ibis Paris Bagnolet (M), tel. 43–60–02–76. 414 rooms, all with bath. Restaurant. MC, V.

Bougival

Forest Hill (M), 12 rue Yvan-Tourgueneff (tel. 39–18–17–16). 175 rooms. Pretty setting overlooking the Seine. Less impersonal than others in this section. Well-placed for Malmaison, Saint-Germain-en-Laye, Marly and Versailles. Value for money. Good buffet restaurant; pool. AE, DC, MC, V.

Courbevoie

Novotel Paris La Défense (E), 2 blvd. Neuilly (tel. 47–78–16–68). 276 rooms, all with bath. Restaurant, bar. Air-conditioned. AE, DC, MC, V.

Paris Penta (E), 18 rue Baudin (tel. 47–88–50–51). 494 rooms. Very well equipped rooms; near La Défense business center. Restaurant. AE, DC, MC, V.

Orly Airport

Pullman (E), at nearby Rungis (tel. 46–87–36–36). 206 rooms, all with bath. Restaurant and pool. Air-conditioned. AE, DC, MC, V.

Hilton Orly (E), (tel. 46–87–33–88.) 380 soundproofed rooms. *Louisiane* restaurant; coffee shop. Air-conditioned. AE, DC, MC, V.

Holiday Inn (E), at nearby Rungis (tel. 46–87–26–66). 168 rooms, all with bath. Restaurant and pool. Air-conditioned. AE, DC, MC, V.

Motel PLM Orly (M), at Orly-Ouest (tel. 46–87–23–37). 200 rooms. Restaurant. Air-conditioned. AE, DC, MC, V.

Arcade Orly-Aéroport (I), at Orly-Sud (tel. 46–87–33–50). 203 rooms, all with bath. Restaurant. V.

Roissy/Charles-de-Gaulle Airport

Holiday Inn (E), (tel. 39–88–00–22). 250 rooms. Restaurant. Air-conditioned. AE, DC, MC, V.

Sofitel (E), (tel. 38–62–23–23). 352 rooms. Restaurant and pool. Air-conditioned. AE, DC, MC, V.

Arcade (I), (tel. 38–62–49–49). 356 rooms, all with bath. Modern, well-run, right by the rail station (direct service to the Gare du Nord); free bus service at regular intervals to airport building. Good value. Restaurant. Air-conditioned. MC, V.

Vanves

Mercure Paris Porte de Versailles (E), rue Moulin (tel. 46–42–93–22). 400 rooms, all with bath or shower. On the very edge of Paris, not far from exhibit center. Has brasserie for light meals. Air-conditioned. AE, DC, MC, V.

RENTALS. Paris is a notoriously overcrowded city, with many applicants for every apartment that comes up for rent. So it isn't surprising that finding short lets is very hard indeed. One of the few opportunities available is afforded by the *Résidence Charles Dullin* in Montmartre, at 10 pl. Charles-Dullin, 75018 Paris. This consists of over 60 studio apartments and a few 2- and 3-room apartments, which can be taken for as little as a week.

Inter-Urbis, 1 rue Mollien, 75008 Paris, does handle rentals, but only for a minimum of two months and at very high rates; and such accommodations are in very short supply.

Résidence Orion rents single rooms, studios, 1- and 2-bedroom apartments, all with kitchens, at reduced prices after the 10th night and during July and August; there is an Orion Résidence in Les Halles area at 4 rue des Innocents, 75001 Paris (tel. 45–08–00–33).

Otherwise you could try looking at the ads in the Paris-based *International Herald Tribune* or in one of the national dailies, particularly *Le Monde* or *Le Figaro.* The trendy English-language fortnightly *Passion* carries ads from people offering to swap a Paris apartment for one abroad, generally in the United States. But we advise you not to count on being able to find anything on these lines.

Where to Eat

Eating out is a major delight for many visitors to Paris—some come only for the food in fact, ignoring museums, theaters and other city occupations so as to concentrate their energies on one of France's world-renowned specialties. Good eating is very important to the French, and as a result you'll find that Paris restaurants generally offer a noticeably high standard of food, at all price levels. Although the city has inevitably suffered from the worldwide boom in fast-food outfits, it still has a very large number of modest little places frequented mostly by the locals where you can get a three- or four-course meal for relatively little. And an interesting backlash against the fast-food vogue has recently emerged, with small places offering fixed-price "formula" meals that represent excellent value.

The great thing about Paris is that there are so many good places to eat, with new ventures constantly springing up, that you could dine in a different restaurant every day for years and still have new discoveries to make. Our lists certainly shouldn't be taken as exhaustive. We've picked out places we think will appeal to you and told you what to expect, giving you a wide range of establishments to choose from. But we'd like to think that you'll branch out on your own too, once you've got your eye in, and followed the tips we'd like to pass on to you.

The first tip is—read the menu! Except for the most luxurious (and expensive) places, restaurants are compelled by law to post up a menu outside, so make sure to have a good look at it before you go in. We have classified our lists into

Expensive (E), Moderate (M), and Inexpensive (I). But prices vary considerably in each category, and your final bill will depend a great deal on what you order and what wine you drink. Fixed-price menus (known in French simply as *menus*) are less common in Paris than in the rest of the country, but are often a lunchtime feature, especially in restaurants frequented by businessmen. They probably won't be served at weekends.

You'll soon see from our lists that, alas, many restaurants are closed for all or part of every weekend. In spite of the huge numbers of tourists in Paris, most restaurateurs are basically catering for Parisians, who flock away from the city at weekends in increasing numbers. So as legislation compels them to give staff two consecutive days off, they find it preferable simply to shut at the weekend. Fish restaurants, as in many countries, are however more likely to close on Sunday and Monday. Incidentally, the weekend closure applies more to Expensive restaurants than to the other categories, so this may be a good time to experiment with one of the more modest little spots that can be such a joy.

Annual closures are another problem. Like most businesses, Parisian restaurants generally close for at least four weeks each year. Those with a predominantly local clientele will usually shut in July and/or August. Those popular with tourists are more likely to shut in January or February. And you should note that the school mid-semester vacations in February, when many French people take off for the ski slopes, generally lead to a number of closures for at least a week. Public holidays again see many closures, particularly among Expensive restaurants. But we advise you to check locally, as decisions on whether or not to close may well be taken at the last minute.

We must also warn you that many of the less expensive restaurants are not keen to take telephone reservations. Try by all means, but it may be better to call by and make the reservation in person earlier in the day, or better still a day or so ahead of time. You should also be warned that some of Paris's top restaurants operate a quota system where tourists are concerned—trying to keep a balance between visitors and locals and thus maintain the atmosphere of their establishments. Don't feel slighted by this; there are masses to choose from.

As for last orders, you'll find a wide variety here. The average neighborhood restaurant will serve lunch between 12 and 2, dinner between 7.30 (in the more tourist-frequented spots) or 8 and around 10 or even 9.30. The chic places will stay open till 11 or 11.30 and a number keep going into the early hours. Our lists specify restaurants that stay open till 11.30 or later, and mention too those few that serve meals all day, not just at meal-times.

Lastly, we must emphasize that snacks are expensive in France. You'll generally fare far better if you eat a full three- or four-course meal that if you fuel up at intervals with snacks. And we advise you not to ask for an omelet and salad, say, in a proper restaurant, though this is of course perfectly acceptable in a café. Quite apart from being rewarded with disapproving stares, you'll probably find the bill comes to as much as for a full meal. If you prefer a light lunch, much better eat a sandwich in a café or buy some delicious goodies from one of the city's many street markets and eat an al fresco meal in an atmospheric spot.

In the following lists, which do not include hotel restaurants, our selections are grouped by district or *arrondissement,* with a few suggestions for the two inner suburbs of Boulogne and Neuilly. They are classified by price, into three categories. As a rough guideline, a three-course meal selected from the *carte* (i.e. not a fixed-price *menu*), without wine, will cost 300 frs. and upwards in an Expensive (E) restaurant (prices in the top places go up to 650–750 frs); 150–300 in a Moderate (M) restaurant; and 100–150 frs in an Inexpensive (I) restaurant.

Credit Cards. As in our hotel listing, AE stands for American Express, DC for Diners Club, MC for Mastercard, V for Visa.

Cookery Courses. For those who are seriously interested in the art of French cuisine, there are excellent courses available. Among the best are those run at Anne Willan's *École de Cuisine La Varenne,* 34 rue St.-Dominique, 75007 Paris. The school offers a range of courses, short and long. Contact for fees and other details.

First arrondissement

Le Carré des Feuillants (E), 14 rue Castiglione (tel. 42–86–82–82). Opened by Alain Dutournier, longtime chef of the *Trou gascon* (Twelfth *arrondissement*), right by the Place Vendome. Good *nouvelle cuisine,* some of it inspired by the hearty southwestern dishes that made Dutournier's reputation. Closed weekends. V.

L'Escargot Montorgueil (E), 38 rue Montorgueil, in the middle of what used to be Les Halles food market (tel. 42–36–83–51). Opened in the 1830s and still going strong, with delightful 19th-century decor of mirrors and traditional wall sofas. Chic clientele. Snails, of course, but other well-cooked dishes too. Closed May 1st and one week mid-Aug. Good-value lunchtime *menu* AE, DC, MC, V.

Le Grand Véfour (E), 17 rue de Beaujolais, behind the Palais-Royal gardens (tel. 42–96–56–27). Still one of Paris's finest restaurants, though no longer owned by the great Raymond Oliver. Now belongs to Jean Taittinger who runs the world-famous Concorde hotels and is keeping up the long-standing tradition of excellent food and superb service. Closed Sun. and Aug. Air-conditioned. AE, DC, V.

Mercure Galant (E), 15 rue des Petits-Champs (tel. 42–97–53–85). Fashionable restaurant with turn-of-the-century decor. Good mixture of traditional and new cooking. Good-value evening *menu.* Closed Sat. lunch and Sun.

L'Absinthe (M), 24 pl. du Marché-St.-Honoré (tel. 42–60–02–45). Friendly service in this chic little restaurant near the pl. Vendome and the av. de l'Opéra. The cooking is mostly "new" with delectably fresh ingredients from the market opposite. Attractive decor with *art nouveau* bits and pieces. Closed Sat. lunchtime and Sun. Some tables outside in fine weather. Open till 11.30 P.M. AE, DC, V.

Barrière Poquelin (M), 17 rue Molière, near the Comédie Française (tel. 42–96–22–19). Small, intimate and chic. New-style cuisine (particularly good fish) and excellent game in season. Good value *menu.* Closed Sat., for dinner on Sun. and most of Aug. AE, DC, V.

Le Caveau du Palais (M), 19 pl. Dauphine (tel. 43–26–04–28). Attractive place on a summer's evening, when you can sit outside in the peace and quiet of this leafy square. Good classical cooking. Closed weekends. AE, V.

Joe Allen (M), 30 rue Pierre-Lescot. A favorite with homesick Americans, but also popular with Paris's smart young things. Generous helpings. Nonstop service from midday to 1 A.M. V.

Louis XIV (M), 1 bis pl. des Victoires (tel. 40–26–20–81). A delightful bistrot in this attractive *place,* though the cuisine (mostly Lyon specialties), can be uneven. Closed weekends and Aug.

Pharamond (M), 24 rue de la Grande Truanderie, in the Les Halles area (tel. 42–33–06–72). Specializes in tripe, but has plenty of other good dishes (mainly Norman) to tempt you, too. Turn-of-the-century decor. Closed Sun., Mon. lunchtime and July. AE, DC, V.

Au Pied de Cochon (M), 6 rue Coquillière. (tel. 42–36–11–75). Re-painted *trompe-l'oeil* decorations to match the chic ambiance of the old market district. You can still enjoy the grilled pigs' trotters and onion soup that made it famous. Open all day and all night. AE, DC, V.

Willi's Wine-Bar (M), 13 rue des Petits-Champs (tel. 42–61–05–09). Good home cooking and desserts, but everybody goes there for the wine list. Wine by the glass. Closed Sun. and public holidays.

André Faure (I), 40 rue du Mont-Thabor, near the Tuileries and the pl. de la Concorde (tel. 42–60–74–28). Good place for a simple, home-style lunch or a special "farmhouse dinner." Good value. Closed Sun.

Bistro de la Gare (I), 30 rue St.-Denis (tel. 42–60–84–92). Fashionable *art nouveau*-style decor and "formula" meals to which you can add delicious desserts and reasonable wines.

Chez Paul (I), 15 pl. Dauphine (tel. 43–54–21–48). In a delightful little square behind the law courts and the Sainte Chapelle. Charming, crowded, unpretentious bistrot with genuine marble counter and straightforward home cooking, presided over by a very Parisienne *patronne.* A few tables outside. Closed Mon., Tues. and Aug.

Le Soufflé (I), 36 rue du Mont-Thabor (tel. 42–60–27–19). Specializes, as its name suggests, in soufflés of all kinds, both sweet and savory. Closed Sun. AE, DC, MC, V.

La Tour de Montlhéry (I), 5 rue des Prouvaires (tel. 42–36–21–82). Crowded, bustling bistrot specializing in steaks and good, home-style cooking. Lively atmosphere, redolent of the old days of Les Halles food market. Closed weekends and mid-July to mid-Aug. Otherwise open 24 hrs. a day.

Second arrondissement

Drouant (E), 18 rue Gaillon (tel. 47–42–56–61). A long-established, comfortable restaurant, popular with old faithfuls, and famous as the place where France's top literary prize, the Goncourt, is awarded. Perfect service, traditional cooking, well-known for seafood, including oysters in season. Also has grill room (M). Open to midnight. AE, DC, MC, V.

Le Petit Coin de la Bourse (M), 16 rue Feydeau (tel. 45–08–00–08). Owned by well-known restaurateur Claude Verger. Lively atmosphere, some "new" cuisine. Closed weekends and public hols. AE, DC, V.

Pile ou Face (M), 52bis rue Notre-Dame-des-Victoires (tel. 42–33–64–33). Tiny upstairs dining room popular with stockbrokers from nearby Bourse at lunchtime, with couples seeking romance in the evening. Mostly *nouvelle cuisine*. Closed weekends and Aug. Terrace. Air-conditioned.

Vishnou (M), 11 bis rue Volney (tel. 42–97–56–54). There aren't many Indian restaurants in Paris, but this is a good one, specializing in Tandoori dishes. Also has takeaway service. Closed Sun. for lunch and Mon. AE, DC, MC, V.

L'Amanguier (I), 110 rue de Richelieu (tel. 42–96–37–79). Near the Bourse and quite close to the Opéra. The delightful green-and-white decor—with parasols and garden chairs—is like a summer's day in the garden or by the sea. Short but imaginative menu, very reasonably priced, with particularly good desserts. Open to 11.30 P.M. AE, DC, V.

Jéroboam (I), 8 rue Monsigny (tel. 42–61–21–71). Attractive bistrot halfway between Opéra and the Bourse. Best known for excellent wines, reliable home cooking. Closed weekends, end of July and most of Aug. V.

Third arrondissement

L'Ami Louis (E), 32 rue du Vertbois (tel. 48–87–77–48). Genuine Paris bistrot (though the prices are far from being bistrot-like) with traditional home-style cooking and lots of atmosphere. Closed Mon., Tues. and July through Sept. AE, DC, V.

Guirlande de Julie (E), 25 pl. des Vosges (tel. 48–87–94–07). Pleasant atmosphere in this flower-filled restaurant in the lovely pl. des Vosges in the heart of the Marais. Good-value lunch *menus*. Closed Mon., Tues. and Feb. AE, V.

L'Ambassade d'Auvergne (M), 22 rue du Grenier-St.-Lazare (tel. 42–72–31–22). Hearty country-style dishes from the Auvergne, in a spacious tavern near the Centre Beaubourg. Open to 1 A.M. Closed Sun. V.

Taverne des Templiers (M), 106 rue Vieille du Temple (tel. 42–78–74–67). Don't be put off by the somewhat overdone medieval decor, as the food, cooked mostly in the classical style, is really good. Closed weekends and Aug. AE, V.

Fourth arrondissement

Benoît (E), 20 rue St.-Martin (tel. 42–72–25–76). Going strong since the turn of the century and has barely changed since. Excellent home-style cooking. Closed weekends and Aug.

Quai des Ormes (E), 72 quai de l'Hôtel-de-Ville (tel. 42–74–72–22). Nice setting close to the Hôtel de Ville. Rather chic, mostly "new" cuisine. Good-value lunch *menus*. Closed weekends and Aug. V.

Les Ursins dans le caviar (E), 3 rue Colombe (tel. 43–29–54–20). Marvelous old building on Ile de la Cité near Notre Dame, with furnishings to match; cuisine has an interesting "new" flavor. Good (M) *menu*. Closed Sun. and Aug. Open to 12.30 A.M. AE, DC, V.

Le Beaubourgeois (M), 19 rue Ste.-Croix-de-la-Bretonnerie (tel. 42–72–08–51). Fashionable bistrot-type spot near the Centre Beaubourg/Pompidou. Open evenings only, until 1 A.M. AE, DC, MC, V.

Bofinger (M), 7 rue de la Bastille (tel. 42–72–87–82). A genuine *brasserie*, though it tends to be pricey. Splendid *art nouveau* decor. Open daily to 1 A.M. for after-theater suppers. AE, DC, MC, V.

Coconnas (M), 2bis pl. des Vosges (tel. 42–78–58–16). Delightful setting in the heart of the Marais. Good-value, interesting cuisine. Under same management as the famous Tour d'Argent. Closed Mon., Tues. and mid-Dec. to mid-Jan. AE, DC, V.

La Colombe (M), 4 rue de la Colombe (tel. 46–33–37–08). Tucked away in a little street near Notre-Dame with open-air dining beneath a vine trellis. Service can be a bit slapdash, but you can linger till midnight in the delightful atmosphere (17th- and 18th-century music too!) and then wander romantically back past Notre-Dame. Closed Sun., Mon. for lunch, Feb. and most of Aug. AE, DC, MC, V.

Le Domarais (M), 53bis rue des Francs-Bourgeois (tel. 42–74–54–17). Worth coming for the decor alone; once the annexe of the Crédit Municipal pawn-brokers—red-velvet seats and intimate atmosphere make it truly special. Good food too, at reasonable prices. Closed Sat. for lunch, Sun., and Mon. for lunch. AE, V.

L'Excuse (M), 14 rue Charles-V (tel. 42–77–98–97). Small, quiet and elegant in the southern section of the Marais near the Seine. Good newish cuisine, pleasant ambiance. Open till midnight. Closed Sun. V.

Julien (M), 1 rue du Pont-Louis-Philippe (tel. 42–78–31–64). Attractive, one-time bakery, hence the beautiful old ceramic tiles. Now serves subtle *nouvelle cuisine,* in rather small portions. Closed Sat., Sun. and Mon. for lunch, and Christmas period. AE, DC.

La Brasserie de l'Ile (I), 55 quai Bourbon, Ile St-Louis (no telephone reservations). Crowded *brasserie* with cheerful, lively waiters who manage to keep smiling in spite of the crush. Traditional Alsatian dishes and fruity Alsatian wines. Popular for Sunday lunch but you must get there early. A good place to go after visiting Notre-Dame. Open to 1.30 A.M. Closed Wed., Thurs. for lunch and Aug.

Jo Goldenberg (I), 7 rue Rosiers (tel. 48–87–20–16). Paris's best-known Jewish restaurant, in the heart of the city's main Jewish district. Bustling and cheerful, with good delicatessen attached. Air-conditioned. AE, DC, V.

Au Gourmet de l'Ile (I), 42 rue St.-Louis-en-l'Ile (tel. 43–26–79–27). Delightful and good-value little restaurant on the Ile St.-Louis. Must reserve. 17th-century cellar setting, country-style dishes. Closed Mon., Thurs. and Aug.

Le Tourtour (I), 20 rue Quincampoix (tel. 48–87–82–48). Fashionable restaurant near the Centre Beaubourg/Pompidou. Charming 17th-century building, now amusingly redecorated to look like a sidewalk café, with genuine Parisian paving stones underfoot. Good-value meals.

Trumilou (I), 84 quai de l'Hôtel-de-Ville (tel. 42–77–63–98). Fashionable with the "in" crowd, so reserve or get there early. Closed Mon. and Sept.

Fifth arrondissement

La Tour d'Argent (E), 15 quai de la Tournelle (tel. 43–54–23–31). A world-famous restaurant is once again living up to its reputation. Extremely expensive, of course, but worth it if you can afford it, for the elegant decor and service, the views of Notre-Dame, the attention to detail at every level, the magnificent wines and not least the cooking which is French *haute cuisine* at its best, with some excellent *nouvelle cuisine* dishes. Good news for the less affluent is that La Tour d'Argent offers a fixed-price *menu* at lunchtime (except. Sun. and public hols.); it works out at less than half the price of an à la carte meal. Closed Mon. AE, DC, V.

Villars-Palace (E), 8 rue Descartes (tel. 43–26–39–08). In the rue Mouffetard area and fashionable, with garden. Mostly fish cooked new-style (i.e. very lightly poached or steamed) and shellfish. Closed Sat. for lunch. AE, DC, MC, V.

Auberge des Deux Signes (M), 46 rue Galande (tel. 43–25–46–56). Wonderful medieval setting with views of Notre-Dame. The cooking is good too, with some Auvergnat dishes. Closed Sun. and public hols. AE, DC, MC, V.

La Bûcherie (M), 41 rue da la Bûcherie (tel. 43–54–78–06). An old favorite, with log fires, classical music and relaxed atmosphere. Good "new" cooking though some people find the portions rather small. Lovely view of Notre-Dame from tables by the window. Located in the section of the rue de la Bûcherie near the Petit Pont. Open to 1 A.M. Closed Mon. for lunch AE, DC, V.

Le Coupe-Chou (M), 11 rue Lanneau (tel. 46–33–68–69). Fashionable, attractive restaurant in an old house with beams. The cooking can be uneven but the atmosphere is enjoyable and it's a good place for eating late—open to 1 A.M. Closed Sun. for lunch. V.

Dodin Bouffant (M), 25 rue Frédéric-Sauton (tel. 43–25–25–14). No longer run by the excellent Jacques Manière, but still very fashionable. Air conditioned; outdoor meals in summer. Serves until 12.45 A.M. Closed weekends, Aug. and over Christmas and New Year. DC, V.

Au Pactole (M), 44 blvd. St.-Germain (tel. 46–33–31–31). Careful cooking blends new and classical cuisine. Discreet atmosphere. Good value lunchtime *menu*. Closed Sat. lunch and Sun. AE, V.

Balzar (I), 49 rue des Ecoles (tel. 43–54–13–67). A genuine *brasserie* with waiters in long white aprons and traditional home-style cooking. Open to 12.30 A.M. Closed Tues. and Aug.

Le Grenier de Notre-Dame (I), 18 rue de la Bûcherie (tel. 43–29–98–29). Good spot for vegetarians, with macrobiotic specialties and even "bio-natural" wines. Closed Tues.

Sixth arrondissement

La Closerie des Lilas (E), 171 blvd. du Montparnasse (tel. 43–26–70–50). Some people find it overrated, but this is still a very popular spot and is always crowded. Lovely open-air terrace is as delightful as it was in the 1930s and dining here is slightly less expensive (M). The food is good, if unoriginal, but the atmosphere is what counts. Open to 1 A.M. AE, DC, V.

Joséphine (E), 117 rue du Cherche-Midi (tel. 45–48–52–40). Good atmosphere and friendly service in unpretentious bistrot. Mostly classical cuisine from the southwest of France. Good house wine. Closed weekends, July and Christmas period. V.

La Méditeranée (E), 2 pl. de l'Odéon (tel. 43–54–98–64). Good setting opposite Odéon theater, marvelous paintings, good seafood. AE, DC, V.

La Petite Cour (E), 10 rue Mabillon (tel. 45–26–52–26). Delightful little courtyard set below sidewalk level on a narrow street a bit away from the bustle of blvd. St.-Germain makes for perfect summer meals. Mostly "new" cuisine. Good value (M) menu at lunch. Closed Sun. and Mon. in winter, Sun. only in summer. Also mid-Dec. to mid-Jan. V.

Relais Louis XIII (E), 8 rue des Grands-Augustins (tel. 43–26–75–96). Wonderful old building near the Seine but very modern cuisine. Closed Sun. and for lunch on Mon. AE, DC, V.

Chez Bébert (M), blvd. Montparnasse, opposite the monster tower. Excellent North African restaurant, delicious *couscous*, beautifully presented, lots of atmosphere.

Dominique (M), 19 rue Bréa (tel. 43–27–08–80). The best-known Russian restaurant in town, started 50 years ago and still going strong, though many of its thirties patrons have died long since, and the atmosphere is perhaps more Parisian than Russian these days. But the caviar and the blinis are still good. Closed school hols. in Feb., and July. AE, DC, MC, V.

La Foux (M), 2 rue Clément (tel. 43–25–77–66). Extremely good cooking, with specialties from the Lyon and Bresse regions. Closed Sun., Christmas and New Year. AE, DC, V.

Chez Hansi (M), 3 pl. du 18-juin-1940 (tel. 45–48–96–42). Large, bustling Alsatian *brasserie* opposite the Tour Montparnasse. Open till 3 A.M. daily. AE, DC, V.

Lipp (M), 151 blvd. St.-Germain (tel. 45–48–53–91). A Parisian institution, always crowded and a favorite haunt of politicians, writers and film people. Fair home-style cooking (marvelous *pot-au-feu* and *choucroute*). Reserve ahead. Open till 12.45 A.M. Closed Mon., Easter, July, first week in Nov. and Christmas period.

Le Muniche (M), 27 rue de Buci (tel. 46–33–62–09). Another crowded spot, but the patrons are more Bohemian than *chez* Lipp. Much more French than German, despite its name. A bit noisy, some tables outside. Open daily to 3 A.M. AE, DC, MC, V.

Le Petit Zinc (M), 25 rue de Buci (tel. 43–54–79–34). An old favorite, ever-popular, ever-crowded. Tables outside in summer. Traditional home-style cooking, plus excellent oysters. Same management as *Le Muniche*. Open till 3 A.M. AE, DC, MC, V.

Tante Madée (M), 11 rue Dupin (tel. 42–22–64–56). An old favorite, now back on form, for home-style cuisine. Good value, especially the lunch *menu*. Closed Sat. for lunch and Sun. AE, DC.

Vagénende (M), 142 blvd. St.-Germain (tel. 43–26–68–18). Charming turn-of-the-century decor in this popular restaurant which is a favorite with our readers. It boasts old-fashioned fare and portions are generous. Good game in season. Open till 2 A.M. AE, DC, MC, V.

Assiette au Boeuf (I), 22 rue Guillaume-Apollinaire (tel. 42–60–88–44). Good-value meals and modish decor attract rather chic young locals. Air-conditioned. Open to 1 A.M. V.

Charbon de Bois (I), 16 rue Dragon (tel. 45–48–57–04). An old favorite in the heart of St.-Germain. Now back on form, and still specializing in charcoal-grilled meat. Always busy. Closed Sun. and for lunch on Mon. Air-conditioned. DC, V.

Aux Charpentiers (I), 10 rue Mabillon (tel. 43–26–30–05). Typical Parisian bistrot, unpretentious and altogether delightful. Used to be the headquarters of the Carpenters' Guild (the walls are covered with fascinating period photographs of the guild members at their get-togethers). The food is good too—plain straightforward homely dishes, very reasonably priced. Open till midnight. Closed Sun. and New Year vacations.

Echaudé St.-Germain (I), 21 rue de l'Echaudé (tel. 43–54–79–02). Very pretty spot in the heart of St.-Germain-des-Prés. Chic and lively; simple cuisine, but good ambiance and good-value *menu*. Open till 1 A.M. AE, DC, V.

Petit St-Benoît (I), 4 rue St.-Benoît (no telephone reservations). Amazingly low prices in this popular bistrot in the heart of St.-Germain-des-Prés. Closed weekends and about mid-July to mid-Aug.

Polidor (I), 41 rue Monsieur-le-Prince (tel. 43–26–75–34). Old-established genuine Paris bistrot with literary associations (André Gide and Paul Valéry used to come here, among many others). Good home cooking, in generous helpings. Closed Sun., Mon. and Aug.

Le Procope (I), 13 rue de l'Ancienne Comédie (tel. 43–26–99–20). Large, crowded, bustling café-restaurant with a famous past (Voltaire and Balzac knew it as a coffee house). Food is adequate. Open till 1.30 A.M. Closed July. AE, DC, V.

Restaurant des Saints-Pères (I), 175 blvd. St.-Germain (tel. 45–48–56–85). An old favorite. You'll love this genuine Parisian bistrot, but go soon—there aren't many of them left, and the slightly grumpy waitresses in their black dresses can't go on for ever. Tables outside in summer. Closed Wed., Thurs., and roughly mid-Aug. to mid-Sept.

Seventh arrondissement

Chez Les Anges (E), 54 blvd. de Latour-Maubourg (tel. 47–05–89–86). Spacious and comfortable; near the Invalides with a judicious mixture of classical, mostly from Burgundy, and "new" dishes. Closed Sun. evening and Mon. AE, DC, MC, V.

Le Divellec (E), 107 rue de l'Université (tel. 45–51–91–96). A recent recruit to Paris's greatest eating places, specializing in mouthwateringly fresh fish. Good-value lunch *menu*. Closed Sun., Mon. and Aug. AE, DC, V.

Au Quai d'Orsay (E), 49 quai d'Orsay. This pleasant spot has long been fashionable and now has a new chef specializing in imaginative potato and mushroom dishes. Closed Sun. and Aug. AE, DC, MC, V.

Le Récamier (E), 4 rue Récamier (tel. 45–48–86–58). Intimate and elegant with first-class food, mainly Burgundian. Closed Sun. DC, MC, V.

Le Jules Verne (E), on the 2nd floor of the Eiffel Tower (tel. 45–55–61–44). At last a restaurant has opened that's worthy of Paris's most famous landmark. Very popular so reserve well ahead. Lovely views, of course, but good, stylish cuisine too, and live piano music at times. AE, V.

Le Bellecour (M), 22 rue Surcouf (tel. 45–51–46–93). Mostly classical Lyonnaise cuisine. Closed Sat. for lunch, (all day Sat. in June and July), Sun. and Aug. AE, DC, MC, V.

Le Bourdonnais (M), 113 av. de la Bourdonnais (tel. 47–05–47–96). Chic little restaurant with "new" cooking. Friendly, candlelit. Closed Sun. and Mon. AE, DC, V.

Chez Françoise (M), in the Invalides Air Terminal (tel. 47–05–49–03). Popular with diplomats and politicians from the nearby Foreign Ministry and National Assembly. Good newish cuisine and excellent wine list. Very Parisian, old-style. Closed Sun. for dinner, Mon. and Aug. AE, DC, V.

Ferme Saint-Simon (M), 6 rue St-Simon (tel. 45–48–35–74). Excellent *nouvelle cuisine;* light and delicious. Closed Sat. for lunch, Sun. and most of Aug. V.

Sologne (M), 8 rue Bellechasse (tel. 47–05–98–66). Specializes in superb game from the famous Sologne forests and marshland in central France. Closed weekends. AE, DC, V.

Vin sur Vin (M), 20 rue Montessuy (tel. 47–05–14–20). Delicious wines by the glass are offered in this cheerful bistrot near the Eiffel Tower; good homestyle cuisine. Open 11.30 A.M.–11 P.M. Closed Sat. for lunch, Sun. and for about a week mid-Aug.

Chez l'Ami Jean (I), 27 rue Malar (tel. 47–05–86–89). Good hearty cuisine from the Pays Basque. Very good value. Closed Sun. and Aug.

La Fontaine de Mars (I), 129 rue St.-Dominique (tel. 47–05–46–44). Near the Eiffel Tower, and popular with local residents. No frills, but straightforward home cooking and friendly service. Tables outside in summer beside a delightful fountain set in a little square. Closed Sat. evening, Sun. and Aug. V.

La Petite Chaise (I), 36 rue de Grenelle (tel. 42–22–13–35). One of the oldest restaurants in Paris. Charming, slightly shabby and traditional, and always full. Excellent value. Open daily. V.

Annexe du Quai d'Orsay (I), 3 rue Surcouf. Small, club-like atmosphere, excellent value. Closed weekends. AE, DC, MC, V.

Thoumieux (I), 79 rue St.-Dominique (tel. 47–05–49–75). French home-style cooking, with specialties from southwestern France, in typically Parisian bistrot. Closed Mon. AE, V.

Eighth arrondissement

Chiberta (E), 3 rue Arsène-Houssaye (tel. 45–63–72–44). Wonderfully fresh ingredients, stylish decor, chic diners make this a must if you can afford it. Closed weekends, public holidays., Aug. and Christmas and New Year periods. AE, DC, MC, V.

Fouquet's (E), 99 av. des Champs-Elysées (tel. 47–23–70–60). Overpriced, but the food is basically good in this eternal landmark. A place to be seen. Open to midnight. AE, DC, MC, V.

Lamazère (E), 23 rue de Ponthieu (tel. 43–59–66–66). Chic and expensive, with particularly good dishes from the southwest of France, including splendid *cassoulet* and *foie gras*. Open till 12.30 A.M. Closed Sun. and Aug. AE, DC, MC, V.

Lasserre (E), 17 av. Franklin-Roosevelt (tel. 43–59–53–43). Usually thought to be one of Paris's finest restaurants. Pretty and smart, and correspondingly expensive. Especially good on summer evenings due to the sliding roof. Closed Sun., Mon. and Aug. Air-conditioned.

Le Lord Gourmand (E), 9 rue Lord-Byron (tel. 43–59–07–27). In a quiet side street off the Champs-Elysées. The still-lifes of game and fish on the walls seem to spring to life as you contemplate your food! Delicious, basically "new" cuisine with a lot of fish. Closed weekends, Aug. and over Christmas. AE, V.

Lucas-Carton (E), 9 pl. de la Madeleine (tel. 42–65–22–90). The brilliantly inventive Alain Sendrens—once of L'Archestrate—now presides over the old-established Lucas-Carton, with its splendid *art nouveau* decor and turn-of-the-century aura. *Nouvelle cuisine* at its subtle best, definitely for aficionados. Extremely expensive. Closed weekends, most of August and over Christmas–New Year period. V.

Le Marcande (E), 52 rue Miromesnil (tel. 42–65–19–14). Recent, elegant and spacious with pleasant service and newish cuisine. Closed weekends and for most of Aug. AE, DC, V.

La Marée (E), 1 rue Daru (tel. 47–63–52–42). One of Paris's top restaurants for superbly cooked traditional dishes, especially fish and shellfish. Closed weekends and Aug. AE, DC

Marius et Janette (E), 4 av. George-V (tel. 47–23–41–88). Excellent fish restaurant, given a facelift in 1985 and now rather fashionable. Specializes in Mediterranean dishes like *bouillabaisse* and *bourride*. Closed Sun. and Sat., Christmas and New Year period. V.

Maxim's (E), 3 rue Royale (tel. 42–65–27–94). Turn-of-the-century and world-famous. This ultra-chic restaurant has belonged to couturier Pierre Cardin since the early 80s and has been revitalized from top to toe. Prices are very high but (M) meals are served on the first floor and there are also fixed-price after-theater suppers served from 11 P.M. Open to 1 A.M. Closed Sun. AE, DC, V.

Pavillon de l'Elysée (E), 10 av. Champs-Elysées (tel. 42–65–85–10). After various changes of management this elegant restaurant, set in a delightful 19th-century "pavilion" in the Champs-Elysées gardens, is now run by the great

Gaston Lenôtre. The cuisine is as superb as you would expect. On the ground floor is the less expensive *Jardins* (M). Air-conditioned. Closed weekends and Aug. (*Jardins* stays open). AE, DC, V.

Au Petit Montmorency (E), 5 rue Rabelais (tel. 42–25–11–19). Very imaginative cuisine, though not yet well known. (M) *menu.* Closed weekends and Aug. V.

Taillevent (E), 15 rue Lamennais (tel. 45–63–39–94). One of France's top restaurants, now specializing in *nouvelle cuisine,* with amazing choice of wine (500 vintages no less!). For a memorable dining experience in what was once an elegant private mansion. Air conditioned. Closed weekends, school vacations in Feb., and Aug.

Alsace (M), 39 av. des Champs-Elysées (tel. 43–59–44–24). Chic *brasserie* with *choucroute,* beautifully fresh seafood and superb fruit tarts as well as the delicious light wines for which Alsace is famous. Has shop selling regional goodies next door. Open all day and all night. AE, DC, V.

Androuët (M), 41 rue d'Amsterdam (tel. 48–74–26–93). There are no fewer than 300 cheeses and cheese dishes on offer in this restaurant attached to a celebrated cheesemonger's. Excellent wines to bring out their full flavor. Closed Sun. AE, DC, V.

Chez Edgard (M), 4 rue Marbeuf (tel. 47–20–51–15). Always crowded, popular with the after-theater crowd. Specializes in fish and shellfish. Open to 1 A.M. Closed Sun. AE, DC, MC, V.

La Fermette-Marbeuf (M), 5 rue Marbeuf (tel. 47–20–63–53). Another useful address if you're going to the theater or cinema. Good-value set *menu,* and one room with genuine *art nouveau* decor discovered during renovations (the other is a copy). Open till 11.30 P.M. AE, DC, MC, V.

Moulin du Village (M), 25 rue Royale (tel. 42–65–08–47). Owned by British wine expert Steven Spurrier. Newish cuisine, good wines and ideal setting in a little passageway just off the rue Royale. Closed Sat. for dinner and Sun. V.

La Cour St.-Germain (I), 19 rue Marbeuf (tel. 47–23–84–25). *Menu-carte* specialties; pleasant décor. Open daily to midnight. AE, DC, MC, V.

Bar des Théâtres (I), 6 av. Montaigne. In the heart of couture and theater land. Basic bistrot-type cooking. Chic clientele. Open till 2 A.M. Closed Sun. and Aug.

Chez Bébert (I), 33 rue Marbeuf (tel. 43–59–57–22). A favorite place for couscous. Lively ambiance full of local color. Open till 1 A.M. AE, DC, MC, V.

L'Hippopotamus (I), 6 av. Franklin-Roosevelt (no telephone reservations). Efficient chain of 11 restaurants (in Les Halles, Bastille, Montparnasse, etc.), serving good food at very reasonable prices. Not a gastronomic experience, but fun, and cheerful atmosphere. Open to 1 A.M. V.

Ninth arrondissement

Opéra (Café de la Paix), (E), 3 pl. de l'Opéra (tel. 47–42–97–02). Superb Napoleon III decor. Refined *nouvelle cuisine;* very good wines and desserts. Closed Aug. AE, DC, MC, V.

Auberge Landaise (M), 23 rue Clauzel (tel. 48–78–74–40). Specializes in cooking from the Bordeaux region and does it beautifully. One of the best *cassoulets* in Paris. Rustic decor to go with the food, though the cooking's full of subtlety too. Closed Sun. and Aug. AE, DC, V.

Le Grand Café (M), 4 blvd. des Capucines (tel. 47–42–75–77). Close to the Opéra. Excellent seafood restaurant, very typical of Paris with its aproned waiters and splendid display of shellfish outside. Open day and night. AE, DC, V.

Au Petit Riche (M), 25 rue Le Peletier (tel. 47–70–68–68). Late 19th-century decor, home-style dishes. Good-value *menu*. Open to 12.15 A.M. Closed Sun. and Aug. AE, V.

Ty-Coz (M), 35 rue St.-Georges (tel. 48–78–42–95). Well-known Breton fish restaurant. Closed Sun., Mon. and part of Aug. AE, DC, V.

Bistro de la Gare (I), 38 blvd. des Italiens (no telephone reservations). Same formula as its namesake in the 6e. Open to 1 A.M.

Chartier (I), 7 rue du Faubourg-Montmartre (tel. 47–70–86–29). Turn-of-the-century decor, great atmosphere, and ludicrously low prices.

Le Roi du Pot-au-Feu (I), 34 rue Vignon (tel. 47–42–37–10). Plain but hearty *pot-au-feu* makes a welcome change if you've been indulging in rich cuisine. Closed Sun. and July.

Tenth arrondissement

Chez Michel (E), 10 rue Belzunce (tel. 48–78–44–14). Excellent Norman cuisine. Air-conditioned. Closed Fri., Sat., part of Feb., most of Aug. and at Christmas. AE, DC, V.

Brasserie Flo (M), 7 cour des Petites-Ecuries (tel. 47–70–13–59). A genuine Alsatian *brasserie* set in a courtyard. Always full so reservation is absolutely essential, especially for late-evening dining. Open till 1.30 A.M. AE, DC, V.

Julien (M), 16 rue du Faubourg St.-Denis (tel. 47–70–12–06). Fashionable, *art nouveau* decor and traditional French cuisine. Clientele is fashionable too, particularly in the evening, when it stays open till 1.30 A.M. AE, DC, V.

P'tite Tonkinoise (M), 56 rue fbg. Poissonnière (tel. 42–46–85–98). Genuine Vietnamese cuisine, delicately spicy. Closed Sun., Mon., Aug. and first half of Sept. V.

La Table d'Anvers (M), 2 pl. d'Anvers (tel. 48–78–35–21). Newly opened with well-known chef (Conticini) and good-value *menu* Open daily to 10.30 P.M. V.

Terminus-Nord (M), 23 rue de Dunkerque (tel. 42–85–05–15). Large and very lively bistrot, opposite the Gare du Nord. Decorated in outrageous *art nouveau* style and under the same ownership as the Brasserie Flo and Julien. Good value; you may have to wait for your table. Open to 12.30 A.M. AE, DC, V.

Eleventh arrondissement

Chez Philippe (Auberge Pyrénées-Cévennes), (M), 106 rue de la Folie-Méricourt (tel. 43–57–33–78). Old café with exquisite food from the southwest. Serves until 10.30 P.M. Closed weekends and Aug. AE, V.

Sousceyrac (M), 35 rue Faidherbe (tel. 43–71–65–30). Bustling family-run restaurant serving specialties from the Perigord region with wonderful *foie gras*. Generous portions and good service. Closed weekends. AE, V.

Twelfth arrondissement

La Gourmandise (M), 271 av. Daumesnil (tel. 43–43–94–41). Light, inventive cuisine by the owner/chef, Alain Denoual, formerly of Maxim's and the Tour d'Argent. Good-value *menu* for lunch (I) and dinner (M). A real find, recommended by an enthusiastic reader. Closed Sat. for lunch, Sun., one week in Apr., Aug. AE, DC, V.

Au Trou Gascon (M), 40 rue Taine (tel. 43–44–34–26). Genuine turn-of-the-century bistrot with inventive "new" cuisine of regional cooking from Gascony, plus superb wines. Closed weekends, mid-July to mid-Aug. and Christmas. V.

La Connivence (I), 1 rue de la Cotte (tel. 46–28–46–17). Simple cooking, and good value. Just behind picturesque Marché d'Aligre. Closed Aug. AE, V.

Thirteenth arrondissement

Aux Vieux Métiers de France (E), 13 blvd. Auguste-Blanqui (tel. 45–88–90–03). Light and modern cuisine (mainly fish), served by candlelight in 17th-century decor. Closed Sun. and Mon. AE, DC, MC, V.

Les Algues (M), 66 av. Gobelins (tel. 43–31–58–22). Typical old Paris bistrot setting; specializes in delicious fish cooked "new" style. Closed Sun., Mon., first half of Aug. and Christmas and New Year period. AE, V.

Fourteenth arrondissement

Le Duc (E), 243 blvd. Raspail (tel. 43–20–96–30). One of Paris's finest seafood restaurants, firmly anchored in the "new" cuisine so don't come here if you're against the idea of raw scallops or underdone *loup de mer*. But we are willing to bet that chef Jean Minchelli will convert you if you're prepared to try. Anyway, *nouvelle cuisine* addicts will adore it, but do make sure to reserve. Closed Sat. through Mon.

Lous Landès (E), 157 av. du Maine (tel. 45–43–08–04). Excellent specialties from southwestern France, with particularly good fish, served in rustic setting. Music to accompany your dinner on Wednesday evenings. Closed Sun. and lunch on Mon. V.

Aux Armes de Bretagne (M), 108 av. Maine (tel. 43–20–29–50). One of the city's best fish restaurants. Good value as long as you stick to the *menus*. Open to midnight. Air-conditioned. Closed Sun. for dinner, Mon., first week in both Jan. and May, and most of Aug. AE, DC, MC, V.

Auberge de l'Argoat (M), 27 ave. Reille (tel. 45–89–17–05). Inventive cooking of fish and shellfish; great *terrines de poissons;* cider from Britanny. Closed Sun., Mon. and Aug.

La Coupole (M), 102 blvd. Montparnasse (tel. 43–20–14–20). Large, famous and long-standing *brasserie* that looks like an arty railway station. Fun people, sound classical cooking. Open all day from 8 A.M. to 2 A.M., with dancing too. Closed Aug. V.

Le Dôme (M), 108 blvd. Montparnasse (tel. 43–35–34–82). Large, bustling restaurant in the middle of Montparnasse specializes in fish dishes. Air-conditioned. Open to 1 A.M. Closed Mon. AE, DC, V.

Pinocchio (I), 124 av. Maine (tel. 43–21–26–10). Delicious homemade pasta and other Italian specialties. Air-conditioned. Closed Sat. for lunch and Sun. AE, DC, V.

Fifteenth arrondissement

Bistro 121 (E), 121 rue de la Convention (tel. 45–57–52–90). Bistrot with a mixture of traditional and new cooking. Closed Sun. evening, Mon., mid-July to mid-Aug., and Christmas and New Year period. AE, DC, MC, V.

Olympe (E), 8 rue Nicolas-Charlet (tel. 47–34–86–08). Run by well-known young female chef. Inventive cuisine, rather small portions. Closed Sat. and Sun. for lunch, Mon., most of Aug. and Christmas period. AE, DC, V.

La Maison Blanche (M), 82 blvd. Lefèbvre (tel. 48–28–38–83). Very plain decor, and short, simple menu offers some of the best value in Paris. Closed Sat. for lunch, Sun., Mon. and 2 weeks in Sept. AE.

Aux Senteurs de Provence (M), 295 rue Lecourbe (tel. 45–57–11–98). A charming old bistrot, recently renovated and specializing in tasty Mediterranean fish dishes (including *aïoli*). Closed Sun., Mon., around Easter and Aug. AE, DC, V.

L'Amanguier (I), 51 rue du Théâtre (tel. 45–77–04–01). Identical to its twin in the 2e—equally interesting menu, equally reasonable prices. AE, MC, V.

Boeuf Gros Sel (I), 299 rue Lecourbe (tel. 45–57–16–33). Good place for mouthwatering home cooking. Closed Sun., Mon. and Aug. V.

Sixteenth arrondissement

Faugeron (E), 52 rue de Longchamp (tel. 47–04–24–53). One of the very best restaurants in Paris serving delicious "new" cuisine. Smart and popular, so do reserve. Good wine list. Closed weekends, Aug. and Christmas.

La Grande Cascade (E), in the Bois de Boulogne (tel. 45–27–33–51). Attractive leafy setting near the famous Longchamp racecourse. Classical cuisine, but also a good place for a delicious ice cream after the races or a stroll in the Bois. Closed from just before Christmas to the end of Jan. AE, DC, V.

L'Ile de France (E), pt. Debilly, opposite 32 av. de New-York (tel. 47–23–60–21). A barge-restaurant moored opposite the Eiffel Tower and bearing a distinct resemblance to a Mississippi paddle steamer with its colonial-style decor. Rather unexpectedly, you can eat well here too, mostly *nouvelle cuisine,* while admiring the delightful view. Closed weekends.

Jean-Claude Ferrero (E), 38 rue Vital (tel. 45–04–42–42). In charming *Hotel Particulier,* with tiny garden. Excellent *nouvelle cuisine* created from fresh produce. Closed weekends, last 2 weeks in Aug., Christmas period. AE, DC, V.

Michel Pasquet (E), 59 rue la Fontaine (tel. 42–88–50–01). Chic and tiny, so you must reserve ahead. Stylish cuisine, with some "new" touches. Good value menu. Closed Sat. for lunch (May to Sept.), Sun., Aug. and Christmas. AE, DC, V.

Pré Catalan (E), rte. de Suresnes, Bois de Boulogne (tel. 45–24–55–58). One of Paris's best and most sought-after restaurants. Very expensive, but very beautiful, especially if it's fine enough to sit out 'neath the spreading chestnut trees. Wonderfully ingenious, mainly "new," cuisine. Closed Sun. evenings, Mon. and part of Feb. AE, DC, V.

Prunier-Traktir (E), 16 av. Victor-Hugo (tel. 45–00–89–12). Long-established seafood restaurant with elegant clientele and twenties decor. Outdoor meals in summer. Closed Sun., Mon. and all July and Aug. AE, DC, V.

Robuchon (E), 32 rue de Longchamp (tel. 47–27–12–27). Young chef-owner Joel Robuchon is an excellent practitioner of the *nouvelle cuisine* and a worthy successor to the great Jamin. Good value *menus.* Must reserve well ahead. Air-conditioned. Closed weekends and July. AE, DC, V.

Le Vieux Galion (E), 10 allée du Bord-de-l'Eau (tel. 45–06–26–10). A 16th-century galleon moored opposite Longchamp racecourse and just right for open-air dining in summer (but it is open all year round), with a view over the Seine. Specializes in fish and shellfish. Open to 12.30 A.M.

Au Clocher du Village (M), 8 rue Verderet (tel. 42–88–35–87). Home-style cooking, chic bistrot ambiance. Closed Sat. for lunch, Sun., and Aug. V.

A la française (M), 120 rue Pompe (tel. 45–53–47–18). Popular with the fashionable residents of this sought-after area; good home-style cooking. Closed Sun., Mon. and Aug.

Ramponneau (M), 21 av. Marceau (tel. 47–20–59–51). Quiet and distinguished. Particularly good for seafood, but offers full range of traditional French cuisine. Open-air tables are very pleasant. Closed Aug. AE, DC, V.

Relais d'Auteuil (M), 31 blvd. Murat (tel. 46–51–09–54). Attractive bistrot near the Bois de Boulogne, good traditional cuisine. Closed Sat. for lunch and Sun. AE, DC, V.

Brasserie Stella (I), 133 av. Victor-Hugo (tel. 47–27–60–54). The favorite meeting place for residents of this well-heeled neighborhood. Particularly lively after-theater crowd, but rather cramped. Open to 2 A.M. Closed Aug.

Seventeenth arrondissement

La Coquille (E), 6 rue du Débarcadère (tel. 45–72–10–73). Ultra-traditional cooking, beautifully done, specializing in game in season. Rather elegant. Closed Sun., Mon. and Aug., and Christmas period. V.

Manoir de Paris (E), 6 rue Pierre-Demours (tel. 45–72–25–25). New venture by chef-owner of the excellent *Ferme St.-Simon* in the Seventh arrondissement. Delicious *nouvelle cuisine*, rather fasionable clientele. Closed weekends and July. AE, DC, V.

Petrus (E), 12 pl. du Maréchal-Juin (tel. 43–80–15–95). Specializes in seafood, cooked in the "new" way. Twenties decor. Closed Sun., Mon. and Aug. AE, DC, MC, V.

Michel Rostang (E), 20 rue Rennequin (tel. 47–63–40–77). Well-known for *nouvelle cuisine* versions of homey dishes, so must reserve. Air-conditioned, and with very friendly service. Closed Sat. lunchtime (but open for lunch May–Sept.), Sun. and Aug. V.

La Barrière de Neuilly (M), 275 blvd. Pereire. Owned by lively restaurateur Claude Verger, serving newish cuisine at not too horrific prices.

Baumann (M), 64 av. des Ternes (tel. 45–74–16–66). A lively crowd patronizes this cheerful restaurant busily eating *choucroute* till 1 A.M. So many different versions you won't know which to choose. Other Alsatian dishes too, plus modish *art nouveau*-style decor. AE, DC, MC, V.

Brasserie Lorraine (M), pl. des Ternes (tel. 42–27–80–04). Long-standing and popular with literary and artistic crowd for its excellent oysters and other shellfish, plus good game in season. Open till 2 A.M. AE, DC, V.

Chez Georges (M), 273 blvd. Pereire (tel. 45–74–31–00). Huge portions of traditional French home-cooking, very popular with the habitués of this distinguished part of Paris. Good for Sunday lunch. Closed Aug.

La Toque (M), 16 rue de Tocqueville (tel. 42–27–97–75). Tiny but comfortable bistrot serving excellent food (chef worked with Michel Guérard). Good-value *menu*. Closed Sat., Sun., Aug. and Christmas vacation. V.

Charly de Bab-el-Oued (I), 95 blvd. Gouvion-St.-Cyr (tel. 45–74–34–62). Popular North African restaurant conveniently sited near the Porte Maillot hotels and the Bois de Boulogne. Air-conditioned. Open to midnight. AE, DC, MC, V.

La Grosse Tartine (I), 91 blvd. Gouvion-St.-Cyr (tel. 45–74–02–77). Family-type cuisine, with specialties from southwestern France. Good wine list, tables outside in summer. Closed Sun., Mon., Tues. for dinner and Aug. AE, DC,

Eighteenth arrondissement

Beauvilliers (E), 52 rue Lamarck (tel. 42–54–54–42). New chef for this charming and well known restaurant just behind Montmartre. Little terrace for sunny days. Closed Sun., for lunch on Mon. and Sept. V.

Clodenis (E), 57 rue Caulaincourt (tel. 46–06–20–26). Small and elegant, with particularly delicious fish and very good value (M) *menus*. Air-conditioned. Closed Sun. V.

Le Consulat (M), 18 rue Norvins (tel. 46–06–50–63). Has been going as a cabaret-cum-restaurant for the last 400 years and shows no sign of fading away! Once a mill, now a cheerful, friendly spot open daily non-stop from noon to 2 A.M. with live pianist in the evenings. AE, DC, V.

Au Cadet de Gascogne, L'Auberge du Village (M), 4 pl. du Tertre (tel. 46–06–71–73). Quite elegant and less "villagey" than some Montmartre restaurants, but still open late (2 A.M.) and with live accordion music in the evenings; a few tables outside, if you don't mind being jostled by the crowds in the square. Closed part of Jan. and Feb.

Clair de Lune (M), 9 rue Poulbot (tel. 42–58–97–03). High up on Montmartre's hill but seems far away from the tourist hordes. Interesting cuisine, including some medieval recipes. Closed Sun., for lunch on Mon. and part of Feb. AE, DC, V.

Chez ma Cousine (M), 12 rue Norvins (tel. 46–06–49–35). Small and friendly, with cabaret in the evening, pancakes in the afternoon. AE, DC, MC, V.

Chez Plumeau (M), 7 pl. du Calvaire (tel. 46–06–70–67). On pretty leafy square with views over Paris. Has Brazilian as well as traditional French music and dancing in the evenings. Tables outside in fine weather. AE, DC, MC, V.

La Crémaillère 1900 (M), 15 pl. du Tertre (tel. 46–06–58–59). Very pretty *art-nouveau*-style decor, tiny garden, delicious *nouvelle cuisine* (specializing in fish), live pianist in the evening. Open daily in summer, but closed Mon. and Tues. from Nov. to Easter. AE, DC, MC, V.

Da Graziano (M), 83 rue Lepic (tel. 46–06–84–77). Charming little Italian restaurant, overshadowed by the huge arms of the Moulin de la Galette and with an adorable tiny garden. And the food's good too. Open till 12.30 A.M. V.

Marie Louise (M), 52 rue Championnet (tel. 46–06–86–55). Long-standing bistrot, off the beaten track but worth it for good value traditional French cuisine. Closed Sun., Mon., July and Aug. V.

Wepler (M), 14 pl. Clichy (tel. 45–22–53–24). Large, long-standing restaurant which makes a change from the more trendy places in Montmartre. Particularly good for seafood. Open daily to 1.30 A.M. AE, DC, MC, V.

Chez La Mère Catherine (I), 6 pl. du Tertre (tel. 46–06–32–69). Small and picturesque. Has been going since 1793, in what was previously a presbytery attached to the church of Saint-Pierre de Montmartre. Tiny garden and tables on square in fine weather. Music in the evenings through till midnight. AE, DC, MC, V.

Au Pichet du Tertre (I), 10 rue Norvins (tel. 46–06–24–19). Good choice of *menus* at reasonable prices. Villagey atmosphere. Open to 11.30 P.M. at weekends. Closed Tues. V

Le Tournant de la Butte (I), 46 rue Caulaincourt (tel. 46–06–39–86). Very inexpensive fixed-price *menu*, cheerful atmosphere and live music at times. Crowded, even though this isn't the touristy part of Montmartre. Closed Mon. and Sept.

Nineteenth arrondissement

The av. Jean-Jaures, close to where the slaughterhouses used to be has several fine restaurants close together and all specialize, of course, in meat. Among them are:

Au Cochon d'Or (E), at no. 192 (tel. 46–07–23–13). Huge portions of traditional French meat dishes and is generally thought to be the best of these restaurants; offal dishes are a specialty. Open all week. AE, DC, MC, V.

Au Boeuf Couronne (M), at no. 188 (tel. 46–07–13–55). Large and cheerful with equally large portions and particularly delicious tripe. Closed Sun. AE, DC, MC, V.

Aux Deux Taureaux (M), at no. 206 (tel. 46–07–39–31). Traditional meat and offal dishes. Closed weekends. AE, DC, V.

Ferme de la Villette (M), at no. 184 (tel. 46–07–60–96). Long-established. Serves shellfish as well as meat specialties. Open till midnight. Closed Sun. and Aug. AE, DC, V.

Neuilly

Jacqueline Fénix (E), 42 av. Charles-de-Gaulle (tel. 46–24–42–61). Elegant little restaurant by Neuilly's open-air market. Also near the Porte Maillot. Imaginative cuisine. Closed weekends, Aug., and Christmas and New Year period. V.

Bourrier (M), 1 pl. Parmentier (tel. 46–24–11–19). Set in a pretty square well away from the traffic at the Porte Maillot. Fine "new" cuisine served by the chefs as there are no waiters. Rather elegant. Closed weekends (but open for Sat. lunch May through Sept.), most of Aug., Christmas and New Year, V.

Café de la Jatte (M), 67 blvd. de Levallois (tel. 47–45–04–20). Huge terrace of this trendy new restaurant on the "ile de la Jatte" is a pleasant place to have lunch or dinner, to see and be seen. Serves until midnight. Closed Sat. for lunch. AE, V.

Sébîllon-Paris-Bar (M), 20 av. Charles-de-Gaulle, just by Porte Maillot (tel. 46–24–71–31). Long-standing and always busy restaurant. Good traditional cooking. Now redecorated and air-conditioned. Open to 1 A.M. AE, DC, MC, V.

La Boutarde (I), 4 rue Boutard (tel. 47–45–34–55). This might look like a modest provincial café, but in fact it has a very unprovincial clientele. Crowded with expense-accounters at lunchtime. Straightforward home-style cooking; very tasty though portions can be small. You can eat outside in summer. Cheerful waiters. Closed Sat. for lunch and Sun. DC, V.

Boulogne-Billancourt

Au Comte de Gascogne (E), 89 av. Jean-Baptiste-Clement (tel. 46–03–47–27). One of the best restaurants in the Paris area. Specialties from southwestern France and some "new" cuisine. Closed weekends and Aug. AE, DC, V.

L'Auberge (M), 86 av. Jean-Baptiste-Clément (tel. 46–05–22–35). Typical 19th-century inn decor, with outdoor service in fine weather. Specialties from the Franche-Comte region, of course, plus some *nouvelle cuisine* dishes. Closed Sun. and Aug. AE, DC, V.

Laux à la Bouche (M), 117 av. Jean-Baptiste-Clément (tel. 48–25–43–88). Despite its punning name (the chef-owner is Monsieur Laux), this is a serious little restaurant with carefully cooked traditional French dishes and particularly good fish. v.

L'Avant-Seine (I), 1 rond-point Rhin-et-Danube (tel. 48–25–58–00). Under the same ownership as the two best-known restaurants in Versailles. Very good value. Closed Sun. and Mon. v.

 CAFÉS. Cafés are an important feature of the Paris scene, both by day and by night. People-watching from a sidewalk café is one of the traditional delights savored by generations of visitors and one you'll never grow tired of. There are hundreds—maybe thousands—of cafés all over the city, ranging from chic places on the Champs-Elysées or near the Opéra and intellectual haunts in Saint-Germain-des-Prés or Montparnasse to neighborhood corner cafés where the locals get together to exchange gossip, play cards, even watch television. The prices vary greatly according to the location, but as no one will stop you lingering for hours over a single cup of coffee or a drink (except in some student places on the blvd. St.-Michel, where you'll be made to reorder every hour or so), you'll find even the more expensive spots won't break the bank.

A word of warning: many cafés have a counter at which you can stand to have a drink or a light snack such as the hard-boiled eggs traditionally found there, or a sandwich. The prices are lower if you are served at the bar than if a waiter or waitress serves you when you're sitting at a table. So don't do as you would in a British pub and pay for your drinks at the bar and then go and sit down—the manager will certainly come over and rebuke you.

Here are a few ideas for the better-known places. You will notice that several of them are grouped on the boulevard Saint-Germain, a traditional place for sidewalk life.

Café de la Paix, 12 blvd. des Capucines, 9e, just by the Opéra. Popular with wealthy foreign visitors.

La Coupole, 102 blvd. du Montparnasse, 14e. An old favorite in Montparnasse.

Aux Deux Magots, 170 blvd. St.-Germain, 6e. Not the intellectuals' mecca it used to be in the heyday of existentialism, when Sartre and Co. practically lived here, but still very fashionable and probably the best place for people watching. You even get street entertainment thrown in at times—fire-eaters, acrobats, mimes and the like.

Le Dôme, 108 blvd. du Montparnasse, 14e. Another well-known Montparnasse spot, but the new decor is a bit overdone (fake *art nouveau*).

Le Flore, 172 blvd. St.-Germain, 6e. Next door to Deux-Magots, though it doesn't share its unbeatable corner location. Changed hands in the mid-'80s, but the new owners had to sign an undertaking to leave it just as it is!

Fouquet's, 99 av. des Champs-Elysées, 8e. Very chic and expensive, on the corner of the avenue George-V. A place to be seen. Has a good bar, too.

Lipp, 151 blvd. St.-Germain, 6e. Officially a brasserie (see *Restaurants*) but has a few tables out front.

La Rhumerie, 166 blvd. St.-Germain. Another Saint-Germain favorite. Always crowded. Specializes in a huge range of punches.

Le Sélect, 99 blvd. du Montparnasse, 6e. Has kept something of the old Montparnasse atmosphere in spite of the rebuilding that has transformed this area. Open late.

 BARS. Cafés are so Parisian in spirit that bars are less common and less frequented than in many other capitals. Among the more attractive bars are those in skyscrapers, where you can enjoy fabulous views while you sip your late-night drinks—or early ones, for that matter.

Café Beaubourg, Plaza of the Pompidou Center. Recently opened; interior designed by Philippe Stark.

Café Coste, 4 rue Berger, 1er. A recent arrival in the Les Halles area. Trendy.

La Calvados, 40 av. Pierre-Ier-de-Serbie, 8e. A favorite spot with the smart-set drinking until the early hours—or later (it stays open all night). Good pianist.

Ciel de Paris, on top of the Tour Montparnasse, 14e. Superb views.

La Closerie des Lilas, 171 blvd. Montparnasse, 6e. Some people say this firmly literary and artistic spot—it's been frequented by writers and painters since the thirties—is overrated. But the pleasant bar is very popular for a latish drink. Sometimes there's a live pianist, too.

Harry's Bar, 5 rue Daunou, 2e. Opened as long ago as 1911 and has never looked back, even though the Hemingway era is well and truly over. Popular with Parisians as well as expatriate and visiting Americans, it stays open year-round till the wee small hours. The idea has been parleyed into an international chain and you'll find Harry's Bars all over Europe.

Montgolfier, 'panoramic bar' in the Sofitel-Paris hotel (you are whisked up there by an outside elevator); even has a swimming pool.

Pacific Palisades, 51 rue Quincampoix, 4e. In the Beaubourg area, *art déco* decor and mood. Very chic, lots of genuine Parisians.

Petit-Opportun, 15 rue Lavandières-Ste.-Opportune, 1er. In the Châtelet area, above a well-known jazz spot of the same name. Open late.

Plein-Ciel, Concorde-Lafayette hotel at the Porte Maillot; lovely views over the Bois de Boulogne.

Rosebud, 11 bis rue Delambre, 14e. Long-established bar in Montparnasse, open daily to around 2 A.M.

Toit de Paris, Hilton hotel; the view isn't all that marvelous, but you can dance here as well as drink.

 WINE BARS. As a general rule, the French prefer to eat their main meal in the middle of the day. It can therefore be difficult to find places to enjoy a light lunch if you're not in the mood for a mere sandwich or other café food. But it has suddenly become fashionable among Paris's well-heeled younger set to go to a wine bar, and the result is a great boon to visitors to Paris who like the idea of relaxing at lunchtime or in the early evening with a glass of wine and a tasty light meal such as pâté, a plate of cold cuts, or a delicious cheese dish. Wine bars of this type are springing up in some parts of Paris, though it is important to note that the old-style *bistrot à vin* is more a place for hardened local drinkers than the newer breed of wine bar, and rarely offers anything very interesting in the way of food.

The typical new-style wine bar is full of fairly chic patrons of the Young Aspiring Professional type, plus a sprinkling of old-timers who've lived in the district for years. The majority don't stay open late, so don't count on them for an evening meal, and few are open on Sundays; in fact many are closed all weekend. The following list offers a few suggestions, but you'll find that there are plenty more to choose from:

Blue Fox, Cité Berryer, 25 rue Royale, 8e. Run by Steven Spurrier who also presides over the Moulin du Village and the Académie du Vin. Closed Sat. evening and Sun.

L'Ecluse, 15 quai des Grands-Augustins, 6e. Once a typical Left-Bank cabaret, now a slick wine bar with converted gas lamps, art nouveau posters and a distinctly upmarket clientele. It's been such a success that it's spawned a minichain with the same name all over Paris and even in chic Neuilly. You'll find others at rue Mondétour, 1er; rue du Pont-de-Lodi, 6e; 15 pl. de la Madeleine, 8e; 64 rue François-Ier, 8e; 2 rue du Général Bertier, Neuilly. All are open to 1.30 A.M. (last orders at 1) and closed Sun. v.

Le Petit Bacchus, 13 rue du Cherche-Midi, 6e. Here you can buy wine to take out as well. Closed Sun. and Mon., and open only until 7.15.

Le Rubis, 10 rue du Marché St.-Honoré, 1er. An old favorite with a huge choice of wine, good lunchtime food too. Closed weekends and most of Aug.

La Tartine, 24 rue de Rivoli, 4e. Typical Parisian spot, with regular clientele, good range of wines, and a friendly atmosphere. Open to around 10 P.M. Closed Tues. and for lunch on Wed.

Taverne Henri IV, 13 pl. Pont-Neuf. Attractive setting right by the lovely place Dauphine on the edge of the Ile de la Cité. Closed weekends.

 JUICE BARS. A newcomer to the Paris eating scene is the juice bar, which is quickly catching on among the younger generation of Parisians, who are more into health foods than their elders. The majority of these pleasantly casual places are near the place Saint-Michel, several of them beside the Seine. They're good places for a refreshing stop between sightseeing visits, and many also serve good homemade ices and milkshakes.

L'Afruitdisiaque, 3 rue du Bourg-Tibourg, 4e. A popular place near the Beaubourg Center and open every day of the week, from 11 A.M. to 2 A.M. Live pianist at times. Also at 5 rue du Cygne, 1er, just by Les Halles. v.

Le Paradis du Fruit, 28bis rue Louis-le-Grand, 2e. Conveniently near the Opéra, also serves salads and some tasty pâtisseries. Open 12 noon to 1 A.M.

Le Paradis du Fruit, 17 quai des Grands-Augustins, 6e. Overlooking the Seine, handy if you're exploring the Latin Quarter. Open 11 A.M. to 2 A.M., closed Tues.

La Passion du Fruit, 71 quai de la Tournelle, 5e. Opposite the Ile St.-Louis on the Left Bank and convenient for Notre Dame. Open daily, 11 A.M.–1 P.M. and 6 P.M.–2 A.M.

Sightseeing

CITY TOURS. The key place for bus tours of Paris enabling you to get the feel of the place is the place des Pyramides, 1er, at the Palais-Royal end of the Tuileries Gardens. That's where the buses start out from, and the various companies running tours can all be found in the area:

American Express, 11 rue Scribe, 9e (tel. 42–66–09–99).

Cityrama, 4 pl. des Pyramides, 1er (tel. 42–60–30–14).

Paris Vision, 214 rue de Rivoli, 1er (tel. 42–60–30–01).

Tours are generally in double-decker buses, with either a live guide or a taperecorded commentary (English available of course), and take around three hours. Paris-by-Night tours also available, generally finishing up at the Lido on the Champs-Elysées for the floor show.

For a more personal tour, contact *Hans Forster's Limousine Guide Service,* 202 rue de Rivoli, 1er (tel. 42–96–40–02 for answering machine with message in English). Guides with cars taking up to 7 passengers will take you round Paris or the surrounding area for a minimum of 3 hours at a charge of around $25–30 per hour all told (no additional mileage charge). *Must reserve.*

The *RATP (Paris Transport Authority)* has many guide-accompanied excursions in and around Paris. Inquire at their Tourist Service in the place de la Madeleine, 8e (to the right of the church when you're facing it), or at their office at 53 quai des Grands-Augustins, 6e; both are open daily, even on public holidays.

Walking Tours. There is a wealth of guided tours of a specific part of Paris, such as the Marais or the Ile Saint-Louis or Saint-Germain-des-Prés, generally concentrating on a specific topic—for instance private walled gardens in Saint-Germain, synagogues or restored mansions in the Marais, or a specific historic building, such as the Hôtel de Lauzun on the Ile Saint-Louis. Tours are often restricted to thirty or so people and are popular with Parisians as well as French and foreign tourists. They are accompanied by guides whose enthusiasm and dedication are often exemplary, but the great majority are in French. However, as this may be the only way you can get to see some private buildings or gardens, you may well find it worth while even if you don't understand all the guide says. Charges vary, depending on whether or not the guide has to pay a fee to the owner of any places visited, but are usually in the region of 20–45 frs per person. Tours are mostly held in the afternoons and generally last around 2 hours.

Full details are given in *Pariscope* and *L'Officiel des Spectacles* (under the heading *Conférences*), and in most cases you must merely turn up at the appointed time (given as *RV* or *rendez-vous*). Best get there early in case there is a restriction on numbers. You can sometimes reserve ahead of time for walking tours organized by the *Caisse Nationale des Monuments Historiques* (Bureau des Visites-Conférences, Hôtel de Sully, 62 rue St.-Antoine, 4e, tel. 42–74–22–22), which publishes a small booklet every two months listing all tours planned for the next two months.

Warning: in the case of visits to some private mansions you may be asked to show identification, so be sure to have your passport on you.

River Trips. Sightseeing trips along the River Seine are a must for most visitors to Paris. Times and prices correct at our press time, but do check locally.

Bateaux Mouches (tel. 42–25–96–10) start out from the Right Bank (i.e. north) end of the Pont de l'Alma, 8e. Departures daily every half hour between 10 and 12 and 2 and 6, with additional evening cruises most of the year between 9 and 10. Prices 20 frs daytime, 25 frs evenings. Cruises including lunch daily except Monday, leaving at 1 P.M. Price for adults, 250–300 frs, for children under 12, 120 frs. Evening cruises including dinner, again daily except Monday, at 8.30. Cost: 450 frs, no children under 12 allowed, must be respectably dressed.

Bateaux Parisiens-Tour Eiffel (tel. 45–51–33–08 or 47–05–50–00) start out from the Port-La Bourdonnais, Pont d'Iéna, Left Bank, 7e. Departures daily every half hour between 9.30 and 6, with evening "illuminations cruises" Sat. only up to 10 P.M. Prices: 25 frs, children under 10, 15 frs. Cruises including lunch Fri., Sat. and Sun. only, at 1 P.M. Price: 230 frs. Cruises including dinner Fri. and Sat. only at 8. Price: 420 frs. Reservations for meals: tel. 47–05–09–85.

Vedettes Paris Ile-de-France (tel. 47–05–71–29) start out from the Port de Suffren, 7e. Departures daily every half-hour between 10.30 and 5, with evening cruises up to 11 P.M. Mon. and Tues., up to midnight other evenings. Prices: 25 frs, children under 10, half-price.

Vedettes du Pont Neuf (tel. 46–33–98–38) start out from the Square du Vert Galant, in the middle of the Pont-Neuf. Departures daily at 10.30, 11.15 and 12, and every half hour between 2 and 5. Prices: 25 frs, children under 10, 12 frs.

Canauxrama (tel. 46–24–86–16) has canal tours in flat-bottomed barges along the Canal Saint-Martin to the Villette in northeastern Paris or vice versa. Departures from 5bis quai de la Loire, 19e (*Métro:* Jaurès) or Port de l'Arsenal, 12e (*Métro:* Bastille). Times vary depending on the river traffic, so you must call them to find out for the day you plan to take the trip. Prices: 55 frs mornings, 70 frs afternoons; students and over-65s, 50 frs and 60 frs; children under 12, 40 frs; no charge for under-6s. Also day cruises on the Canal de l'Ourcq, with return journey in special bus. Departures from Bassin de la Villette, 19e. Price around 160 frs. Check times locally.

Quiztour, 19 rue Athènes, 93 (tel. 48–74–75–30) runs the famous "Patache Eautobus" which plies Paris's canal. Check schedules and prices locally.

Air Tours. *Hélicap* (tel. 45–57–75–51) organizes helicopter trips overflying Paris, or the Défense on the western edge of the city, or Versailles; or you can have a long panoramic flight. Approximate costs: Paris tours 430 frs; Versailles, 270 frs; Versailles and Paris 600 frs; panoramic trip, 1075 frs. Reductions for groups of 10 or more. *Reservation essential.*

 MUSEUMS AND GALLERIES. Museum opening times in Paris vary considerably. Those belonging to the **City of Paris** (marked *CP* in our sightseeing checklists) are closed on Monday, but otherwise open 10 to 5.40. No admission fee for children under 7 or anyone over 65 at any time (passport may be required to prove your age). No admission charge for anyone on Sundays to permanent collections; but you may still have to pay to visit special temporary exhibits.

National or State-owned Museums (marked *N* in our checklists) are closed on Tuesday, except for the Musée d'Orsay, which closes Monday. However opening times are not standardized, with some still closing over the lunch break. Our checklists give opening times for each museum. No admission charge for anyone under 18, or for professional artists, journalists and teachers with documentation to prove their status. Half-price is the general rule on Sundays for everybody, and on other days for young people aged between 18 and 25, over-65s and those attending (and therefore paying for) lecture tours.

Private Museums again have widely varying opening hours, detailed in our checklists. However you should bear in mind that when a special exhibit is on show opening hours may be quite different from the standard times for the main collection; for instance museums that are normally shut on Sunday may stay open when they're staging a special exhibit. Check this out with *Pariscope* or *L'Officiel des Spectacles.*

Unless otherwise stated in our lists, all Paris museums charge an admission fee to most visitors. If you belong to any of the categories enjoying free or reduced admission in the state-owned museums it is always worth politely inquiring at private museums if they offer concessions to your particular category. It is also worth proffering a student card if you have one—that may well result in a reduced charge. We can't give you a rule of thumb about the cost of getting into museums, as admission charges vary so much. The *Direction des Musées de France,* Palais du Louvre, Cour Visconti, 34 quai du Louvre, 75001 publishes a brochure every two months giving details of all Paris museums, including admission charges for the next two months. You can also ask for it at the city's tourist offices. But make sure to have an up-to-date issue: admission charges are liable to shoot up when special exhibits are showing.

Public holidays are a problem as there are no hard-and-fast rules. We advise you to buy *Pariscope* or *L'Officiel des Spectacles* if a public holiday falls during your visit: they publish lists of museums open on the relevant holiday. Beware particularly of May, which has a public holiday every week most years: 1 May, 8 May, Ascension Day and Whit Monday.

Galleries in Paris are a law unto themselves, as far as opening times are concerned. They may well not open until 10 A.M. but there's a good chance they'll be open till 7 P.M.; the smaller ones may close between around 12.30 and 2. They are normally closed on Sundays and public holidays and some are also closed on Monday mornings, or even Monday all day. They do not normally charge for admission, as they are mostly there to sell what they have on display. The main areas to head for are Saint-Germain-des-Prés, especially the little streets between the boulevard and the river Seine.

CHURCHES. Many of Paris's historic churches are full of beautiful paintings and other objects that you'll want to admire. In these days of widespread thefts from churches they are no longer open all day and all night. Most open quite early in the morning, around 7 A.M. when early masses are held. They may be closed between around 12.30 and 3, then reopen until around 7. You should naturally maintain a respectful attitude when masses are in progress and it would be ill-mannered to wander round sightseeing at such times. But no one will object if you stay quietly at the back admiring the architecture and perhaps slipping into the side chapels. Although dress rules are not as rigidly enforced as in, say, Spain, we recommend that you avoid shorts and skimpy barebacked beach-style wear. However you do not need to cover your head.

SPECIAL EXHIBITS. Public libraries, cultural centers, even business firms and banks sometimes stage interesting exhibits of paintings, photographs or sculpture, or historical exhibits consisting of items connected with the history of one particular district in Paris. Such exhibits are usually free and are often of exceptional interest. Check if anything of the kind is on during your visit by studying the lists in *Pariscope* or *L'Officiel des Spectacles* and keep an eye open for posters advertising this type of one-off display.

You may also find it interesting to visit one of the big fairs held in Paris throughout the year. For instance there's the *Foire de Paris* in May (a huge exhibit with big sections on France's regions and on regional food and wines), the *Salon du Livre* in March or April (a must for book-lovers) and the *Antiquarian Book Fair* in June or July. There is usually an admission charge to such fairs, in the region of 35 frs per person, but foreign visitors are sometimes allowed in free (take your passport).

PARIS

Entertainment

FINDING OUT. As you'd expect from its reputation, Paris nightlife is colorful and varied. There's a huge choice on offer, ranging from chic nightclubs frequented by the international jet set to tiny dives popular with kids. And if Paris by Night isn't really your scene, you'll find a whole host of other entertainments on offer, some expected, some less so, and most of it available year-round too.

Your first move should be to buy one of the weekly "What's On" publications, *Pariscope* or *L'Officiel des Spectacles,* both of which come out on Wednesday (the day the movie programs change). They list everything you can think of in the way of entertainment, cultural, sexy and just plain fun. Your hotel may have a copy of *Paris Sélection,* a free publication produced by the Paris Tourist Office. Another useful aid to successful planning is the *Sélection Loisirs* telephone service—call 47–20–88–98 for the English-language version. The recorded message covers the week's happenings in the capital. Watch out, too, for posters displayed by the City Hall all over Paris; they'll tell you about one-off events such as firework displays, open-air dances etc.

OPERA AND BALLET. Fortunately, you don't need a knowledge of French to enjoy the excellent productions at the **Paris Opéra,** the opulent building in the place de l'Opéra, now generally considered to be one of the great houses. But you'll probably have a lot of trouble getting tickets.

The **Opéra Comique** (also known as the **Salle Favart**), 5 rue Favart, 2e, is Paris's second opera house specializing in opera with spoken dialogue (which is what the term *opéra comique* means in French).

The Opéra is also the home of the state-subsidized ballet company, which has a fairly high reputation. Rudolf Nureyev became its main director in 1983, for an indefinite period. But you'll find that much of the most interesting ballet in Paris comes during the annual November–December Ballet Festival held in the **Théâtre des Champs-Elysées** in the avenue Montaigne. Major foreign companies and guest stars perform during this excellent festival. Other places where ballet is staged are the **Théâtre de la Ville,** pl. du Châtelet, the huge **Palais des Congrès** at the Porte Maillot and the **Palais des Sports** at the Porte de Versailles—not as atmospheric as the Opéra, but able to seat thousands of people. The **Théâtre Musical de Paris,** in the place du Châtelet, offers opera and ballet designed for a more popular audience with much lower seat prices than at the Opéra. A "popular opera house" at the Bastille is due to open on 14 July 1989 for the Bicentennial of the French Revolution.

Keep an eye open for ballet performances during the *Festival du Marais* in the early summer and the *Festival Estival* (Summer Festival), which runs from mid-July to around mid-September. And outside Paris, opera (and occasionally ballet) is staged in the pretty opera house in Versailles.

THEATER. National Theaters. The shows are naturally in French, so if your command of the language isn't great, you may find them heavy going. Paris's best-known "national" (i.e. state-subsidized) theaters are:

The **Comédie Française** near the Opéra and beside the Palais-Royal in the place André-Malraux. The company specializes in performances of the great dramatists of the 17th century, Corneille, Molière and Racine, but also ranges well beyond the classical repertoire, staging plays by modern playwrights from France and all over the world. Seats can be reserved in person a maximum of 1 week in advance.

The **Théâtre de Chaillot,** in the place du Trocadéro 16e, has some interesting experimental shows from time to time.

The **Odéon,** in the place Paul-Claudel in the Latin Quarter, is used mainly as an overspill for the Comédie Française, but also houses visiting companies, including major foreign troupes (such as Britain's Royal Shakespeare Company) playing in their own language.

The **Théâtre de la Ville** in the place du Châtelet stages a major international theater festival, plus opera and ballet at times.

Commercial Theaters. For the many commercial theaters, most of which are in the Opéra area, you'll need to study lists of what's currently on. A surprising number of plays turn out to be translations of American or British hits, but you may find such well-known French dramatists as Jean Anouilh, Henri de Montherlant or the ever-green Ionesco running. Many English-speaking visitors think French acting rather declamatory and "theatrical" compared to what they are used to at home.

Experimental Theaters. You may well find that one of the experimental theaters is more to your taste. True theater buffs should certainly check out what's showing at places such as the following:

Cartoucherie, av. de la Pyramide, on the edge of Paris at Vincennes. Several resident companies here, with invariably interesting, sometimes way-out shows. At our presstime these three separate mini-theaters were operating, but be sure to check the latest position: **Théâtre de la Tempête,** tel. 43–28–36–36; **Atelier du Chaudron,** tel. 43–28–97–04; **Théâtre de l'Aquarium,** tel. 43–74–99–61.

Epicerie, 12 rue du Renard, 3e, tel. 42–72–23–41, near Beaubourg and the Hôtel de Ville.

Lucernaire, 53 rue Notre-Dame-des-Champs, 6e, tel. 45–44–57–34, with two separate theaters, the **Théâtre Noir** and the **Théâtre Rouge,** each generally offering two different shows nightly.

Rond-Point, av. Franklin-Roosevelt, 8e, tel. 42–56–70–80; the **Petite Salle** in this very attractive former ice-skating palace now housing the world-famous Madeleine Renaud–Jean-Louis Barrault company often has interesting semi-experimental shows.

Café-Theaters. Originally an import from the United States, café-theaters have now been thoroughly absorbed into the cultural life of Paris and often display that spark of invention that is missing in more conventional theater.

Shows are generally short and in some several different plays or shows are staged each evening. They are usually crowded, often uncomfortable, but at some you can get a good dinner too. Most are closed Sundays. They tend to come and go, but the following are usually reliable:

Au Bec Fin, 6 rue Thérèse, 1er (tel. 42–96–29–35). Here you can get a good dinner before, after or between the shows (two different ones nightly).

Les Blancs-Manteaux, 15 rue des Blancs-Manteaux, 4e (tel. 48–87–15–84). Has 2 separate mini-theaters, each offering 3 different shows nightly.

Le Café d'Edgar, 58 blvd. Edgar-Quinet, 14e (tel. 43–20–85–11). 3 different shows nightly.

Le Café de la Gare, 41 rue du Temple, 3e (tel. 42–78–52–51). Bigger than the others (can seat 400).

Le Point Virgule, 7 rue Croix de la Bretonnerie, 8e (tel. 42–78–67–03). Several shows nightly. Closed Mon.

La Vieille Grille, 1 rue Puits-de-l'Hermite, 5e (tel. 47–07–60–93). Dinner about 8, show at about 10.30.

Chansonniers. These have been superseded to a certain extent by the café-theaters, especially for young people, but they are still very popular with Parisians. The material is topical and frequently satirical, so you'll need to be pretty familiar with the current French political and social scene, as well as knowing French really well. The best two are:

Caveau de la République, 1 blvd. Saint-Martin, 3e (tel. 42–78–44–45).

Deux-Anes, 100 blvd. de Clichy, 18e (tel. 46–06–10–26).

CONCERTS. Paris is one of Europe's liveliest cities for contemporary music these days, thanks partly to the influence of Pierre Boulez, France's greatest living composer-conductor, who returned to the country to head the contemporary music section at the **Pompidou/Beaubourg Center.** Interesting concerts are given there most of the year. Fine classical concerts are often held in the city's concert halls and, perhaps more interestingly for foreign visitors, in her historic churches. This is a splendid way of combining the delights of sightseeing with listening to music. Have a look to see if there's a concert being performed in **Notre-Dame, Saint-Louis-des-Invalides, Saint-Germain-l'Auxerrois, Saint-Merri** or the **Sainte Chapelle,** all of which provide the most stunning settings. The concerts in the marvelous Gothic Sainte Chapelle are out of this world, especially if you're lucky enough to hit a time when they're performed by candlelight. Leaflets covering six months of programs can be obtained from the Paris Tourist Office or the Sainte Chapelle itself, and you'd be well advised to reserve well ahead if possible.

In the summer months the excellent *Festival de l'Ile-de-France* stages fine concerts of classical music in churches, abbeys, châteaux and town halls all over the Ile de France. This again gives you an opportunity to combine an evening's concert going with a spot of sightseeing. And during the *Festival du Marais* in Paris concerts are often performed in the courtyards of the area's beautifully restored mansions.

MOVIES. Paris has hundreds of movie houses, some huge and palatial, some tiny and uncomfortable. Parisians are far more addicted to the cinema as an art form than Londoners or New Yorkers, and you'll find that the latest films, French or foreign, are widely discussed. The letters "v.f." (*version française*) beside a foreign film in a newspaper or magazine listing mean that it has been dubbed into French; the letters "v.o." (*version originale*), that it is showing in the original language with French subtitles.

The bigger movie houses are mostly on the Champs-Elysées or around the Opéra, the smaller art houses in the Latin Quarter or Saint-Germain-des-Prés. Programs change on Wednesdays. The standard program has movies showing at two-hourly intervals between around 2 P.M. and midnight (later on Fri. and Sat.). Prices are 30% lower on Mondays, except public holidays.

Paris has two **cinémathèques,** showing classics from all over the world, one in the Beaubourg/Pompidou Center, 4e, the other at the Palais de Chaillot in the Place du Trocadéro, 16e.

Programs can be found in the "What's On" publications, and in the daily press.

CIRCUSES. The circus is a popular form of entertainment in Paris and has the great advantage that you don't need to know the language. Don't miss the splendid **Cirque National Gruss** if it's playing when you're in town. This is true traditional circus, with the emphasis on brilliant equestrian acts. In fact, there has been a tendency to go back to traditional circus, rather than spectacular numbers better suited to television, and you'll find a number of small family circuses in town at frequent intervals, especially during the school vacations. Again, check the "What's On" publications.

SHOWS. Dinner plus floor show is one of the traditional ways of spending an evening on the town in Paris. But nightclubs are expensive and you'll usually find you're expected to drink champagne, though this doesn't stop them being full to bursting most nights. Best reserve several days ahead of time to make sure you get a good table, and don't be disappointed if your fellow guests are mostly other tourists.

Alcazar de Paris, 62 rue Mazarine, 6e (tel. 43–29–02–20). A well-known spot in Saint-Germain-des-Prés. Dinner at 8, show around 9.30.

Le Don Camilo, 10 rue des Sts.-Pères, 6e (tel. 42–60–25–46). An old favorite in Saint-Germain-des-Prés. Dinner and show from around 8.30. Prices more reasonable than most.

Folies-Bergère, 32 rue Richer, 9e (tel. 42–46–77–11). The best-known name and it deserves its reputation. Extravagant sets, showy costumes, elaborate sound effects, spectacular semi-nude dancers. Show at around 8.45.

Lido, 116 av. des Champs-Elysées, 8e (tel. 45–63–11–61). Very lavish, full of dazzling technical tricks and sound-and-light effects, plus very professional entertainers. The food is adequate, but the show's the thing, and you can dance before and between the shows, too. Dinner-dance at 8 or 8.30, shows at around 10.30 and 12.30 (A.M. natch).

Moulin Rouge, pl. Blanche 19e (tel. 46–06–00–19). Still cashing in on the most famous name in Montmartre's night life, thanks to Toulouse-Lautrec and a whole string of famous and talented artists; and still specializing in the one and only one can-can. Very professional. Dinner-dance at 8, shows at about 10 and midnight.

Le Paradis Latin, 28 rue du Cardinal-Lemoine, 5e (tel. 43–25–28–28). Lively, crowded, very "in"; attracts some big names. Dinner and show at about 8. "Champagne revue" at about 10.30 or 11. Closed Tues.

Raspoutine, 58 rue Bassano, 8e (tel. 47–20–04–31). Russian in the grand style, with red velvet, mirrors, the lot. Not exactly "in," but marvelously luxurious. Dinner and show from about 9. Stays open till dawn.

Shéhérazade, 3 rue de Liege, 9e (tel. 48–74–85–20). Atmospheric Russian cabaret; very plush setting.

Les Girls. A lot of the shows that were once merely titillating are frankly pornographic nowadays, but these two strip shows have proved their worth and can be safely recommended:

Crazy Horse Saloon, 12 av. George-V, 8e (tel. 47–23–32–32). Claims to be the world's top nude show and many of its regular patrons would agree, which is why it's always crowded. Well-run place, with two slick shows at around 9.30 and 11.45 Sun.–Thurs., and three on Fri. and Sat., the last at around 1 A.M. Air-conditioned.

Milliardaire Club, 68 rue Pierre-Charron, 8e (tel. 42–25–25–17). Used to be called "Le Sexy" and is still just that. Not as stylish as the Crazy Horse, but a pretty good show for nude-fans. Two separate shows at around 10.30 and 12.30, plus "night Show" at 2 A.M.

CLUBS. Parisian "private clubs" are both expensive (a bottle of whiskey might be in the region of 1,000 frs) and notoriously hard to get into. "Club" is really a misnomer, it's their way of keeping out people they don't like the look of. The best *entrée* is, inevitably, knowing the right people. Failing that, do your best to look interesting yet respectable, and see how you make out. If it doesn't work, never mind, Paris has thousands of other opportunities to offer.

L'Apocalypse, 40 rue du Colisée, 8e (tel. 42–25–11–68). Popular with the affluent jet set.

Castel's, 15 rue Princesse, 6e (tel. 43–26–90–22). Extremely chic and certainly the hardest to get into, unless you happen to be a friend, or a friend of a friend, of the great Jean Castel, king of Paris's night life. On three floors and very plush, with good food too, mostly enjoyed by a very young and trendy set.

Club 79, 79 av. des Champs-Elysées, 8e (tel. 47–23–68–75).

Elysées-Matignon, 2 av. Matignon, 8e (tel. 42–25–73–13). Ultra-fashionable with the show-biz crowd.

Le Garage, 41 rue Washington, 8e (tel. 42–25–53–20). Dazzling strobe lighting, rather flashy decor.

Keur Samba, 79 rue La Boétie, 8e (tel. 43–59–03–10). Long-standing, open very late, popular with the hardened night owls.

Régine's, 49 rue de Ponthieu, 8e (tel. 43–59–21–60). The most chic and luxurious of them all, attracting a slightly older crowd than some. Good food, too.

. . . OR JUST A FUN EVENING OUT. Now let's suppose you want a pleasant evening out but don't feel the urge to rub shoulders with the ultra-fashionable set, and don't want to spend a fortune on a slick show either. Here are some places that should fit the bill. Many are closed on Sundays, but closing days change frequently, so check with *Pariscope* or *L'Officiel des Spectacles* when you are in Paris.

La Canne à Sucre, 4 rue Ste.-Beuve, 6e (tel. 42–22–23–25). Long-established favorite for live West Indian music (two separate bands) and rum punches.

Le Caveau de la Bolée, 25 rue de l'Hirondelle, 6e (tel. 43–54–62–20). One of the oldest and still one of the best, in a roomy cellar close to the place Saint-Michel. Modern and traditional French songs plus some jazz.

Le Caveau des Oubliettes, 1 rue St.-Julien-le-Pauvre, 5e (tel. 43–54–94–97). This famous medieval cellar seems to have been going for ever, but the picturesque atmosphere and the jolly French songs are as much fun as ever they were.

Chapelle des Lombards, 19 rue de Lappe, 11e (tel. 43–57–24–24). Partly discs, but good live music too, mostly African.

Chez ma Cousine, 12 rue Norvins, 18e (tel. 46–06–49–35). Colorful Montmartre cabaret, with singers and poets and entertainers of all kinds. Reasonably genuine atmosphere, unlike some places in Montmartre. You'll enjoy dinner or late supper here too (see Restaurant section).

Club des Poètes, 30 rue de Bourgogne, 7e (tel. 47–05–06–03). Two shows nightly (except Sun.) with poems and songs. Charming, but you need to know French pretty well.

Félix, 23 rue Mouffetard, 5e (tel. 47–07–68–78). In the picturesque Contrescarpe area. Light-hearted ambiance, where you can have a drink or a pleasant candlelit dinner and enjoy listening to music, dancing, watching the odd *chansonnier* or whoever happens to be on the bill. Live Brazilian music to dance to in the atmospheric cellars.

Le Lapin Agile, 22 rue des Saules, 18e (tel. 46–06–85–87). Won its reputation in the days when Montmartre's artist colony spent their nights here. But still great fun, with its wooden tables and lively atmosphere. It's perched high up above Paris and you'll enjoy sipping the traditional glass of cherries preserved in brandy and listening to the show (mostly old French songs, with a handful of newer ones). The prices are reasonable too.

Michou, 80 rue des Martyrs (tel. 46–06–16–04). Great show with dinner every evening. Reserve well in advance.

Peanuts, 51 rue Lucien-Sampaix, 10e (tel. 46–07–46–17), by the picturesque Saint-Martin canal. Cheerful thirties atmosphere, with songs and sketches in English as well as French. Dinner around 9 to midnight, show 10–1 A.M. Closed Sun., Mon. and Aug.

Péniche des Arts, on a barge moored opposite 116 av. du Président-Kennedy, 16e (tel. 45–27–77–55). Charcoal grilled meals, bat, cabaret, plus lots of splendid old movies.

La Rôtisserie de l'Abbaye, 22 rue Jacob, 6e (tel. 45–62–68–04). This one's been going since Quasimodo was a boy. Folk songs—usually in French and English—and guitar playing make a lively accompaniment to your dinner or late-night supper. Closed Aug.

Villa d'Este, 4 rue Arsène-Houssaye, 8e (tel. 43–59–78–44). Nicely varied entertainment, with singers, conjurors, sketches and plenty of dancing to a good band. You can dine well, if expensively. Closed in August.

The Jazz Spots. The French take jazz seriously and Paris is one of the great jazz cities of the world, with several specialist record shops and an array of clubs, often ephemeral. Every branch of the music is provided, from the stolidly traditional through classic bebop to jazz-rock and, increasingly, South American and African offshoots. A major change in recent years is that European jazz has developed its own distinctive character and can be of a very high standard, so don't insist on American stars.

For precise details of who's on when, see either of the excellent specialist magazines, *Jazz Hot* or *Jazz Magazine,* and listen to the jazz programs on France Musique. Remember that nothing gets going until 10 or 11 P.M., credit cards are almost never accepted, and although prices are generally reasonable, they do vary according to the attraction.

Le Caméléon, 57 rue St.-André-des-Arts, 5e (tel. 43–26–64–40). There was a time when you could be sure of an enthusiastic crowd in this dark record bar with its downstairs cellar for live music and dancing. It's quieter these days, though the choice of records is still discriminating. Decent range of beers and whiskies but no exotic cocktails. Inexpensive.

Le Caveau de la Huchette, 5 rue de la Huchette, 5e (tel. 43–26–65–05). Large stone cellar in student (and tourist) quarter. An illustrious history but now a little past its prime, and mainly featuring traditional French bands. Good for dancing and, if you're young, making contact. Stays open especially late on Fridays and Saturdays. Entrance 45–55 frs; cheap drinks.

Le Montana, 28 rue St.-Benoît, 6e (tel. 45–48–93–08). An informal bar in the heart of Saint-Germain-des-Prés which sometimes has live piano jazz.

New Morning, 7–9 rue des Petites Ecuries, 10e (tel. 45–23–51–41). A large room (seats over 400) with excellent sound and visibility. Although it's only been going since 1981, this is now the best club in Paris, if not in Europe, and the premier venue for visiting American musicians, top French groups and fashionable *salsa* bands. A serious place, for aficionados only. Entrance prices range from 85–110 frs, but include either a free soft drink or reduction on first alcoholic drink. Moderate range of cocktails, spirits and beers.

Le Petit Journal, 71 blvd. St.-Michel, 5e (tel. 43–26–28–59). Well run, mature club, opposite the Luxembourg Gardens, specializing in live traditional and mainstream. Individual booths, unusual cocktails, lavish salads and ice-creams. Entrance and first drink 65–70 frs, second drink around 40 frs. Closed Sun. and August.

Le Petit Opportun, 15 rue des Lavandières-Sainte-Opportune, 1e (tel. 42–36–01–36). Converted bistro with cramped atmospheric basement (seats 50) often featuring top-flight American soloists with French rhythm sections. Entrance and first drink up to 100 frs. At street level there's a pleasant bar with recorded music and cheaper drinks.

Slow Club, 130 rue de Rivoli, 1e (tel. 42–33–84–30). Long-established dancing club often presenting Maxim Saury's well-known traditional band. Open especially late at weekends. Entrance 50–60 frs, cheap drinks.

Le Sunset, 60 rue des Lombards, 1e (tel. 42–61–46–60). In the reinvigorated Les Halles area: a small whitewashed cellar with first-rate live music. Clientele is young, chic and there to listen. Open very late and stays crowded. Entrance, including first drink, about 70 frs, second drink 40 or 50 frs. Long list of cocktails.

Rock. Unlike French jazz, French rock is generally not considered to be up to much, and certainly has never achieved an international reputation. You should get to hear live rock music in the following places, most of which charge in the region of 75–100 frs entrance money, including the first drink, and around 40–50 frs for subsequent drinks. Prices often rise on weekends, when they get pretty crowded. Most don't get going properly till 11.30 or midnight, then stay open through to dawn or thereabouts.

Les Bains (see *Disco* section) usually has live rock on Wednesday nights.

Bus Palladium, 6 rue Fontaine, 9e (tel. 48–74–54–99). On the edge of Montmartre, youthful clientele, mostly live rock, some discs.

Gibus, 18 rue fbg. du Temple, 10e (tel. 47–00–78–88), has been *the* place for rock for many a long year.

Le Palace 999 (see *Disco* section) has live rock at times.

Rose Bonbon, 34 rue de la Roquette, 11e (tel. 48–06–69–58). Near the Bastille in downmarket eastern Paris, has live rock every night of the week.

Gay's the Word. Paris seems to be full of gay locales these days, some fairly rough. Here are two of the more respectable:

Madame Arthur, 77bis rue des Martyrs, 18e (tel. 42–64–48–27). The forerunner of many later men-only cabaret joints. Atmospheric, with just a whiff of Berlin in the '30s.

Moune, 54 rue Pigalle, 9e (tel. 45–26–64–64). The best known of the "female cabarets." Opens from around 4.30 P.M. on Sun. and public holidays, otherwise from around 10 P.M.

Discos. As you'd expect, Paris is full of discos and many a little bar or club that once offered live music now throbs to the latest discs, more often than not accompanied by strobe lighting and special effects, some stylish, some frankly tasteless. The audience is mostly very young. As is the way with such places, they come and go, sometimes enjoying a meteoric rise to fame then dying a quick death, sometimes carrying steadily on as fashions wax and wane. Some are chic and elegant, others are on the seedy side. The ones we list here should be still on the go by the time you read this, but don't blame us if some of them have changed their name—it seems that some places get an urge to change every few months, which makes life pretty confusing, though the décor and the ambiance often weather the changes. Discos usually open about 10 or 10.30 P.M. and stay on the boil till around dawn. Some are closed on Mondays but a fair number open Sunday afternoons; virtually all of them stay open during the summer, but check locally to be on the safe side. Quite a few let girls in free of charge during the week.

Adison Square Gardel, 23 rue du Commandant-Mouchotte, 14e (tel. 43–21–54–58). Good place for dancing, with rather respectable clientele. Also has what the French quaintly still refer to as *thés dansants* on Mon., Tues. and Fri. (from 4 P.M.), plus occasional "pancake evenings."

Les Bains, 7 rue du Bourg-l'Abbé, 3e (tel. 48–87–01–80). Once a public bath-house, then a wildly popular spot specializing in New Wave music ("Les Bains-Douches"). In 1985 it became merely "Les Bains" after extensive redecorations and started having live music on Weds.

Balajo, 9 rue de Lappe, 11e (tel. 47–00–07–87). Crowded, lively, lots of fun, with plenty of nostalgic '60s discs some nights.

Cherry Lane, 8 rue des Ciseaux, 6e (tel. 43–26–28–28). All the latest sounds, plus video show.

La Main Jaune, pl. Porte Champerret, 17e. A good place to meet young Parisians. Dancing on roller skates.

Martine's, Pavillon Royal, Bois de Boulogne (tel. 45–00–51–00). Chic private club popular with well-heeled set (must be respectably dressed). Discs plus dinner to 2 A.M.

Le Palace 999, 8 fbg. Montmartre, 9e (tel. 42–46–10–87). Went through a bad patch after the death of its founder in the early '80s, but is now back on form and again attracting a way-out young crowd. Has a good brasserie next door.

Navy-Club, 58 blvd. de l'Hôpital, 13e (tel. 45–35–91–94). Good for dancing, with three separate dance floors. Popular Sun. afternoons, too.

Whisky à Gogo, 57 rue de Seine, 6e (tel. 46–33–74–99). Has special "psychedelic evenings" from time to time. Popular with Left Bank crowd (it's below the Alcazar nightclub).

Wonder Club, 38 rue du Dragon, 6e (tel. 45–48–90–32).

Zed Club, 2 rue des Anglais, 5e (tel. 43–54–93–78). Purely disco these days, with plenty of lively dancing and some rock-only evenings. Closed Mon., Tues. and Aug.

 RACING. Going to the races in and around Paris has long been a fashionable pastime, for visitors as well as the French. Paris has two racecourses, Auteuil and Longchamp, both in the Bois de Boulogne. On the eastern edge of town at Vincennes is a famous trotting course, called simply Vincennes. Just outside Paris to the west is Saint-Cloud. Further out are Chantilly—with its major races the *Prix de Diane* and the *Prix du Jockey* held in June and attracting a very chic crowd—Enghien and Maisons-Lafitte,

Traveling outside Paris

 EXCURSIONS. Excursions to the area round Paris are organized by the *Paris Transport Authority* (*RATP*), 53 quai des Grands-Augustins, 6e or in the pl. de la Madeleine, 8e (a kiosk beside the church); guides are normally French-speaking only, but some will be able to do some explaining in English. For guided tours in luxury buses with commentary in English you have a choice of *American Express,* 11 rue Scribe, 9e (tel. 42–66–09–99); *Cityrama,* 4 pl. des Pyramides, 1er (tel. 42–60–30–14); or *Paris Vision,* 214 rue de Rivoli (tel. 42–60–30–01). All of these organize half-day or whole-day excursions to such places as Chartres, Giverny (sometimes combined with Rouen), Fontainebleau, Malmaison, Versailles, or to two destinations combined (Versailles with Chartres, Fontainebleau or Malmaison; Fontainebleau and Barbizon with Malmaison); *Cityrama* also offers Chantilly.

The very full program of lecture tours organized by the *Caisse Nationale des Monuments Historiques,* Hôtel de Sully, 62 rue St.-Antoine, 4e (tel. 42–74–22–22), includes a few traveling by coach to lesser-known museums and historic buildings, some of them not normally open to the public. The commentary is normally in French and presumes on a fairly detailed knowledge of art history and architectural terms.

 BY TRAIN. Paris has six mainline rail termini:

Gare d'Austerlitz: for trains to the southwest, going to Bordeaux and on to Spain via Orléans, Tours and Poitiers, and to Toulouse via Limoges.

Gare de l'Est: trains going eastwards to Nancy and Strasbourg and on to Germany.

Gare de Lyon: for trains to the southeast, including the TGV (high-speed train) to Lyon, Grenoble, Marseille, Nice and Montpellier.

Gare de Montparnasse: for trains to the west (especially Brittany) via Chartres, Angers and Le Mans.

Gare du Nord: for trains northwards and on to Britain, and also to Belgium, Holland and the Scandinavian countries.

Gare Saint-Lazare: for trains to Normandy, and to Britain via Dieppe.

For **passenger enquiries** in English call 43–80–50–50 for all destinations.

BY EXPRESS MÉTRO. The *RER (réseau régional exprès)* has fast trains slotted into the ordinary métro (subway) inner-city system and going out to such places as Versailles, Saint-Germain-en-Laye and Saint-Rémy-les-Chevreuse, as well as to the two Paris airports, Orly and Roissy/Charles de Gaulle.

BY CAR. The main highways or motorways (*autoroutes*), marked with blue signs, out of Paris are the A1 northwards; the A4 eastwards to Metz and Strasbourg; the A6 southwards through Dijon and Lyon to the Riviera (by which time it has become the A7); the A10 southwards to Bordeaux via Orléans and Tours; and the A13 westwards to Normandy.

EXPLORING PARIS

A Safari Around Parnassus

by
VIVIENNE MENKES

Conveniently enough, the geographical center of Paris and its historical heart more or less coincide on the one spot that is known to every visitor to Paris—the Ile de la Cité crowned by the twin towers of the mighty Gothic cathedral of Notre Dame. Like all great metropolises, Paris is changing fast and this chapter describes some of the futuristic buildings that are giving other parts of the city—especially the outskirts—a new look. But there is little doubt that this island, which was the first inhabited part of the ancient city of Lutetia—the forerunner of Paris—is the right place to start the rewarding voyage

137

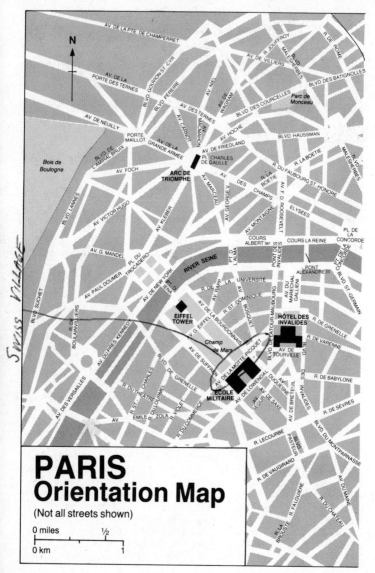

PARIS
Orientation Map
(Not all streets shown)

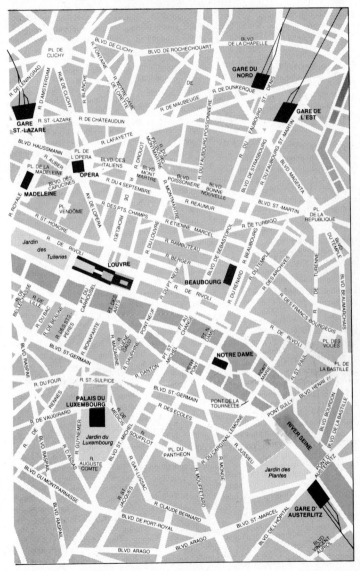

of discovery that every tourist can enjoy, however tight his purse strings.

Indeed one of the major plus points of Paris from the tourist's point of view is that so much of interest is in walking distance of the center—there's no need to spend a fortune on taxis or tourist coaches, just put your best foot forward and you'll soon be steeped in the delights of one of the world's most beautiful cities.

Getting Your Bearings

Where better to get your bearings than the boat-shaped Ile de la Cité, where the ancient Parisii, a race of fisherfolk who set up their huts here in about 200 B.C., must have done just that as they took out their primitive version of the compass and surveyed the marshy countryside to the north (still known as Le Marais—The Marsh) and the open wastes to the south where the bustling Latin Quarter now stands?

A good place to start your travels is at the tip of the island, at the place du Pont-Neuf in the middle of what is, despite its name (The New Bridge), the oldest of Paris's bridges spanning the Seine. A delightful medieval-style fair, complete with jesters and tumblers and street musicians, was held here in 1978 to celebrate the 400th anniversary and was such a success that it has now become an annual event, held during a weekend towards the end of June. Facing you is an equestrian statue of Henri IV, the Protestant Bourbon king who converted to Catholicism and did much to shape the city known today before falling victim to a fanatical assassin. This statue was the first to be built in a public place in France (though the original was destroyed during the Revolution and subsequently replaced by the one you see today). Behind the king is the peaceful treelined square du Vert-Galant (a nickname given to Henri because of his reputation for gallant adventures with women). The square is the starting-point for the Vedettes du Pont-Neuf, the glass-topped motorboats that will take you for a pleasant and instructive ride along the Seine.

Once you've admired the view up and down the river, with the many bridges spanning it in either direction, you can start spotting the landmarks that will help you chart the next stages of your voyage of discovery. The first bridge to the west is the romantic Pont des Arts, a graceful cast-iron structure that has long been a favorite spot for strollers.

Slightly upriver to the north-west you can see the Louvre, now one of the world's great museums but once a royal palace. Beyond it stretch the leafy Tuileries Gardens leading into the place de la Concorde, with the avenue des Champs-Elysées, dominated by the glassy roof of the Grand Palais, running in a straight line up to the Arc de Triomphe.

To the north beyond the Louvre lie the Palais Royal, the Opéra, and in the far distance the gleaming white Sacré-Coeur basilica perched high up in Montmartre. On the other bank of the river but still looking westwards come first the place de l'Institut, with the glittering dome of the Académie Française, then the old Orsay station, now refurbished to house a splendid museum of 19th- and 20th-century art; round the bend in the river and out of sight is the dome of the Invalides, beneath which Napoleon Bonaparte's remains are enshrined, but the spindly Eiffel Tower beyond it is clearly visible.

Turning due east you're pointing towards the Palais de Justice and the Sainte-Chapelle, with beyond them the towers of Notre Dame (just visible from the southern tip of the Pont Neuf) and Paris's other island, the Ile Saint-Louis. On the north bank lie the Hôtel de Ville, the City Hall, part of its roof visible above the rooftops, and the controversial Pompidou Center. Slightly further north is the renovated Marais district, with its elegant 17th- and 18th-century mansions and squares.

Now turn to face south, where the once-aristocratic boulevard Saint-Germain runs roughly parallel to the Seine, bisected at right angles by the bustling boulevard Saint-Michel, the highway of the student district or "Latin Quarter," leading up to first the Luxembourg Gardens, the Sorbonne and the Panthéon, then on to artistic Montparnasse. Downriver to the southeast lie the Jardin des Plantes, the capital's attractive Botanical Gardens, and the Natural History Museum.

And now, with your mental compass set correctly and a rough sketch map of Paris taking shape inside your head, you can decide which area you're going to explore first. Our choice would be the obvious one—the Ile de la Cité itself.

The Ile de la Cité

Heading east you come first to the delightful place Dauphine, triangular in shape and with a few 17th-century houses still standing, plus several pleasant restaurants. At the far end looms the monumental façade of the law courts, the Palais de Justice, part of a huge complex of buildings including the Conciergerie and the Sainte Chapelle, on the site of the palaces of the city's Roman governors and her earliest kings, and later the seat of parliament. The Palais is open to the public on weekdays, so you can wander round the corridors watching the important-seeming bustle of the law-givers, or even attend a court hearing.

Aficionados of detective fiction will also want to have a look at the quai des Orfèvres, haunt of Simenon's Maigret and home of the *police judiciaire,* the equivalent of the CID at Scotland Yard in London.

But most tourists prefer to head for the Sainte-Chapelle, one of the finest examples of Gothic architecture with breathtakingly beautiful stained glass—so light and airy that the stone work seems to melt away and you feel as though you're floating inside a brilliantly polished jewel. The chapel originated with the sale of what was said to be the authentic Crown of Thorns to the French king Louis IX, known as Saint Louis—he bought it from emperor Baldwin I of Constantinople, who was drastically short of funds. Louis then acquired a number of other sacred relics and decided to have a fitting shrine, a true jewel case in stone and stained glass, built to house them. The new chapel was consecrated in 1248 and two-thirds of the original stained-glass windows are still intact over 700 years later—not surprisingly they are the earliest in Paris to have survived. (During World War II they were removed and stored in a safe place.) The chapel is made up of two halves, but it is the Chapelle Haute or Upper Chapel that acts as a magnet for visitors. Try to attend one of the magical candlelit concerts held here at frequent intervals.

Another piece in the jigsaw of this large complex of buildings on the Ile de la Cité is the Conciergerie, best known as a prison during the Revolution (Marie Antoinette was imprisoned here before being led off to the guillotine) but originally part of the royal palace. It was presided over by the Concierge or Governor of the palace, whose considerable income was increased by the special privilege he enjoyed of leasing out

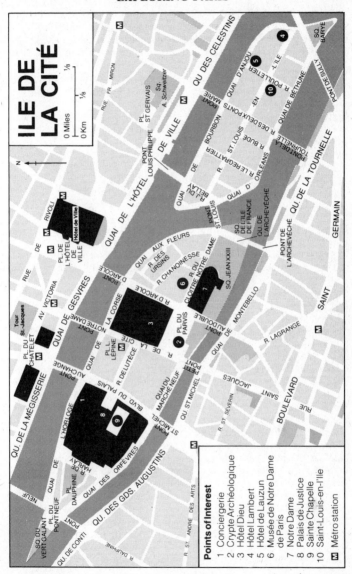

ILE DE LA CITÉ

0 Miles   ⅛

0 Km   ⅛

N

Points of Interest

1 Conciergerie
2 Crypte Archéologique
3 Hôtel Dieu
4 Hôtel Lambert
5 Hôtel de Lauzun
6 Musée de Notre Dame de Paris
7 Notre Dame
8 Palais de Justice
9 Sainte Chapelle
10 Saint-Louis-en-l'Ile

M Métro station

individual shops and showrooms. The building is easily recognized by its four towers overlooking the Seine, the best known being the 14th-century Clock Tower or Tour de l'Horloge on the corner of the boulevard du Palais. The clock itself—the earliest public clock in Paris—has been ticking away since 1370. Inside the Conciergerie (conducted tours only) you'll be shown the guardroom, with Gothic vaulting and columns with intricately-carved capitals, but finer still is the huge Salle des Gens d'Armes. A short corridor leads to the kitchens with four vast fireplaces. You can rent them out for private receptions nowadays, if you feel like throwing a really memorable party! Also on view are the prisoners' gallery, various cells, including the one where Marie Antoinette was incarcerated before her execution, and the chapel, where objects connected with the ill-fated queen are displayed.

From the Conciergerie you can walk along by the Seine until you come to the picturesque flower market (if you're there on Sunday, however, you'll find it's been transformed into a bird market). Then follow the rue de la Cité, which runs alongside the Hôtel Dieu, a hospital dating only from the Second Empire but built close to the site of a hospice originally founded twelve centuries earlier.

And so to the magnificent Gothic cathedral of Notre Dame, one of the finest religious buildings in the world and thought by many to be the pinnacle of French architecture. Building started in 1163, with an army of stonemasons, carpenters and sculptors working on a site that had previously seen a Roman temple, an early Christian basilica and a Romanesque church. The chancel and altar were consecrated in 1182, but the magnificent sculpture surrounding the main doors was not put into position until 1240 and the north tower was completed ten years later. In spite of various changes in the 17th century, including the removal of the rose windows, the cathedral remained much the same until the Revolution, when the statues of the kings of Judah on the façade were hacked down because the mob thought they represented the despised royal line of France. Everything inside and out that was deemed to be "anti-Republican" was stripped away. An interesting postscript to this destruction occurred in 1977, when some of the heads of the kings of Judah were discovered buried beneath what is now a bank in the boulevard Haussmann. They'd apparently been hidden there for safe keeping by an ardent royalist who owned the small mansion and courtyard that now form part of the bank's premises. The restored heads are now on display at the Musée de Cluny.

By the early 19th century the excesses of the Revolution were over and the cathedral could fulfil its religious function once again. Napoleon Bonaparte crowned himself emperor here in 1804—you can see David's famous painting of this lavish ceremony in the Louvre. Full-scale restoration work started in the mid-19th century, and at this time too the famous city planner Baron Haussmann had the medieval buildings surrounding it demolished and replaced with a large square known as the *parvis*. Beneath the square is the Archeological Crypt museum, which displays the results of excavations ranging from the foundations of the city's 3rd-century ramparts to remains of medieval houses.

You can gaze at the cathedral in all its splendor from the pedestrians-only place du Parvis. The façade divides neatly into three, with at the base the three portals, each a different size: the Portal of the Virgin on the left, the Portal of the Last Judgement in the center and the Portal of St Anne on the right. All three are surrounded by magnificent carvings of biblical figures and scenes, plus foliage, fruit and other motifs. The portals are surmounted by the Galerie des Rois, though the kings are of course copies since, as we have seen, the originals were victims of the Revolution. Above the gallery is the rose window, though its true beauty can be experienced only from inside the cathedral. The Grande Galerie above the rose window lies at the base of the twin towers, between which you can glimpse the spire crowning the chancel, which was added during the 19th-century restorations. The south tower houses the great bell of Notre Dame, familiar to readers of Victor Hugo's novel, *Notre Dame de Paris*. It was recast in the 17th century and still tolls today, though only on ceremonial occasions.

The interior of the cathedral, with its vast proportions, soaring nave and the gentle multicolored light filtering in through the stained-glass windows manages to inspire awe in spite of the inevitable throngs of tourists. If you're able to attend a mass you'll find it an unforgettable experience, and the organ concerts held here are another great attraction. You come first to the massive 12th-century pillars supporting the twin towers and from them can look down the long nave to the transept with its stained glass, most of it original, and a particularly-beautiful 14th-century statue of the Madonna and Child generally known simply as Notre Dame de Paris, Our Lady of Paris, at the south side of the entrance to the chancel. The chancel or choir itself owes some of its decoration to a vow made by Louis XIII in 1638—still childless after 23 years of marriage, he promised to dedicate the whole of France to the Virgin if his queen produced an heir. When the longed-for event happened and the future Louis XIV was born the fulfilment of the vow was symbolized by new adornments to the chancel—the choir stalls, a Pietà by Nicolas Coustou and sculptures of the king and his heir.

South of the choir is the old sacristy, now the treasury, which has a display of chalices and other ecclesiastical objects, plus manuscripts. If you're there on Good Friday or one of the Sundays in Lent you'll also be shown a nail and splinter of wood allegedly from Christ's Cross.

If you're feeling hale and hearty, make your way to the north aisle near the Portal of the Virgin and embark on the stiffish climb up the

387 steps to the very top of Notre Dame. You'll be rewarded by one of the finest views in Paris, with the spire and flying buttresses against a backdrop of first the Ile de la Cité and then all of Paris, the whole magnificent scene framed by the highly photogenic gargoyles.

Talking of views, no visit to Notre Dame is complete without a walk round to the back of the cathedral, to the attractively laid out square Jean XXIII (called after the much-loved Pope John), which offers a breathtaking view of the east end of the cathedral ringed round by the splendid flying buttresses and surmounted by the spire and finally by the towers at the west end. From here Notre Dame seems to float above the Seine like the magnificently decorated hull of a boat. In the nearby rue Cloître Notre-Dame you can visit the Notre-Dame Museum, with its paintings, engravings, medallions, and other objects and documents connected with the cathedral's history.

As you move towards the eastern tip of the island, with the views of Notre Dame becoming lovelier all the time, you come to the square de l'Ile de France, which housed the city's lugubrious morgue until early this century but now has a modern crypt dedicated to the memory of those who were deported during the Nazi occupation of France and died in the concentration camps. A visit to this most moving memorial is highly recommended. You may well find the peaceful garden above it a good place to rest and muse on the mysterious dichotomy that enables the human race to construct buildings of infinite beauty and yet on other occasions to treat their fellow men with infinite cruelty.

The Ile Saint-Louis

A narrow bridge, the Pont Saint-Louis, crosses over from the edge of the square de l'Ile de France to link the Ile de la Cité to the smaller Ile Saint-Louis, one of the most peaceful parts of Paris and much sought after as a residential area.

The island was originally made up of two separate islands, one called Notre Dame Island and the other Cow Island (L'Ile aux Vaches), apparently because it was used for grazing land. The two were joined together in the 17th century by an engineer called Christophe Marie (whose name survives in the Pont Marie, linking the Ile Saint-Louis to the mainland). He also had a whole series of classical mansions built here as a speculation. This explains why the Ile Saint-Louis gives such a strong impression of being all of a piece—its narrow streets and quays are full of noble buildings all dating from the same period, and a period when French architecture was particularly elegant, with a wealth of beautiful decorative elements.

The two finest examples are the Hôtel Lambert, at the eastern end of rue St Louis-en-l'Ile, which unfortunately isn't open to the public, and the Hôtel de Lauzun, which can be visited about once a week when special guided tours are held there. As well as its magnificent painted ceilings, tapestries and gilded carvings, it has interesting literary associations—in the 19th century the "Hashish-Eaters' Club," founded by the poet Théophile Gautier and frequented by Baudelaire, among others, met here regularly. Nowadays the mansion is the scene of far more respectable goings-on, as it belongs to the City of Paris and is used for official receptions, albeit extremely lavish ones.

The island's only church, Saint-Louis-en-l'Ile, is also worth a visit, with its exceptionally rich fittings and decoration. And before you leave this oasis of calm in the heart of the city, don't miss the wonderful view of the east end of Notre Dame from the quai d'Orléans.

SIGHTSEEING CHECKLIST. Look under *Sightseeing* in the *Practical Information* section for general points on museums and places of interest.

Conciergerie, 1 quai de l'Horloge, 4e (tel. 43–54–30–06). Open daily 10–5. Half-price Sun. and public holidays. *Métro:* Châtelet, Cité.

Crypte archéologique de Notre-Dame, pl. du Parvis Notre-Dame, 4e (tel. 43–29–83–51). Open daily 10–5. Half-price Sun. and public holidays. *Métro:* Cité.

Hôtel de Lauzun, 17 quai d'Anjou, 4e. Guided tours only, generally on Tues. at 3. Check dates with the *Caisse Nationale des Monuments Historiques,* 62 rue St.-Antoine, 4e (tel. 48–87–24–14) or look at lists in the *Caisse*'s bi-monthly bulletin or one of the weekly "What's on in Paris" publications. Get there early as tours are restricted to thirty people. *Métro:* Pont-Marie.

Mémorial de la Deportation, square de l'Ile de France, at the tip of the island. Open permanently.

Musée Notre-Dame de Paris, 10 rue du Cloître Notre-Dame, 4e (tel. 43–25–42–92). Open only Wed., Sat. and Sun., 2.30–6. Closed Easter Sun.

Notre-Dame, pl. du Parvis de Notre-Dame, 4e (tel. 43–54–22–63). Cathedral open daily but visits not allowed during masses. You can climb up the towers daily 10–5; half-price Sun. and public holidays. *Métro:* Cité.

Sainte-Chapelle, blvd. du Palais, 4e (tel. 43–54–30–09). Open daily 10–5. Half-price Sun. and public holidays. *Métro:* Cité.

LUNCH SPOTS. The following places are all reasonably priced and suitable for a fairly quick meal during a sightseeing tour. You will find more restaurants in our Restaurant Listing if you are interested in a more leisurely lunch.

Bar du Caveau, 17 pl. Dauphine, 1er. Pleasant wine bar in attractive setting on the place Dauphine, close to the Ste.-Chapelle, the Pont Neuf and Notre Dame. Closed weekends.

Brasserie de l'Ile, 55 quai Bourbon, on the Ile St.-Louis. A few steps across the bridge behind Notre Dame and you've reached this cheerful, crowded spot with its Alsatian specialties. Closed Wed., Thurs. and Aug.

Aux cinquante jardins de thé, rue St.-Louis-en-l'Ile, 4e. Attractive little tearoom on the Ile St.-Louis, diagonally opposite the Brasserie, serving light meals with unusual flans and salads. Open non-stop from noon, so you can pop in when it suits you.

Au Franc Pinot, 1 quai de Bourbon, 4e, again on the Ile St.-Louis. Ground floor is a good wine bar; basement a more elaborate restaurant.

Chez Paul, 15 pl. Dauphine, 1er. An old favorite in the pl. Dauphine— another entrance on the quai by the river. Typical Parisian bistrot with good home cooking.

La Samaritaine Pont-Neuf, 19 rue Monnaie, 1er. Top-floor restaurant in this popular department store on the Right Bank is good for views while you enjoy a light lunch.

Taverne Henri IV, 13 pl. du Pont-Neuf, 1er. Old-established wine bar in the middle of the Pont Neuf.

The Marais, Beaubourg and Les Halles

The Pont-Marie takes you back to the mainland and to the Marais district, a must for anyone interested in the history of Paris and in architecture, and well worth a whole day's exploration if you can find the time.

Once ultra-fashionable, the district endured a long period of neglect that nearly proved fatal, but from which it was rescued in the early 1960s by an enlightened government decision to designate it a "protected area." Many of the splendid mansions known in French as *hôtels particuliers* have been beautifully restored, yet at the same time care has been taken to make sure that the Marais does not become merely a museum district—crumbling apartment buildings have been restored to provide low-cost housing (the funds usually coming partly from private developers and partly from the state or the City of Paris), and the craftsmen who used to inhabit the area have been encouraged to stay. Where only a few years ago dilapidated tenement buildings and squalid courtyards teeming with dark and unhygienic workshops housed some of the poorest citizens of Paris you will now find well-planned housing units, airy studios and attractive little shops. Inevitably some people grumble that the local inhabitants have been driven out to make way for "trendy culture," but in fact many of the former population have been able to stay and their living conditions are now infinitely better.

Quite apart from the restoration of buildings dating from the golden age of the Marais, the Festival du Marais, held in June and July, has brought back some of the elegance of former days with its concerts and theater and ballet performances in illuminated mansions and churches throughout the district. And the area is becoming even more attractive as several major streets are closed to traffic.

The ascendancy of the Marais as a fashionable place to live started in the 14th century with Charles V's decision to leave the royal palace on the Ile de la Cité, which held too many unhappy memories after the bloody riots led by the cloth merchant and provost of Paris, Etienne Marcel. He moved to the Marais and most of his successors on the throne followed his lead. But the district didn't really come into its own as a fashionable place to live until Henri IV had the place Royale (now called the place des Vosges) built in the early 17th century and rich and noble families flocked to build their own mansions nearby.

On the mainland side of the Pont-Marie you can see ahead of you the beautifully-restored Hôtel de Sens, one of the few private buildings in Paris to have survived from the Middle Ages. With its pointed corner towers, Gothic porch and richly-carved decorative details it is an authentic mixture of fairytale château and defensive stronghold. Built in the late-15th and early-16th centuries, it was originally lived in by the archbishops of Sens—hence the name—though Queen Margot, the worldly-wise first wife of Henri IV, was a more famous occupant and the old walls have seen many an amorous adventure. The building now houses a fine and applied arts library called the Bibliothèque Forney, with good temporary exhibits.

Now walk a little way east along the quai des Célestins and turn left into the rue des Jardins-Saint-Paul, part of a successful redevelopment scheme involving a judicious mixture of restoration plus demolition and rebuilding. Several of the courtyards now house attractive craft workshops and small antique shops. Here you can see a part of Philippe Auguste's ramparts, built in the 12th century and surrounding what was then Paris (it was only about an eighth the size of Paris today). At the far end of this street, by the Lycée Charlemagne, turn left and follow the rue de Jouy till you reach the Hôtel de Beauvais, with amazing vaulted cellars dating from the 13th century, and try to imagine the infant prodigy, Wolfgang Amadeus Mozart, giving several concerts here at the age of only seven. Now walk along the rue Saint-Antoine to the church of Saint-Paul-Saint-Louis, built by the Jesuits in the 17th century and modeled on the Gesù church in Rome.

The busy rue Saint-Antoine, well-known for its furniture workshops for centuries, is a good place for spotting ordinary Parisians about their daily business, perhaps the descendants of the infuriated mob who emerged from the narrow streets round about to storm and destroy the hated Bastille, not far from here. Cross over and turn right until you come to the Hôtel de Béthune-Sully at no. 62. It was one of the first large 17th-century mansions to be restored and now houses the Caisse Nationale des Monuments Historiques, which organizes excellent guided visits to this and other parts of historic Paris. You can buy an attractively-illustrated plan of the Marais from the porter's lodge just inside the gates. Good exhibits, usually connected with architecture, are held here too. The beautiful formal garden is now open to the public. A bit further on the narrow rue de Birague on the left leads to the delightful place des Vosges, commissioned by Henri IV and now restored to much of its former glory. You'll be impressed by the harmonious lines of the square and by its symmetry, with its rows of pinkish brick houses, covered arcades running all round for comfort-

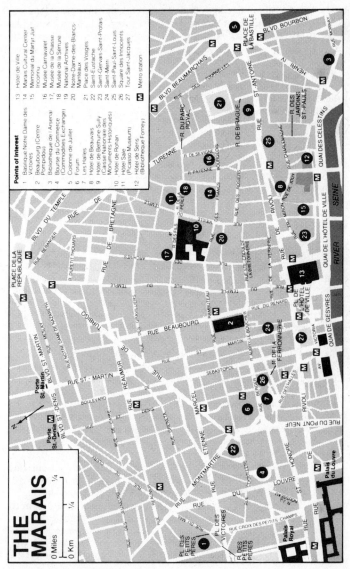

THE MARAIS

0 Miles   1/4
0 Km   1/4

Points of Interest

1 Basilique Notre Dame des Victoires
2 Beaubourg (Centre Pompidou)
3 Bibliothèque de l'Arsenal
4 Bourse du Commerce (Commodities Exchange)
5 Colonne de Juillet
6 Forum
7 Les Halles
8 Hôtel de Beauvais
9 Hôtel de Béthune-Sully (Caisse Nationale des Monuments Historiques)
10 Hôtel de Rohan
11 Hôtel Salé (Picasso Museum)
12 Hôtel de Sens (Bibliothèque Forney)
13 Hôtel de Ville
14 Maras Cultural Center
15 Memorial du Martyr Juif Inconnu
16 Musee Carnavalet
17 Musee de la Chasse
18 Musee de la Serrure
19 National Archives
20 Notre-Dame-des-Blancs-Manteaux
21 Place des Vosges
22 Saint-Eustache
23 Saint-Gervais-Saint-Protais
24 Saint Merri
25 Saint-Paul-Saint-Louis
26 Square des Innocents
27 Tour Saint-Jacques

Ⓜ Metro station

able window shopping in wet weather, and the king's and queen's pavilions facing each other on the north and south sides. There are several restaurants and cafés here, but you may prefer to sit under the trees in the middle of the square, watching the lively children at play and thinking back to the days when the square echoed to the sound of carriage wheels and swordfights (this was a great dueling spot once).

The *place* wasn't solely the preserve of the nobility—it's had its fair share of literary lions too, including Victor Hugo, whose former home can be visited at no. 6, Madame de Sévigné (she was born at no. 1) and Alphonse Daudet, author of the delightful *Letters from my Windmill*. The equestrian statue in the middle of the square is of Louis XIII, though this is a copy as the original was—yet again—melted down during the Revolution. You'll be glad of the shade offered by the trees around the statue if you visit the area on a typically hot and dusty summer's day. Incidentally, the square is now called after the Vosges mountains for the distinctly unromantic reason that that was the first part of France to cough up the taxes imposed by the Revolutionaries in 1800.

Before continuing your visit of the Marais, make a short detour to another square that has little left to see, but is full of historical associations. In fact the whole point of the place de la Bastille, where the course of French history changed for ever, is that there *isn't* anything much to see! Why? Because the infamous Bastille prison (which once held the mysterious Man in the Iron Mask) was destroyed on 14 July 1789, by a furious mob who had decided that it symbolized the tyranny of the *ancien régime*. And ever since, on 14 July, the people of Paris have danced in the streets on their national holiday (also known as Bastille Day) to celebrate the toppling of royal authority.

To find the square, retrace your steps to the rue Saint-Antoine and continue eastwards, or walk round from the north side of the place des Vosges via the rue des Tournelles. The July Column in the center was built in memory of the men and women who lost their lives during the uprising of July 1830 that put the "bourgeois monarch," Louis Philippe, on the throne. If you walk south beside the Canal Saint-Martin, then take the rue Mornay, you come to the Bibliothèque de l'Arsenal, a library in what was once the royal arms manufactory. If you're interested in the theater you'll find the library particularly fascinating, as it includes the text of every French play, as well as thousands of books and manuscripts connected with the history of the theater.

Now return to the place des Vosges. The continuation of the north side of the square running westwards is the rue des Francs-Bourgeois, the Street of the Free Citizens (the name comes from the people lodged in alms houses here in the 14th century, who were so poor they were allowed to be "free" of tax). Probably its best-known building is the

16th-century Hôtel Carnavalet, now a fascinating museum specializing in the history of Paris and once the home of the no less fascinating Madame de Sévigné, whose letters paint such a vivid picture of life in 17th-century France. Don't miss a little stroll in the pretty gardens. Madame de Sévigné gave her name to the street running beside the museum, which takes you past several restored mansions to the rue du Parc Royal, with another garden and lined by more imposing 17th-century mansions. Continue till you come to the Hôtel Libéral-Bruand in the rue de la Perle.

This too has been restored and now houses the unusual Musée de la Serrure (Lock Museum) or Musée Bricard, which traces the history of locks and locksmiths from Roman times. The restoration of the Hôtel Chassepot next door has been completed, and the nearby Hôtel Salé or Hôtel de Juigné, in the rue de Torini, has been drastically redesigned to house the splendid new Picasso Museum. The mansion was built for the royal collector of the salt tax, one of the most hated taxes in pre-Revolutionary France, hence its nickname, "the salted (or pickled) mansion." The large collection of paintings and drawings in the new museum was accepted by the State from Picasso's heirs in lieu of death duties.

Somewhat unexpectedly, the elegant mansion from a more dignified age seems to work perfectly as a background for the ever-exuberant Picasso and for once there has been total agreement that the Picasso Museum was an inspired idea. Be prepared for huge crowds at any time of year.

The street running down the other side of the Musée Carnavalet, the rue Payenne, has a little garden full of stone monuments and sculpture. The mansion at no. 11 is now the Swedish Cultural Center and well-designed art exhibits are often held here. Turn right into the rue des Francs-Bourgeois, where at no. 26 you'll see the Marais Cultural Center; it, too, stages good art exhibits. Further along on the same side you come to the Palais Soubise, housing the magnificent National Archives, invaluable to historians and now spreading into several other restored mansions nearby, and the well-designed Museum of French History, where you can pore over such precious exhibits as letters written by Joan of Arc. Both the Palais Soubise and the Hôtel de Rohan in the rue Vieille du Temple (with a famous carving by Robert Le Lorrain over what was once the stable door) can be visited. If you know about the famous, or rather infamous, story of the "Queen's Necklace" you'll be interested to know that Cardinal de Rohan, who featured so largely in it, lived here.

In the rue des Archives itself is the little-known Musée de la Chasse (Hunting Museum) in the Hôtel Guénégaud, one of the most beautiful mansions in the whole district. But you'll soon realize that the Marais is studded with historic houses, many of them now restored and far too many to describe in detail here. If you keep your eyes open and peer into courtyards you'll be rewarded with a wealth of elegant staircases, wrought-iron decoration, carved doorways, intricate balconies, pretty lamps and so on—and you'll understand why this is once again an ultra-fashionable area to live in. This is one place where you really can say the wheel has turned full circle—from elegance to degradation and back to elegance again.

Just one more recommendation: visit the church of Notre-Dame-des-Blancs-Manteaux (55–67 rue des Francs-Bourgeois), with its elaborate inlaid pulpit, and try to attend a concert there. And before leaving the Marais, a word about Paris's picturesque Jewish quarter, centered on the rue des Rosiers (the scene of a tragic massacre in 1982), with many tiny synagogues and shop and restaurant signs in Hebrew. Since the French withdrawal from North Africa and the ensuing exodus of many Franco-Jewish families, the predominantly Eastern European atmosphere previously conjured up by the presence of so many Russian, Hungarian and Polish exiles has been superseded by a more typically North African ambience—indeed several Ashkenazi synagogues are now Sephardic. Guided tours of some of these little synagogues are occasionally organized.

The Hôtel de Ville

For some time now the area round the City Hall or Hôtel de Ville has been enjoying a new lease of life. This can be partly explained by the reinstatement in the late 1970s of the office of mayor of Paris—for just over a century the city had been the only place in France without its own mayor. The man elected to the post in 1977 was a former prime minister, the dynamic Gaullist party leader Jacques Chirac, and he made the most of the opportunity, acting as something very much more than a figurehead. Reelected prime minister in 1986 he also decided to remain Mayor of Paris, and has so far shown no loss of interest in the city's affairs. He has revived a number of old customs and traditions, staging many popular festivals and fairs. As a result the Hôtel de Ville is now a focus of interest, with exhibits connected with the history of Paris often staged there.

Two other explanations for the renaissance of this once run-down part of Paris should be mentioned. One is the building of the controversial Pompidou/Beaubourg Center nearby, which has led to a huge influx of art-lovers, avant-gardists in general and tourists of all nationalities. The other is the massive restoration program now nearing completion in the Marais district, which again has attracted large numbers of visitors.

The City Hall may look old but it is in fact a modern copy of its 16th-century predecessor, which was burned down during the Paris Commune in 1871. Parts of it can be visited, but you'll probably find it more instructive to ponder on the stirring events that have taken place over the centuries in this now thankfully peaceful spot. For instance it was the scene of public executions of a particularly blood-thirsty kind (a nasty blend of hanging, drawing and quartering, and burning) for a good 500 years. First, in the 14th century the fierce uprising against royal authority led by Etienne Marcel resulted in his establishing the city's government here. Then when the Bastille was captured the revolutionary mob did a fair amount of damage, while five years later their former hero, the tyrannical Robespierre, took shelter here when his jaw was broken and hastily bound up before he was dragged off to the guillotine. When the short-lived Restoration ended with the fall of Louis-Philippe, the City Hall was temporarily the seat of government and again witnessed violent clashes. Twenty or so years later the most violent act of all saw the total destruction of the building by yet another furious mob. Nearer the present time it was here that in 1944 the returned hero, General de Gaulle, calmly took over the city—and the country—from the Resistance leaders. Just about the only reminder of all this, however, is the equestrian statue of Etienne Marcel in a little garden on the south side of the City Hall overlooking the Seine. The square in front of the City Hall has been splendidly restored, and is now mercifully traffic free, so it is a good place for a stroll during evening floodlighting.

Behind the building you'll see the impressive three-tiered classical façade of the church of Saint-Gervais-Saint-Protais, set at a slightly peculiar angle. This church is well known for its music, both during masses and in special concerts, and has a particularly fine organ—the Couperins, the distinguished musical family of whom the composer François Couperin is best known, were organists here for generations. The 16th-century stained glass and the paneled Chapelle Dorée are among the church's other points of interest.

Many buildings in the old streets just east of the church have recently been restored and here too you'll find the imposing Memorial to the Unknown Jewish Martyr.

This end of the rue de Rivoli is far more popular (dare we say working-class?) than the Concorde end, with the huge department store called Le Bazar de l'Hôtel-de-Ville a major attraction. The extraordinary do-it-yourself department in the basement always seems to be packed with enthusiasts of all ages and walks of life.

To the west, past the shops and pancake stalls, stands the Gothic Tour Saint-Jacques, now used as a weather center and looking rather strange all by itself in the middle of a square garden. The church to which it was once attached was demolished shortly after the Revolution. The great mathematician and philosopher Blaise Pascal used to conduct experiments in the tower, which explains why a statue of him stands at its foot. South of the tower is the place du Châtelet, once the site of a fortress but now dominated by two huge theaters, the one on the west side now offering good opera, ballet and concerts at reasonable prices.

The Plateau Beaubourg

Just north of the Tour Saint-Jacques is the area known as the "Plateau Beaubourg," which was a rather run-down district until the mid-1970s but is now bubbling with life and vigor thanks to a daring project dreamed up by the late President Georges Pompidou—of which more anon.

From the Hôtel de Ville, cross the rue de Rivoli and take the rue Renard and the rue de la Verrerie to the left until you reach the rue Saint-Martin, which is a pedestrians-only street at this point. Turn right and you find yourself looking up at the church of Saint-Merri, built in the 16th century in the Late Gothic style of an earlier age. It has several fine paintings, by Carle Vanloo and Simon Vouët for instance, and a magnificent organ. Concerts are often held here, particularly during the Ile de France Festival.

Some of the attractive houses in the street just north of the church, the rue du Cloître Saint-Merri, have now been restored. Continue along the rue Saint-Martin, which has several restaurants and some fashionable little shops, including one devoted solely to writing equipment old and new, and a very popular baker's where you can treat yourself to a delicious *brioche* still warm from the oven.

A few steps further on and you will be confronted with—yes, really —the most popular building in Europe, the Centre National d'Art et de Culture Georges Pompidou. "Confronted" is the word. Be prepared for a shock when you see the place for the first time—this highly-controversial arts complex is vast, gaudily colored and frequently likened to an oil refinery or an ocean liner!

In order to allow the maximum space inside the building, architects Renzo Piano and Richard Rogers (an Italian and an Englishman) have thrust as much as possible to the outside—stairs, lifts, escalators, ventilation shafts, hot-air pipes, gas and water pipes; and on top of this, at night it's brilliantly lit to resemble a fairground. But love it or hate it—it's a building that seems to inspire extreme reactions—there's no getting away from the fact that this "cultural Disneyland," as *Time Magazine* once called it, has succeeded beyond its planners' wildest dreams in attracting people who are not normally museum-goers. The statistics speak for themselves: in its first year of existence it had 5,558,137 visitors, nearly four times as many as the Louvre, and is now packing in 8 million visitors a year.

So how exactly did this extraordinary phenomenon come about? In 1968 the Plateau Beaubourg, which had been partly cleared of its decaying houses before World War II, was officially included in the redevelopment plan scheduled for the nearby Les Halles sector. A year later President Pompidou was announcing plans for a cultural center that was designed to act as a magnet for all those interested in the arts, and to restore Paris to what he saw as its rightful place as the world's leading art capital. Piano's and Rogers's design was chosen after fierce competition and work started in 1972. In January 1977 the building opened to shrieks of horror from died-in-the-wool Parisians, but also to shrieks of delight, especially from young (and young-at-heart) people who liked its informal, unstuffy atmosphere, its light and airy exhibition rooms, its policy of mingling all the arts (paintings and sculpture, dance and drama, books and films)—and its long opening hours.

But, you may say, just what's inside the building? Well, for a start, Beaubourg, as it's generally called (the French seem to have a built-in resistance to using names attached to heads of state, as witness their refusal to call Charles-de-Gaulle airport anything but Roissy, which is indeed where it is), houses the National Museum of Modern Art. This is the largest collection of modern art in the world and is full of marvelous things. The spacious and uncluttered galleries really seem to lend themselves to the display of contemporary paintings and other works of art. It's difficult to give guidance on what to see and where, as in keeping with the progressive spirit of the place the exhibits are constantly being changed and moved. But you'll no doubt want to spend quite a lot of time looking at the wide range of Matisses on view, and will also find that the museum gives you an excellent overview of the various "-isms" of modern art (fauvism, cubism, expressionism and so on). For those who like to keep up with the latest developments in art there are some very recent works that are pretty far from traditional ideas of art.

But Beaubourg is much more than an art museum. It also has an excellent and popular reference library (one of the few in France with an open-shelf system) including language-learning tapes, slides of works of art, video recorders and television sets; a cinémathèque showing classics from all over the world, with four or five different films every day; a children's painting studio; an acoustics and music research center (headed by Pierre Boulez); a reconstructed version of the studio used by the great sculptor Constantin Brancusi; an industrial design center; and an excellent bookshop selling art books, posters, postcards and so on. Many temporary shows are held here, ranging from large and lavish exhibits to small, specialized and sometimes obscure ones devoted to, say, half-timbered houses in the Auvergne or children's adventure playgrounds, often with a somewhat sociological-cum-ecological commentary. The center also stages theater and ballet performances and concerts, and on the top floor is a good cafeteria with an openair terrace and a fine view over Paris. A good art bookshop has also opened up here.

Don't be put off by the rucksacks and general litter cluttering up the ground floor—it's the inevitable other-side-of-the-coin of the free-and-easy atmosphere of the place. Just wade in and see for yourself. If you've got children in tow they'll adore it all, especially the sloping space in front of Beaubourg, known as "the Piazza," which is thronged at most times of the day (and night—though not so late now, as a result of complaints from outraged local residents) with crowds enjoying the performances given by street musicians, fire-eaters, "Indians" doing the rope trick, clowns and assorted entertainers, even a fully-fledged circus sometimes.

Indeed this whole area has become one of *the* entertainment centers in Paris, with café-théâtres all over the place, not to mention improvised street dancing on occasions such as Bastille Day (14 July).

The narrow streets round Beaubourg are full of fashion boutiques, art galleries, antique shops, smart restaurants, even the occasional sex shop, and the apartments in the restored buildings nearby are changing hands at alarmingly high prices. This phenomenon is partly explained by Beaubourg's proximity to Les Halles.

Les Halles

To get to Les Halles from the Pompidou Center, walk due west along the short rue Aubry-le-Boucher, cross the busy boulevard de Sebastopol and continue along the rue Berger to the renovated square des Innocents, bordered by pedestrian streets, lively pavement cafés, avant-garde boutiques and art galleries. In the middle of the square is a beautiful Renaissance fountain, the Fontaine des Innocents, standing on the site of a former church and what was once Paris's largest cemetery. It was designed by Pierre Lescot and the graceful figures are by the sculptor Jean Goujon, whose work can also be seen in the Louvre and at the Musée Carnavalet.

Running parallel to the south side of the square is the rue de la Ferronnerie, where the course of French history changed abruptly with the assassination of King Henri IV in 1610 by a schoolmaster and mystic called François Ravaillac (the deed was done outside no. 11).

And so to Les Halles, which was for so long what the 19th-century novelist Emile Zola dubbed "the belly of Paris." But in 1979 an astute publicity campaign recoined Zola's famous phrase to claim in jubilation: "The belly of Paris has become the city's heart!"

Why the anatomical slogans? The answer is that for over 800 years Les Halles did indeed cater to the bellies of Parisians—it was the home of the capital's food market, France's equivalent of London's Covent Garden, a magnificent palace of food growing bigger and more unwieldy all the time. Yet in spite of the massive problems raised by the traffic congestion it generated, and the inevitable refuse, not to mention the smell, which didn't exactly fit in with contemporary ideas about preventing environmental pollution, Les Halles was a great magnet. The smart way to finish an evening on the town was to wind up in the early hours drinking onion soup or eating snails in one of the many picturesquely-named bistrots or restaurants fringing the market, part of the charm undoubtedly arising from the idea of the rich going slumming—grand ladies in fur coats rubbing shoulders with the tough market porters.

But by the sixties the planners had sealed the fate of the market originally started during the reign of Philippe Auguste. In 1969 it was moved out to a specially-designed modern complex at Rungis near Orly airport, and two years later the elegant 19th-century pavilions of glass, cast-iron and steel were pulled down, to the dismay of conservationists. All that was left was one big hole.

For years controversy raged over the famous *trou* (hole), which featured in countless cartoons and became something of an attraction in itself as people peered down into the bowels of the earth trying to work out what the cranes and mechanical diggers were up to. Ten years and a great deal of muddle and indecision later, plus much-publicized disagreements between President Giscard d'Estaing and the mayor of Paris, long-time rivals, about how the hole was to be filled, the first stage of Les Halles Mark 2 was unveiled with the official opening in September 1979 of "the Forum," the much-vaunted new heart of Paris.

The futuristic and grandiose schemes dreamed up in an earlier decade, the towering office blocks and sleek trade center later favored by the powers-that-be, had given way to a scheme better suited to the new climate of energy-saving and environmental awareness. The phoenix that eventually rose from the ashes is a striking and stylish pedestrians-only shopping-and-leisure center built in glass and concrete on several different levels, with plenty of room to stroll and watch the world go by. Such great names as Cardin, Saint-Laurent, Ungaro and Daniel Hechter have flocked to open fashion boutiques here—a sure sign that the cynics' insistence that the Forum would be a gigantic flop was ill-founded. But fashion isn't the only name of the game. Modern furniture stores, a huge branch of the FNAC chain selling books and high-quality audiovisual equipment, plus records and sports goods at discount prices, many shoe and accessory shops, can all be found here. And this shopping center with a difference also has a theater performing plays for children in the afternoon, drama, ballet or concerts in the evening, plus jazz or café-théâtre late at night. There are movie theaters too, a branch of the famous Grevin waxworks museum, the Holography Museum, a post office and several restaurants covering a wide price range. The area round Les Halles has now been completed; it includes a 50-meter pool, a billiards room, a poetry center, a concert hall, more movie theaters, and a tropical garden. With four Métro lines and the RER all converging on the Forum, plus a large carpark, access is no problem.

In the mid-'80s it seems fair to say that the belly of Paris really has shifted upwards and leftwards. Les Halles is full of life and interest. The overall scheme has achieved the planners' aim of making a focal point and recreating "the mosaic of activities that make up the heart of any city." Just as important, fears that all the old-established bars, cafés and restaurants round the edge of Les Halles would die out have proved groundless. They've stayed, and many are still on the go more or less round the clock. And a whole new breed of chic but casual cafés has sprung up, offering many opportunities for watching the world go by as you sip your drink or savor your ice cream.

One landmark that has survived the changing fortunes of Les Halles is the beautiful church of Saint-Eustache on its northern edge, which is well known for the excellent concerts held there. The ground plan is Gothic and similar to that of Notre Dame but much of the decoration dates from the Renaissance and the main façade is an 18th-century addition with classical pillars—a mixture that makes this church a must if you're interested in architecture. If history or literature are more your line, you'll be impressed to know that both the christening and the funeral of the great dramatist Molière took place here, while music lovers might like to note that Berlioz's *Te Deum* and Liszt's *Missa Solemnis* were given their first performances in Saint-Eustache. Among several interesting paintings and sculptures inside the church, don't miss the early Rubens, *The Pilgrims of Emmaus (The Adoration of the Magi* is not by Rubens himself but a copy).

The round building on the west side of Les Halles is the Bourse du Commerce or Commodities Exchange, built in 1765 on the site of a grand 16th-century mansion commissioned and lived in by Queen Marie de Médicis. A tall column is all that is left of the former *hôtel*. West of the Bourse du Commerce runs the rue du Louvre, known to tourists mainly as the home of Paris's only all-night post office (it's open 24 hours a day year-round). If you cross it and turn into the rue Jean-Jacques Rousseau running diagonally south (the great man lived here towards the end of his life), you come to the picturesque Galerie

Véro-Dodat, an early 19th-century version of a luxury shopping arcade where the tragic actress Rachel lived for a while. The arcade has been restored and provides an interesting contrast to the new-style luxury of the Forum.

At the far end of the arcade, turn right into the attractively-named rue Croix des Petits-Champs (Street of the Cross of the Little Fields), which leads to the 17th-century place des Victoires, with a few remaining elegant façades (nos. 4 to 12) and an equestrian statue of Louis XIV (one of the three statues of him remaining in Paris). The circular *place* was built as a special site for a splendid statue of the Sun King that was subsequently melted down during the Revolution. The present statue dates from the early 19th century and is by a sculptor from Monaco called Bosio. The *place* has several avant-garde fashion boutiques and a couple of good restaurants. Just north of here is the 17th-century basilica of Notre Dame des Victoires in the place des Petits-Pères, chiefly of interest for its paintings by Carle Vanloo and its thousands of votive offerings (a pilgrimage to worship the Virgin Mary has been staged here since the early 19th century). During the Revolution the basilica was used as a stock exchange, so don't be surprised to discover that you're now on the edge of Paris's banking and financial district.

 SIGHTSEEING CHECKLIST. Look under *Sightseeing* in the *Practical Information* section for general points on museums and other places of interest.

Archives Nationales, (Museum of the History of France), Hôtel Soubise, 60 rue des Francs-Bourgeois, 3e (tel. 42–77–11–30). Daily except Tues., 2–5. Half-price on Sun.; no admission charge for students and teachers. *Métro:* Hôtel-de-Ville, Rambuteau.

Bibliothèque Forney, Hôtel des Archevêques de Sens, 1 rue du Figuier, 4e (tel. 42–78–14–60). Open Tues. to Sat., 1.30–8. No admission charge. *Métro:* Pont-Maries, St.-Paul.

Centre National d'Art et de Culture Georges Pompidou, Plateau Beaubourg, 4e (tel. 42–77–12–33). Open 12–10 weekdays except Tues.; weekends 10–10. No admission charge to the Center itself, but you must pay to visit the National Museum of Modern Art (except on Sun.) and special exhibits. Special one-day pass (*laissez-passer un jour*) costs around 30 frs. Guided tours at 3.30 on weekdays, 11 on weekends. Frequent guided tours of individual exhibits. *Métro:* Châtelet, Hôtel-de-Ville, Rambuteau.

Hôtel de Bethune-Sully, 62 rue St.-Antoine, 4e (tel. 42–74–22–22). Open daily 10–6. *Métro:* St.-Paul.

Hôtel de Ville, pl. Hotel de Ville, 4e (entrance may be in the rue de Rivoli). Special exhibits generally open 10–6 or 6.30; closed Tues. *Métro:* Hôtel de Ville.

Maison de Victor Hugo (Victor Hugo's House), 6 pl. des Vosges, 4e (tel. 42–72–16–65 or 42–72–10–16). Open Tues. to Sun., 10–5.40. (CP). *Métro:* St.-Paul.

Marais Cultural Center, 28 rue des Francs-Bourgeois, 3e (tel. 42–72–73–52). Special exhibits only, no permanent collection. Opening hours generally 10–7 daily, except Tues., but check locally.

Musée Bricard de la Serrure (Lock Museum), 1 rue de la Perle, 3e (tel. 42–77–79–62). Open 10–12 and 2–5; closed Sun., Mon., and public holidays. *Métro:* St.-Paul.

Musée Carnavalet (History of Paris Museum), 23 rue de Sévigné, 3e (tel. 42–72–21–13). Open Tues. to Sun., 10–5.40. Prints, drawings and photographs section open only Mon. to Fri., 2–7, Sat. 10–12. (CP). *Métro:* Chemin Vert, St.-Paul.

Musée de la Chasse et de la Nature (Hunting Museum), Hôtel Guénégaud des Brosses, 60 rue des Archives, 3e (tel. 42–72–86–43). Open 10–5.30; closed Tues. and public holidays. Half-price for children under 10. *Métro:* Rambuteau.

Musée Grévin (Waxworks Museum), Forum des Halles, Level 1, 3e (tel. 42–61–28–50). Open 10.30–6.45 weekdays; 1–7.15 Sun. and holidays.

Musée de l'Holographie (Holography Museum), Forum des Halles, Level 1, 3e (tel. 42–96–96–83). Mon. to Sat., 11–7; Sun. and holidays 1–7. *Métro and RER:* Châtelet.

Musée Picasso, Hôtel Salé, 5 rue de Thorigny, 3e, (tel. 42–71–25–21). Thurs. to Mon., 9.45–5.15; Weds., 9.45 A.M.–10 P.M.; closed Tues.

Swedish Cultural Center, 11 rue Payenne, 3e (tel. 42–71–82–80). Special exhibits only, no permanent collection. Opening hours generally 12–6 weekdays; 2–6 weekends; but check locally. No admission charge. *Métro:* St.-Paul.

Tour of Synagogues. Check the weekly listings of guided tours.

LUNCH SPOTS. There are many lively cafés around the pretty Square des Innocents, between the Beaubourg Center and Les Halles, and some more ordinary ones in the rue St.-Antoine where Parisians go for a quick drink, coffee or sandwich standing up at the bar. The following places all offer light meals or snacks served quickly so you don't waste precious sightseeing time. If you need a more serious meal, consult our main restaurant listing.

Auberge de Jarente, 4e. Modest small spot in an attractive area of little streets and squares near the pl. des Vosges. Basque specialties. Closed Sun., Mon., most of Aug. and early Sept.

Dattes et Noix, 4 rue du Parc-Royal, 4e. Tearoom-cum-health-food restaurant in the heart of the Marais. Delicious savory tarts.

Hippopotamus, 29 rue Berger, 1er. One of a whole menagerie of cheerful restaurants, with good service and "formula" meals, ideal for non-lingerers.

Jo Goldenberg, 7 rue des Rosiers, 4e. Well-known Jewish restaurant, again in the Marais' heart. DC, V.

Ma Bourgogne, 19 pl. des Vosges, 4e. A popular spot for sitting outside to admire this harmonious square.

Pain Vin Fromages, 3 rue Geoffrey-Langevin, 4e, near the Beaubourg Center. A good place to try out new wines and cheeses—with fabulous country-style bread, of course.

Picasso Museum. Adequate snack bar in entrance pavilion where you get your ticket. Closed Tues.

Quatrième sans ascenseur, 8 rue des Ecouffes, 4e. Good salads, rather trendy. Closed Mon.

Around the Opéra

Just south of the place des Victoires is the massive Banque de France, originally set up by Napoleon Bonaparte in 1800. In the 1920s a vast strongroom was built underground for France's gold reserves, and a number of extensions, with more underground vaults, built later remind us that the French, luckily for them, have long set great store by the yellow metal.

Opposite the bank is a covered arcade called the Galerie Vivienne, a useful place for wet-weather shopping. Follow it round and you come out opposite a huge complex of buildings housing France's most famous library, the Bibliothèque Nationale. It originated with the royal library and is now vast—not surprisingly, considering that since the early 16th century a copy of every single book or booklet printed in France has had to be deposited there. But in the complicated modern world the librarians have to cope with many other things beside the printed word—records, microfilms and so on—and the library also has a huge sheet-music collection. The library itself is open to ticket-holders only, but you can visit the beautiful Galerie Mazarine, which was once filled with the magnificent collection of paintings and *objets d'art* assembled by Cardinal Mazarin and is now used for temporary exhibits, and the Cabinet des Médailles et Antiques with coins and medals, cameos and so on.

Just north of the library and reached via the rue Vivienne is the Bourse, the Paris Stock Exchange, finished in 1825, looking rather like a Roman temple. There's a special visitors' gallery inside, so you can try to follow the mysterious maneuvers of the moneymen on any weekday morning; the well-planned guided visit should help you grasp what's going on. On the other side of the rue Vivienne and running into the rue du 4 Septembre is an unusual street called the rue des Colonnes, with a long, pillared arcade.

The Opéra and the Grands Boulevards

A short walk north from the Bourse along the rue Notre Dame des Victoires and the rue Montmartre brings you out in the boulevard Montmartre, almost opposite the waxworks museum, the Musée Grévin, Paris's equivalent of Madame Tussaud's in London and very popu-

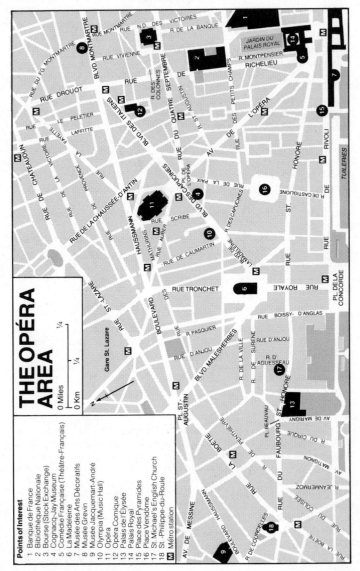

THE OPÉRA AREA

0 Miles ¼

0 Km ¼

Points of Interest

1 Banque de France
2 Bibliothèque Nationale
3 Bourse (Stock Exchange)
4 Cognacq-Jay Museum
5 Comédie Française (Théâtre-Français)
6 La Madeleine
7 Musée des Arts Décoratifs
8 Musée Grévin
9 Musée Jacquemart-André
10 Olympia (Music Hall)
11 Opéra
12 Opéra Comique
13 Palais de l'Elysée
14 Palais Royal
15 Place des Pyramides
16 Place Vendôme
17 St. Michael's English Church
18 St.-Philippe-du-Roule
Ⓜ Métro station

lar with children. You are now on the *Grands Boulevards* (if you know Yves Montand's song of the same name you'll soon find yourself humming it), the semicircle of broad streets running from the place de la République in the east to the church of the Madeleine in the west and following the line of the old city ramparts.

Nowadays the boulevards are inevitably jammed with automobiles, and they aren't a fashionable place to stroll any more. But it's easy to imagine them in their heyday, in the late-18th and early-19th centuries, when fashionable Paris came here to take the air, to dine in the elegant restaurants, to see a show in one of the many theaters, or the circuses that often performed in the eastern half of the semicircle. This is still an important entertainment area, with dozens of movies and theaters, not to mention the extraordinary disco and concert hall called Le Palace (just off the boulevard in rue du Faubourg Montmartre), which attracts a huge crowd of way-out youngsters. There are also plenty of good traditional restaurants—not little "in" places but large, reliable ones (often open late at night) of the type that have been successful for generations.

If you follow the boulevards east you'll come to two triumphal arches, the Porte Saint-Denis and the Porte Saint-Martin. They were both erected here in the 1670s, to commemorate military victories, and are decorated with allegorical groups of sculpture. If you've seen Marcel Carné's much-loved movie *Les Enfants du Paradis* you'll be interested to know that it was in the various theaters hereabouts that the great Frédéric Lemaître made his name as an actor, at a time when melodrama was all the rage. Not far beyond here is the place de la République, which has seen many a stirring event (especially during the Commune) but has little now to interest the tourist.

In fact most tourists don't come in this direction at all but work their way westwards along the boulevards from the Musée Grevin. Opposite here is the Passage des Panoramas, where the American inventor Robert Fulton (creator of the steamship) had two circular buildings put up at the very end of the 18th century to display cycloramas (a kind of early version of vistavision). A bit further along, on the right-hand side, is the Drouot auction house in the street of the same name, now operating in ultramodern buildings (with auctions daily at 2 P.M.).

You are now in the boulevard des Italiens, once thronged with dandies and their ladies in the latest fashions, nowadays lined with movie houses and banks. On the left-hand side is the Opéra Comique (also referred to as the Salle Favart), the home of light opera (Offenbach is particularly well done here). At the end of this boulevard is Paris's other home of opera, *the* Opéra itself, a majestic 19th-century building magnificently—almost theatrically—set off by the huge square in front of it, especially if you're lucky enough to see it glittering against a brilliant blue sky. The architect was an unknown young man called Charles Garnier, whose reputation was swiftly made by his design. After a lot of problems during the construction, including an underground spring, the building was opened in 1875. So typical of the Second Empire with its grandiose proportions, its somewhat curious mixture of styles and its rather florid decorative details. But no such reservations need be voiced about the beautiful ceiling painted for the Opéra in the early sixties by the Russian painter Marc Chagall, who lived in France from the 1920s, or about the dramatic marble staircase. The opera house also has an interesting museum and library, part of which is open to the public during the intervals of performances—for which, by the way, you'll find a wide range of seat prices. You can visit the theater itself on weekday afternoons.

On one corner of the place de l'Opéra is the famous Café de la Paix, a favorite haunt of wealthy foreign visitors and a good place for watching the world go by.

Behind the Opéra in the boulevard Haussmann are Paris's best-known department stores, Printemps and Galeries Lafayette, conveniently alongside one another, facing Britain's Marks & Spencer, which is now an accepted part of the Paris shopping scene.

On down the boulevards (you'll be in the boulevard des Capucines by now) and you'll find yourself in a shopping street with several good shoe shops and the rather staid Trois-Quartiers department store which has attractive silk scarves and gloves, plus an elegant man's shop. Here, too, is the Olympia music hall, which attracts the great names such as Johnny Halliday and Mireille Mathieu, and which once echoed to the evocative voice of Edith Piaf. Closer to the Opéra, on the left-hand side, is the Cognac-Jay Museum, with excellent collections of 18th-century paintings and furniture, including canvases by Fragonard and Boucher and their English contemporaries Gainsborough and Joshua Reynolds. Almost opposite, at no. 14, a commemorative plaque tells you that here the Lumière brothers held the first performance of their new invention, the forerunner of the modern movie. And at no. 11 in the last of the boulevards, the boulevard de la Madeleine, there lived and died Alphonsine Plessis. This was the lady on whom Alexandre Dumas *fils* modeled the consumptive heroine (played by Garbo on celluloid) of his romantic masterpiece *La Dame aux Camélias,* which also provided the inspiration for Verdi's opera *La Traviata.*

The Madeleine

The boulevards end in a flourish with one of Paris's most famous and fashionable churches, the church of Sainte-Marie-Madeleine, generally known merely as "la Madeleine" and looking disconcertingly like a

Greek temple. The reason for this is simple. In 1806 Napoleon decreed that the unfinished building already standing on the spot, which was in fact modeled on the Parthenon, was to be razed to the ground and replaced by a temple consecrated to the glory of his Grande Armée. But at the Restoration Louis XVIII wisely opted for a policy that steered clear of temples and glory and decided that it was to be a church after all, and one dedicated to Mary Magdalen.

The church has nothing of special interest inside, but the Corinthian columns surmounted by a carved frieze running round the outside are most impressive, and the symmetrical effect created by the Palais Bourbon beyond the rue Royale, the place de la Concorde and the Seine, easily explains why this is one of the city's best-known vistas. Society weddings are sometimes held here and a special Thanksgiving Day service is attended by the American community. In the summer parts of the Sunday masses are often said in English. Beside the church is an attractive flower market, and behind it are located Fauchon and Hédiard, Paris's exclusive food stores. Close by is a useful address—one of the two tourist offices of the Paris transport system (the RATP).

The rue Royale, with a number of luxury shops, is best known for the presence here, at no. 3, of Maxim's restaurant, now owned by couturier Pierre Cardin.

Leading west off the rue Royale, before you reach Maxim's, is the rue du Faubourg Saint-Honoré, a mecca for window-shoppers with its fashion houses. Yves Saint-Laurent, Guy Laroche, Lanvin, Courrèges and many other great names are to be found here, as well as Helena Rubinstein and Lancôme, and the world-famous glove and scarf maker, Hermès. Here too is the British Embassy, with a delightful garden, and St. Michael's English church in the rue d'Aguesseau just opposite. Don't be surprised if you spot larger numbers than usual of policemen round here—they're not out to catch smash-and-grab thieves tempted by the beautiful window displays but to protect the President of the Republic, whose official residence, the Elysée Palace, is a little further along, backed by a huge garden. Needless to say, tight security will prevent you actually getting into the imposing courtyard, but you will be able to manage a discreet peek. This is where emperors and royal favorites lived before the breed vanished for ever and France decided to put herself in the hands of presidents. (Mark you, one president did die in the arms of his mistress in this very building, but the incident was swiftly shrouded in discreet silence.)

If you continue along the same street you come to the church of Saint-Philippe-du-Roule, recently restored and with a fine fresco of the Deposition. A short walk from the church along the rue de Courcelles brings you to the boulevard Haussmann and the Musée Jacquemart-André, which stages interesting special exhibits and also has a permanent collection of 18th-century paintings and furniture plus some rooms devoted to the Italian Renaissance. The presentation may seem a little old-fashioned, but this is a museum well worth visiting.

The Place Vendôme

The other side of the rue Royale, opposite the rue du Faubourg Saint-Honoré, is the rue Saint-Honoré, which will take you to the place Vendôme. This street is best known for its expensive shops for women's fashions and accessories, but they now mainly cater to the older *Parisienne,* whose daughters (and indeed grand-daughters) prefer the more trendy boutiques in Saint-Germain-des-Prés or Les Halles or elegant Passy. But this is still a good place for beautifully-made umbrellas or gloves or hand-stitched handkerchiefs if that's your style.

The rue de Castiglione on the northern side leads into the octagonal place Vendôme, a majestic square dominated by a huge stone column covered with bronze melted down from the guns captured at the Battle of Austerlitz, which ended in one of Napoleon's most famous victories. Appropriately enough the figure perched 44 meters (145 feet) above you is Napoleon himself, though it's a copy of the original, which was replaced first by one of Henri IV when the emperor went into exile, then by a huge *fleur-de-lys,* then by another less grandiose figure of Napoleon. This is, in fact, the fifth replacement. The column itself was demolished in 1871, but re-erected during the Third Republic. The somewhat somber, yet discreetly opulent buildings round the square were originally designed as a setting for an equestrian statue of Louis XIV (as so often happened in Paris, political changes led to a complicated game of musical chairs with the city's statues). They form Paris's most perfect group of 17th-century buildings to have survived down to our own day.

Here you'll find the Ritz Hotel (now owned by the same Egyptian family as the great Harrod's store in London), along with several very grand jewelers (Van Cleef & Arpels, Boucheron and Chaumet), a few merchant banks, the Justice Ministry, and, perhaps a symbol of our times when the great multinational companies represent the new élite, the headquarters of IBM. If you're traveling on to Britain you might also like to know that the British Tourist Authority has its office and information bureau here.

Travel and jewelry are also two keynotes of the deluxe rue de la Paix, which leads off from the north side of the *place* and takes you up to the Opéra. Cartier, no less, is at no. 13, and there are several airline offices here too.

The Palais Royal

If you leave the place Vendôme by the southern end and take the rue Castiglione (with a couple of luxury hotels and some good bookshops) towards the Tuileries Gardens you come to the rue de Rivoli, once fashionable but now rather given over to souvenir shops. It's still pleasant to walk along the covered arcade, however, and one or two tearooms have appeared here recently, as well as the famous "English tearooms" at W.H. Smith's English bookshop further along in the direction of the Concorde.

A walk in the other direction along the rue de Rivoli will offer you the pleasure of seeing the dashing bronze-gilt statue of Joan of Arc in the place des Pyramides, close to the spot where she fell wounded in 1429 when the English held Paris and she launched an attack against the gate that once stood here. It's interesting to reflect that over 500 years later, when Paris was in the hands of a new enemy, the Hôtel Meurice in the rue de Rivoli was the headquarters of the Nazi commandant. Most of the tourist buses visiting Paris and the Ile de France leave from here.

Continuing along the rue de Rivoli you will soon see the Musée des Arts Décoratifs on the Louvre side, which has excellent permanent collections, but is perhaps better known for the beautifully-staged temporary exhibits held here. In the same part of the Louvre (the Pavillon Marsan) is the newly opened Musée de la Mode. The Finance Ministry building next door will soon house items from the Louvre's collections that have previously not been on public display for lack of space.

Beyond the Ministry you come to the place du Palais-Royal. The huge building on the far side of the square is a smart antiques emporium. Exhibits of the fine and applied arts are held here.

The Palais Royal itself, on the north side of the square, was built in the 1630s by Cardinal Richelieu, Louis XIII's chief minister. After his death Louis's widow, Anne of Austria, came to live here with her small son, Louis XIV. It continued to be lived in by various members of the royal family, including Louis Philippe's father, known as "Philippe Egalité" (Philip Equality) because of his democratic views. As a member of parliament in the revolutionary period he even voted for the execution of his cousin Louis XVI, though this anti-royalist stance didn't save him from death on the scaffold himself, in the very same year as the king! In keeping with his democratic ideals (or, to be honest, because he was short of cash) he had had shops and apartments built all around the gardens of the palace before the Revolution and let them out for high rents; a few years later he decided to build a theater next door, which was to become France's best-known playhouse.

It was soon ultra-chic to go for a stroll in the Palais Royal gardens, to drink coffee in the coffee houses that were springing up all over the place or gamble in one of the gaming clubs. There were even a circus and a dance hall here at one time. But not everyone who came to the Palais Royal was bent on pleasure. In 1793 that determined young woman Charlotte Corday came here to buy the dagger (some say, more prosaically, that it was a mere bread knife) with which she murdered Marat in his bath.

The gardens are now a peaceful oasis in the heart of Paris, peaceful, that is, except for the area where the new black-and-white pillars called *les colonnes de Buren* have introduced a note of modern outrage to the classically-calm square. The fascinating mixture of perspective, water and lights is a permanent reminder of the heady days of former Minister of Culture Jack Lang.

The typically Parisian square with its fountains and globe-shaped street lamps in front of Philippe Egalité's theater is now called the place André-Malraux in honor of General de Gaulle's culture minister, who did a great deal to restore Paris's decaying buildings to their former splendor. Fittingly, the Culture Ministry is housed in a splendidly restored building overlooking the Palais Royal gardens.

You will now have reached the Théâtre-Français, better known to foreigners as the Comédie Française, and a must if you're at all interested in the French theater. Try to see a play by one of the great dramatists of the Grand Siècle, Molière, Corneille or Racine (incidentally the first two died very close to here), or one of the elegant comedies by Marivaux or Musset. You may find the acting style a bit declamatory, but the sets and costumes are magnificent and there's no better way of appreciating the elegance and grandeur that the French have always set so much store by in all forms of art. Inside the theater are a memorable bust of Voltaire by Houdon and the very chair in which Molière collapsed on stage during a performance of his own play *L'Avare*. Behind the Comédie Française you can see another reminder of the great comic dramatist—the Molière Fountain in the rue de Richelieu, close to where he lived.

From the place André-Malraux you have a splendid view of the Opéra in the far distance, at the end of the avenue de l'Opéra. This part of Paris has changed in recent decades and the avenue now has more airline offices and travel agencies than the luxury shops that once attracted a fashionable, cosmopolitan crowd here. Many of the smart restaurants round about have given way to self-service restaurants and cafés as the concept of chic moves on to new pastures, and even the famous Café de la Régence in the rue Saint-Honoré, where Voltaire and Diderot, Musset and Grimm, Benjamin Franklin and Napoleon himself used to meet friends and to play chess, has vanished, to be replaced by the Moroccan Tourist Office, though you can still admire its splendid façade.

 SIGHTSEEING CHECKLIST. Look under *Sightseeing* in the *Practical Information* section for general points on museums and other places of interest.

Bibliothèque Nationale, 58 rue de Richelieu, 2e (tel. 42–61–82–83). Open daily except public holidays, 12–6. *Métro:* Bourse, Pyramides, 4-Septembre.

Bourse, pl. de la Bourse, 2e. Guided tours every half-hour, 11–1, except Sat., Sun. and public holidays. Also public gallery. *Métro:* Bourse.

Musée Cognac-Jay, 25 blvd. des Capucines, 2e (tel. 42–61–94–54). Open Tues. to Sun., 10–5.40. No admission charge on Sun. (CP). *Métro:* Opéra.

Musée de l'Opéra, pl. de l'Opéra, 9e. Open 10–5; closed Sun., public holidays and the two weeks before Easter. *Métro:* Opéra.

Musée des Arts-Décoratifs, 107 rue de Rivoli, 1er (tel. 42–60–32–14). Has been extensively renovated and is now an excellent example of modern museum presentation. Has boutique selling an attractive selection of modern French design covering a wide price range. Open Wed. to Sat. 12.30–6.30; Sun. 11–7; closed Mon. and Tues.

Musée des Arts de la mode (Fashion Museum), Pavillon Marsan, 109 rue de Rivoli, 1er (tel. 42–60–32–14). Open Wed. to Sat. 12.30–6.30; Sun. 11–5; closed Mon. and Tues. *Métro:* Palais-Royal, Tuileries.

Musée Grévin (Waxworks Museum), 10 blvd. Montmartre, 9e (tel. 47–70–85 –05). Open daily 1–7 (no admittance after 6). *Métro:* Montmartre.

Musée Jacquemart-André, 158 blvd. Haussmann, 8e (tel. 45–62–39–94). Open 1.30–5.30; closed Mon. and Tues. *Métro:* Miromesnil, Saint-Philippe-du-Roule.

 LUNCH SPOTS. This is an excellent area for restaurants. Below we list a few places to consider for a fairly simple lunch. You will find others, some more elaborate, in our regular Restaurant Listing.

Assiette au Boeuf, 20 blvd. Montmartre, 9e. One of a number of restaurants of the same name, good for "formula" meals consisting of *hors d'oeuvre* and grilled meat, with optional extra dessert. Fast service.

Bistro de la Gare, 38 blvd. des Italiens, 9e. Good for "formula" meals, with fast and efficient service.

Fauchon, pl. de la Madeleine, 8e. Open for lunch Mon. through Sat. Excellent sandwiches, light meals and patisseries.

Hippopotamus, 1 blvd. des Capucines, 2e. Another place with a well-planned "formula" system.

Minim's, rue du fbg. St.-Honoré, 8e. Opposite Elysée Palace and attracting a rather chic crowd. Open from 10 A.M. non-stop to 7 P.M.

Smith & Son, 248 rue de Rivoli, 1 er. Well-known English-language bookshop has popular upstairs restaurant.

The Louvre

Not all first-time visitors to Paris realize that before becoming one of the world's major museums the Louvre was the palace of the kings of France, dating originally from the beginning of the 13th century when Philippe Auguste first built it as a fortress complete with towers and high walls. But it was François I, in the early 16th century, who decided to transform the fortress into a palace proper. Although work continued under his successors for another three hundred years, and many changes were made, the bulk of the Louvre as it is today still looks basically as it did when François's architect, Pierre Lescot, designed it.

However, change is in the air for the Louvre. A far-reaching scheme to expand the collections is underway and during your visit you will find building work in progress. The main aim is to spread into the rue de Rivoli (the north wing of the overall complex), taking over buildings currently occupied by the Finance Ministry. Beneath the central square an underground complex of restaurants, libraries, art cinemas and car-and-bus parks is being built. Works above ground include the sci-fi glass pyramid by American-Chinese architect I.M. Pei, and the restoration of the former gardens to their former glory. Completion is scheduled for the middle of 1989.

The Louvre as it is today forms a letter "A" widening from east to west, with the south wing overlooking the Seine, the north wing running along the rue de Rivoli, and the bar of the "A" formed by the grandiose and harmonious Cour Carrée, probably the most interesting part of the building architecturally. To help you work out what dates from when, keep an eye open for the initials carved on the various sections—not graffiti of course, but the initials of the various kings and queens who commissioned them. "He" stands for Henri II and a double "C" for his queen Catherine de Médicis (though many people have noticed that the "C" sometimes looks more like a "D"—no doubt standing for Diane de Poitiers, the king's mistress, who built the lovely château of Anet not far from Paris). "K" means Charles IX; "H" (on the west wing), Henri III; "HDB," Henri IV. "LA" means Louis XIII and Anne of Austria; "LB" (Louis de Bourbon) stands for Louis XIV and "LMT" for the Sun King plus his wife, the Spanish Infanta Maria Theresa.

Step outside the Cour Carrée and you are in the rue de l'Amiral Coligny, which commemorates one of the earliest victims of the terrible Massacre of St Bartholomew in 1572. The signal for the slaughter of thousands of Protestants was given from the belfry of the church you see opposite, Saint-Germain-l'Auxerrois, once the parish church of French kings and now well known for its concerts. But the real point of coming out here is to admire the colonnade designed by Claude Perrault, a 17th-century architect who also designed the Paris Observatory (his brother, incidentally, wrote the first version of Cinderella and many other well-loved fairy stories, as well as being adviser to Louis XIV's minister Colbert, which may well explain why Claude got this important commission).

But let's concentrate on the Louvre as a museum, which is after all how it's best known. It's made up of seven separate sections: Oriental Antiquities, Egyptian Antiquities, the Greek and Roman department, Sculpture, Paintings, Prints and Drawings, and Furniture and *Objets d'Art.* Best advice is to buy a plan or guidebook inside the museum, as rooms are frequently redesigned and exhibits moved. The main entrance, by the way, is the Porte Denon, in the south wing. You can hire a cassette in English from the large room just inside the main entrance where you buy your ticket, and where you can also buy postcards, books, and reproductions of some of the exhibits. In the height of the tourist season this area of the museum is sheer bedlam, so be warned.

What you want to see will depend on your own preferences, but you surely won't want to miss the following highlights. Top of the list for most visitors is Leonardo's *Mona Lisa,* though many are surprised by how small the lady with the enigmatic smile seems. Another surprise is that the painting's surrounded by a glass box—a necessary precaution for what is probably the world's best-known painting and one that has already been attacked by various madmen and vandals. The lady is also known as *La Gioconda* and you'll have much less trouble finding her if you bear in mind that the French version is *La Joconde.* Other highlights include the *Victory of Samothrace,* generally known as the *Winged Victory,* and of course the *Venus de Milo,* both in the Greek and Roman section. The best-known exhibit in the Egyptian department is the *Seated Scribe,* but you will also be enthralled by the Crypt of Osiris in the basement designed to recreate the atmosphere of an embalmer's workshop, with statues of Isis and Osiris, animal mummies, jewelry and tombs.

It's impossible to pick out highlights from the paintings sections, there are so many masterpieces, but the Rembrandts and much of the

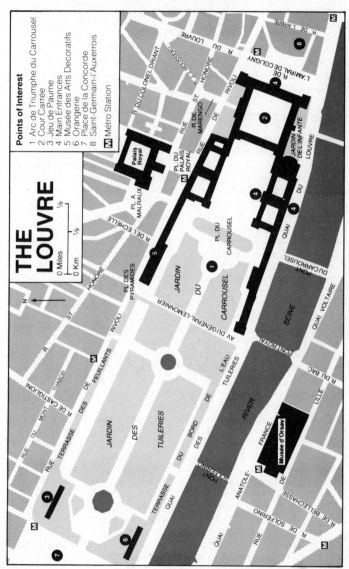

THE LOUVRE

0 Miles 1/8
0 Km 1/8

Points of Interest

1 Arc de Triumphe du Carrousel
2 Cour Carrée
3 Jeu de Paume
4 Main Entrances
5 Musée des Arts Decoratifs
6 Orangerie
7 Place de la Concorde
8 Saint-Germain-l'Auxerrois

M Metro Station

Italian school are particularly popular. The best-known exhibit in the sculpture section is Michelangelo's pair of *Slaves* for the tomb of Pope Julius II, while no one would want to miss the stunning Apollo Gallery, with the magnificent crown jewels of France—a vivid illustration, you may feel, of why the spendthrift royal court was bound to be toppled, and why in these democratic days royal palaces become splendid museums.

The Tuileries Gardens

In the 16th century the widowed Queen Catherine de Médicis commissioned another palace to stand close to the Louvre. This was the Tuileries, so called because the clay soil there was once used for making tiles (the name means "tile kilns"). But this second palace was burnt down during the Commune and only the beautiful formal gardens are left, stretching from the Louvre to the place de la Concorde.

When you leave the Louvre you'll find yourself being drawn as by a magnet to these ornamental gardens laid out by the great landscape artist Le Nôtre, just the place for a soothing stroll after so much magnificence inside the Louvre. They're an excellent example of what is technically known as a *jardin à la française,* a "French-style garden," with fountains and ornamental ponds and statues and little bits of lawn fenced off, and a constant love of symmetry.

Symmetry is indeed the keynote of the extraordinary view that greets you as you enter the gardens—a splendid vista sweeping triumphantly (in fact it's often referred to as "the Triumphal Way") through the small arch known as the Arc de Triomphe du Carrousel, which is modeled on the arch of Septimus Severus in Rome, to the gardens themselves, on to the place de la Concorde with its needle-sharp obelisk, and up the Champs-Elysées to the much bigger triumphal arch known the world over as simply the Arc de Triomphe. (In the far distance, and seeming even to dwarf the majestic arch, can be seen the modernistic skyscrapers of the La Défense business and residential district on the western outskirts of Paris.) Openair concerts are sometimes held in the place du Carrousel. Don't miss one if you're in Paris at the right time, as you'll love the setting, with the arch's pink marble pillars gleaming under the floodlights. The square's name, by the way, comes from an elaborate equestrian display held to celebrate the birth of Louis XIV's first child in 1662.

The gardens are popular with children, who adore sailing boats in the ornamental ponds—so do some adults!—and needless to say with tourists. They can get hot and dusty in summer, but are otherwise the perfect place for a romantic stroll—best not to wander alone here at night, however. It's hard to remember that these peaceful avenues of trees were once the scene of appalling bloodshed when the Swiss Guards were slaughtered here during the Revolution. The gardens have been given a much-needed facelift and are now bright with flowerbeds.

At the western end of the Tuileries are twin pavilions—symmetry again! At the northwestern corner is the Jeu de Paume, originally used for an early version of tennis that was popular in 17th- and 18th-century Paris and subsequently famous as the Museum of Impressionism. The superb Impressionist collection is now in the Musée d'Orsay and the Jeu de Paume, currently closed for renovation, will be used for temporary art exhibits.

The Orangerie, the spacious twin pavilion on the river side of the gardens, was also extensively restored in the early '80s. As well as Monet's famous *Waterlilies* series, it now houses a magnificent collection of Impressionist and modern works bequeathed to the nation by a private collector.

Between the Jeu de Paume and the Orangerie is an ornamental gate flanked by a pair of winged horses carved by the 17th-century sculptor Antoine Coysevox from a single block of marble for the royal château at Marly. And opposite them, on the far side of the place de la Concorde, they are perfectly balanced by another pair of horses, this time by Coysevox's nephew Guillaume Coustou, originally carved to replace their winged predecessors when they were moved to the Tuileries.

 SIGHTSEEING CHECKLIST. Look under *Sightseeing* in the *Practical Information* section for general points on museums and other places of interest.

Jeu de Paume, pl. de la Concorde, 1er (tel. 42–60–12–07 or 42–96–42–73). Closed for renovation.

Musée du Louvre, Palais du Louvre, 1er (tel. 42–60–39–26). Open 9.45–5 (but some rooms stay open till 6.30 on a rota system). Closed Tues. The whole of the museum is open Mon. and Wed., but some rooms are closed on other days on a varying schedule, so check locally. Half-price on Sun.

Main entrance is currently via the ground floor in the Egyptian Antiquities section. Special exhibits in the Pavillon de Flore open 9.45–5 daily except Tues. Entrance hall houses an information bureau, an exchange counter, art bookshop and counters selling postcards and reproductions.

Guided tours of the Greek and Roman antiquities section and Paintings section daily, except Tues. and Sun., between 10 and 4 (frequent tours in English). Many special lecture tours on specific themes (check program locally). *Métro:* Louvre, Palais-Royal.

Orangerie des Tuileries, pl. de la Concorde, 1er (tel. 42–97–48–16). Open 9.45–5.15, daily except Tues. Half-price on Sun. *Note:* Monet's *Waterlilies* cannot be visited between 12 and 2. *Métro:* Concorde.

LUNCH SPOTS. Here the best choices fall in the neighboring areas—notably around the Champs-Elysées and in the rue de Rivoli. We give a couple below, and more, of course, in the main restaurant listings.

Angelina's, 226 rue de Rivoli, 1er. Once the famous Rumpelmayer's, now a fashionable spot for a late breakfast, early, middling or late lunches, teas and so on—a very flexible place, with good light meals and mouthwatering pastries. Closed mid-July to mid-Aug. v.

A la Grille, 15 pl. du Marché St.-Honoré, 1er. Good *menu* for lunch.

Louvre, there is an adequate snackbar in the Pavillon Mollien, open during museum hours, and so shut on Tues.

The Champs-Elysées

So to the place de la Concorde, scene of so many momentous events and often said to be the most beautiful square in the world, its elegance untarnished even by the constant stream of traffic whirling round it. Make your way cautiously to the central island—the traffic is lethal—and as you pivot slowly round you'll soon be gasping in wonder as each 45° turn reveals a new and even more splendid vista. To the east, the Tuileries Gardens framed by the winged horses and stretching leafily through to the Carrousel arch and the Louvre. To the south, your gaze travels over the pont de la Concorde spanning the Seine to the majestic classical façade of the Palais Bourbon, seat of the French parliament, the Assemblée Nationale. Turn to face north and the word "symmetry" will again spring to your lips: there at the end of the rue Royale is the classical façade of the Madeleine church, in a direct line with the Palais Bourbon and framed by a pair of huge colonnaded 18th-century mansions built by Gabriel, who also designed the Petit Trianon at Versailles. One of the mansions is now the headquarters of the French navy, the other the deluxe Hôtel Crillon. Now turn to the west and the most famous vista of all unfolds before you—the avenue des Champs-Elysées, broad and tree-lined, sweeping inexorably up to the huge Arc de Triomphe. But before you make your way up the celebrated avenue, wrench your gaze back from the views and spare a moment for the obelisk towering above you. It came originally from Luxor in Egypt and is well over three thousand years old. To understand what it's doing here you need to know something of the history of the *place*.

It was built to honor Louis XV and bore his name, with a statue of this popular monarch on the very spot where you're standing. But although it was briefly the setting for many a spectacular celebration, it wasn't long before it fell victim to the fervor of the revolutionary mob. In 1792 the king's statue was toppled and the *place* was renamed "the Square of the Revolution." Less than a year later another king was toppled—but this time it was the man himself, not his statue. Louis XVI was one of over a thousand victims whose heads rolled to the sound of drums and the swish of Madame Guillotine's dreaded blade. He was soon followed by his queen, Marie-Antoinette, and in due course—such are the pendulum swings of history—by the leading revolutionaries, Robespierre and Danton, who had set up the guillotine in the first place. When all the blood had been washed away, the Revolution and the Empire had come and gone and a more peaceable age had been ushered in, sensible Louis-Philippe decided that it would be a good idea to steer clear of heads of state for the statue in the center of Paris's finest square, now optimistically renamed "the Square of Concord." Which is why Egypt's offer of the venerable obelisk seemed so opportune—surely no one was going to try to topple that as the symbol of a hated regime!

But now leave the safety of the island with its strictly non-controversial monument and venture across to the Champs-Elysées. The building to your right, by the way, on the corner of avenue Gabriel, is the U.S. embassy.

The Champs-Elysées

Once you have passed the Marly horses you are actually in the Champs-Elysées, in what was originally designed (by Le Nôtre again) as a magnificent garden sweeping away from the Louvre. During the Second Empire fashionable ladies and their escorts would parade up and down here in their carriages, determined to see and to be seen. Today the ladies and gentlemen of leisure have vanished, the crowds are foreign rather than Parisian and the avenue is more a temple to leisure-pursuits spent in far-away places—many airlines and travel agents have their offices here. Also, the avenue has become a haunt of muggers. But the Champs-Elysées is still a name to conjure with, a definite must on every tourist's itinerary. If you're lucky enough to be here on 14 July you'll be thrilled by the splendid military parade held annually to celebrate the fall of the Bastille. The whole area shakes to the passage of huge tanks while troop-carrying helicopters thunder overhead and crack air-display squadrons trail red-white-and-blue smoke.

The great victory processions of modern times have been staged here—in 1919, and when Paris was liberated in 1944, with General de Gaulle leading his followers down the Champs-Elysées before the triumphal mass in Notre Dame. And a couple of decades later, during the "May events" in 1968, the anti- and pro-de Gaulle factions chose the Champs-Elysées for their respective mass demonstrations. When great men die the nation tends to do homage to them here, too—Victor Hugo in 1885, General de Gaulle in 1970. And the avenue is also the scene of a very different sort of triumph every year, when the winner of the world's major cycling event, the Tour de France, flashes past to the acclaim of thousands of fans.

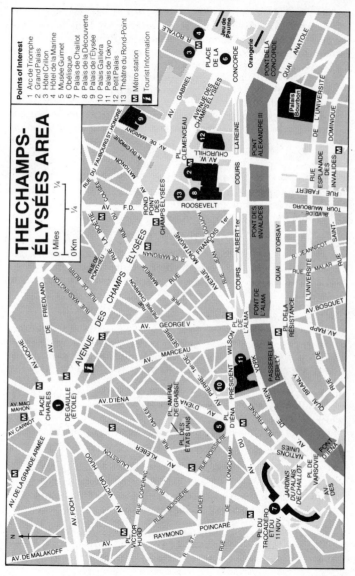

THE CHAMPS-ÉLYSÉES AREA

Points of Interest

1 Arc de Triomphe
2 Grand Palais
3 Hôtel Crillon
4 Hôtel de la Marine
5 Musée Guimet
6 Obélisque
7 Palais de Chaillot
8 Palais de la Découverte
9 Palais de l'Élysée
10 Palais Galliéra
11 Palais de Tokyo
12 Petit Palais
13 Théâtre du Rond-Point

M Métro station
i Tourist Information

0 Miles ¼
0 Km ¼

The first half of the avenue is still flanked by gardens dotted with theaters and expensive restaurants, and just beyond them on the right-hand side are the presidential palace and the British Embassy, both with delightful gardens running down to join the Champs-Elysées gardens. At the first crossroads you come to, on the right-hand side, is the site of Paris's open-air stamp and coin market (old postcards too, these days). The avenue de Marigny on the right leads past the Elysée Palace to the ultra-fashionable rue du Faubourg Saint-Honoré, full of expensive dress shops and art galleries. Opposite is the avenue Winston Churchill, leading to the Pont Alexandre III and the Invalides, and flanked by the huge Grand Palais and its smaller neighbor, the Petit Palais. Both Palais were originally built as pavilions for the Great Exhibition of 1900. They are now used for important art exhibits, though the Petit Palais also has an excellent permanent collection of furniture and applied art, plus the 19th-century paintings belonging to the City of Paris (including an *art nouveau* exhibit). The huge Grand Palais with its glass roof is one of Paris's landmarks and is soon to be refurbished—few people visiting one of the major exhibits staged in parts of the building realize that this splendid pavilion with its steel and iron framework once looked something like London's late lamented Crystal Palace. The west side of the Palais houses the Palais de la Découverte, Paris's well-displayed science museum with an excellent planetarium. Near here is another "palace," the circular Palais de Glace, once an ice-skating rink but now the Théâtre du Rond-Point, the home of Jean-Louis Barrault's and Madeleine Renaud's celebrated theater company.

Beyond the Grand Palais and on the same side of the Champs-Elysées is a deluxe area forming a triangle bordered by the avenue Montaigne and the avenue George V, where you'll find the great couture houses and some of Paris's grandest hotels. If you're visiting Paris during the Christmas and New Year period, you'll be enchanted by the beautifully-lit streets round here, especially the avenue Montaigne, which also has several theaters.

After the Rond-Point des Champs-Elysées the avenue widens and the gardens give way to broad sidewalks lined by cafés with openair terraces, shops, movie houses and offices. If you knew Paris some while ago you'll be surprised to see that the old maxim that anybody who was anybody walked down the northern side (unless they were going to Fouquet's, that is) is no longer valid. Both sides now have elegant cafés and are thronged with a cosmopolitan crowd. Alas, you'll soon spot another change too—gastronomically the Champs-Elysées isn't what it once was and it has been invaded by hamburger joints (McDonald's is to be found here), pizza houses and various other fast-food outfits. But you can still enjoy a cup of coffee or a drink in one of the cafés as you watch the world go by. And some of the elegant shopping arcades—Galerie des Champs-Elysées, Galerie du Rond-Point, Galerie du Lido—leading off the avenue have good restaurants tucked away. For the many tourists who seem to suffer from a different sort of hunger, the famous Lido nightclub, towards the top on the right-hand side, is easily identified by the number of coaches parked outside. Another important landmark, on the other side this time, is the Paris Tourist Office, at no. 127, close to the Drugstore and the Arc de Triomphe.

The Arc de Triomphe

Here at the top of the Champs-Elysées you've reached the place Charles de Gaulle, still better known by its old name of the Etoile (the Star)—not surprisingly, since this huge circular *place* with 12 broad avenues radiating out from it really is like a star (or to be strictly honest, like a wheel). And right in the center is the towering mass of the Arc de Triomphe, a classical structure built to celebrate Napoleon's victorious armies and commissioned by the emperor himself. By the time it was completed, in 1836, the days of imperial glory were well and truly over and the monarchy had been restored. But appropriately enough, the first of many elaborate and emotional ceremonies staged here was the arrival of the carriage bearing Napoleon's remains to their last resting place in Les Invalides. Beneath the huge arch lies the tomb of the unknown soldier, topped by an eternal flame rekindled ceremonially every evening at 6.30 by groups representing one of the French regiments and, on Armistice Day, 11 November, by the president of the republic in person. On national holidays a gigantic flag in the French national colors—red, white and blue—is suspended from the center of the arch and reaches right down to the ground. It's a most dramatic sight, especially at night, when red, white and blue floodlights project their beacons into the sky.

To study the superb groups of reliefs carved on the arch you must take the underpass on the northern tip of the Champs-Elysées—on no account attempt to walk through the surging traffic. The finest sculptures are by François Rude, the masterpiece being, by common consent, the *Departure of the Volunteers in 1792,* generally known as "La Marseillaise" and a stirring symbol of patriotism with the *Patrie,* the Motherland, her wings spread out to exhort the volunteers to fight for France. It's on the right-hand side if you're standing with your back to the Champs-Elysées. The other sculptures depict Napoleon's greatest battles or allegorical subjects with resounding names such as "Resistance" or "Peace." And the names of the emperor's many campaigns are carved in the stone of the arch too.

The Arc contains a little museum which now has an audio-visual presentation of its history. You can also carry on up to the platform on the top, which affords a glorious view over the whole of Paris, with the twelve radiating avenues clearly visible. The one directly opposite the Champs-Elysées, the avenue de la Grande-Armée, leads to the skyscrapers of the modern La Défense district. You won't be surprised, in this symmetry-loving capital, to hear that La Défense was built at exactly the same distance from the Arc de Triomphe as the place de la Concorde, and that another arc is being completed in La Défense; this will house offices and the International Center for Communication. The widest avenue, bordered by lawns and trees, is the luxury residential avenue called after Marshal Foch, and leading to the Bois de Boulogne, Paris's much-needed lung, its biggest park. Follow avenue Kléber, which leads to the Trocadéro, your next port of call.

The Trocadéro

If you were thinking that La Défense, for all its faults, was about all 20th-century Paris had to show of any stature, you'll change your mind when you reach the Trocadéro and see the huge Palais de Chaillot, built in 1937, directly facing the Eiffel Tower on the other side of the Seine and with two curving wings separated by a vast terrace lined by glittering gilded statues. From the terrace a splendid view unfurls at your feet, first formal gardens with fountains playing, then the Seine and the Eiffel Tower and on to the Ecole Militaire, with the bulky Tour Montparnasse in the distance. In recent years a huge firework display has been held here on Bastille Day or the night before. The Palais de Chaillot houses Paris's maritime and anthropological museums (the Musées de la Marine and de l'Homme) in the west wing and in the east wing the Musée des Monuments Français, with life-size reproductions of sections of France's major historic buildings, and the little Cinema Museum, which includes a cinémathèque with daily showings. Also in this building is one of Paris's subsidized theaters, the Théâtre National de Chaillot.

The avenue du Président-Wilson, leading from the Trocadéro to the place de l'Alma, houses several more museums: the Palais de Tokyo, home of the National Museum of Modern Art before it moved to the Pompidou Center, is now mainly used for temporary exhibits; the Museum of Modern Art of the City of Paris, devoted to 20th-century painting; the Musée Guimet, for Far Eastern art, and the Fashion and Costume Museum in the Palais Galliéra, which has particularly good temporary shows.

SIGHTSEEING CHECKLIST. Look under *Sightseeing* in the *Practical Information* section for general points on museums and other places of interest.

Arc de Triomphe, pl. Charles-de-Gaulle-Etoile, 8e (tel. 43–80–31–31). Open daily 10–5. Small extra charge to use the elevator and for the audio-visual presentation of major events in the Arch's history. Half-price Sun. and public holidays. *Métro:* Charles-de-Gaulle-Etoile.

Grand Palais, av. du Général-Eisenhower, 8e (tel. 42–89–54–10). Open Mon. and Thurs. to Sun., 10–8; Wed. 10–10; closed Tues. Reduced admission charge on Sat. Special exhibits only, no permanent collection. (N). *Métro:* Champs-Elysées Clemenceau.

Musée d'Art et d'Essai (Palais de Tokyo), 13 av. du President-Wilson, 16e (tel. 47–23–36–53). Open 9.45–5.15, closed Tues. Some rooms close between 12 and 2. Half-price on Sun. (N). *Métro:* Alma-Marceau, Iéna.

Musée d'Art Moderne de la Ville de Paris, 11 av. du Président-Wilson, 16e (tel. 47–23–61–27). Open Tues. and Thurs. to Sun., 10–5.30; Weds. 10–8.30; closed Mon. No admission charge on Sun. (CP). *Métro:* Alma-Marceau, Iéna.

Musée de la Marine, Palais de Chaillot, pl. du Trocadero, 16e (tel. 45–53–31–70). Open 10–6; closed Tues. and public holidays. Half-price for children under 12. *Métro:* Trocadéro.

Musée de la Mode et du Costume (Fashion and Costume Museum), Palais Galliéra, 10 av. Pierre-1er-de-Serbie, 16e (tel. 47–20–85–46). Open 10–5.40; closed Mon., public holidays and sometimes between exhibitions. (CP). *Métro:* Alma-Marceau, Iéna.

Musée de l'Homme, Palais de Chaillot, pl. du Trocadéro, 16e (tel. 45–53–70–60). Open 9.45–5.15, closed Tues. Films shown at 3 daily, except Tues. and Sun. (no extra charge). *Métro:* Trocadéro.

Musée des Monuments Français, Palais de Chaillot, pl. du Trocadéro, 16e (tel. 47–27–35–74). Open 9.45–12.30, 2–5.15, closed Tues. Half-price on Sun. *Métro:* Trocadéro.

Musée du Cinéma, Palais de Chaillot, pl. du Trocadéro, 16e (tel. 45–53–74–39 or 45–53–21–86). Open daily except Tues. Check times locally as they are liable to change. *Métro:* Trocadéro.

Musée Guimet, 6 pl. d'Iéna, 16e (tel. 47–23–61–65). Open 9.45–12, 1.30–5.15, closed Tues. Half-price on Sun. (N). *Métro:* Alma-Marceau, Iéna.

Palais de la Découverte, av. Franklin-Roosevelt, 8e (tel. 43–59–18–21). Open 10–6, closed Mon. and public holidays. Extra charge for Planetarium. Half-price for under-18s, students and over-65s. *Métro:* Champs-Elysées Clemenceau, Franklin-Roosevelt.

Petit Palais, av. Winston-Churchill, 8e (tel. 42–65–12–73). Open 10–5.40, Tues. to Sun. No admission charge on Sun. (CP). *Métro:* Champs-Elysées Clemenceau.

LUNCH SPOTS. An area absolutely bursting with restaurants of every kind. Apart from the fairly easy, and moderately priced, places below, you might look at our regular Restaurant Listing to find other possibilities.

Assiette au Boeuf, 123 av. des Champs-Elysées, 8e. Specializes in "formula express" meals—in other words, you get served quickly and don't have much choice! But the food is good and the atmosphere a pleasant bustle.

Bistro de la Gare, 73 av. des Champs-Elysées, 8e. Good grills, salads and desserts; nice mock art-nouveau decor.

Boutique à Sandwiches, 12 rue du Colisée, 8e. Often said to be the best sandwich joint in town. Closed Sun. and Aug.

Café de Paris, Galerie du Lido, av. des Champs-Elysées, 8e. Conveniently sited in one of the attractive galleries running off the triumphal avenue.

Le Colisée, 44 av. des Champs-Elysées, 8e. Traditional cafe for people-watching. Serves a *plat du jour,* too.

Ficotière, 17 rue Jean-Giradoux, 16e. Popular bistrot-cum-*salon de thé* with good help-yourself hors d'oeuvres. Closed weekends and most of Aug.

Fouquet's, 99 av. des Champs-Elysées, 8e. A highly fashionable spot with a lot of mileage in the chic stakes. The food's not bad either!

Grand Palais, av. du Général-Eisenhower, 8e. Handy self-service cafeteria upstairs; gets crowded when there's a major exhibit on, so best get there early if you don't want to stand in line.

Théâtre du Rond-Point, av. Franklin-Roosevelt, 8e. Delightful spot inside the theater presided over by Jean-Louis Barrault. Good food, relaxed atmosphere and decor, sprinkling of theatricals among the clientele.

The Eiffel Tower and the Invalides

You won't need telling that Gustave Eiffel's extraordinary iron lady, built in the 1880s, is the symbol of Paris for people the world over who have never even set foot in France's capital. And if the Mona Lisa is smaller than you expected, you'll probably be surprised at how *big* the Eiffel Tower looks—its huge giraffe-like structure can be seen from all over Paris, its top soaring 330 meters (over 1,000 feet) into the sky and often wreathed in clouds or mist. When it was built it was the world's tallest monument, and though it's since been surpassed by various skyscrapers, none of them can compete with the simultaneous impression of solidity and lightness it creates. Many writers have seen this paradoxical aspect as symbolizing the spirit of Paris, which no doubt helps to explain why the tower has long been *the* souvenir of Paris in the form of little scale models, or pendants for charm bracelets, or ashtrays or scarves. In recent years it has also been vitally important to Parisians as the capital's main television transmitter, and before that was already being used for radio transmission and as a weather monitoring station. A local radio station (Radio Tour Eiffel) broadcasts from the Tower, which has been refurbished and now has a huge range of amenities—restaurants, cabaret, audiovisual show, post office, bank and a branch of the Paris Tourist Office.

The Ecole Militaire

At the foot of the Eiffel Tower stretches the Champ de Mars, once used for military maneuvers and later for elaborate national festivals, but now a perfect playground for small children, with donkey rides and puppet shows, and a pleasant place for strolling. At the far end rises the imposing Ecole Militaire, a fine 18th-century building where France's army officers are trained, as Napoleon Bonaparte was before them. It was built on the initiative of a financier called Pâris-Duverney, aided and abetted by Louis XV's mistress Madame de Pompadour and his friend, the playwright and adventurer Beaumarchais, who taught the harp to the royal princesses before becoming famous as the author of *The Marriage of Figaro* and *The Barber of Seville*. Indeed it was Beaumarchais who persuaded the king to pay for the completion of the academy by imposing a tax on playing cards, of all things.

Close to the Ecole Militaire, on the other side of the avenue de Suffren, is a very different tourist attraction—the Village Suisse, a series of small and rather expensive antique shops.

The Invalides

Behind the Ecole Militaire is the UNESCO building, a good example of imaginative mid-20th century architecture and multinationally adorned with paintings by Picasso, a statue by Henry Moore and one of Alexander Calder's more massive mobiles. The building can be visited, but most tourists prefer to take the avenue de Tourville, leading from the place de l'Ecole Militaire straight to the Hôtel des Invalides and the majestic Eglise du Dôme, where Napoleon's remains lie in a series of six coffins within a tomb of red porphyry beneath the highest dome in Paris, a gilded masterpiece 107 meters (350 feet) high by the 18th-century architect Jules Hardouin-Mansart, who also designed the place Vendôme. You may be taken aback by the coloring, the red porphyry contrasting somewhat oddly with the green granite base, but you'll find it hard not to be awed by the majesty of the tomb, indeed a fitting memorial to a man whose short rule left such an indelible mark on France's institutions. The remains of L'Aiglon, the young King of Rome, lie in front of a statue of his father. The body was sent to Paris from Vienna, where it had lain since the youth's death in 1832, by Hitler, in a futile attempt to secure the goodwill of the occupied city.

The *son et lumière* performance here is unforgettable (daily performances in English). The Jardin de l'Intendant, next to the Church of the Dome, is decorated with a statue of Mansart.

The church also contains many other important tombs and monuments, as well as magnificent architectural and sculptural decoration. The other church in the Invalides complex, Saint-Louis-des-Invalides, might seem bare by comparison, if it weren't for the tattered enemy flags hanging from the cornice, a potent reminder of the many battles fought by the Napoleonic armies. In the crypt and the cellars are the tombs of some of France's illustrious generals, including a hero of World War II, Marshal Leclerc, for whom a mass is said annually, but they aren't open to the public.

You can, however, visit the well-planned Musée de l'Armée (Army Museum), with many historical exhibits that will impress even those who aren't normally interested in things military. Also here are the Musée des Plans-Reliefs, with models of French fortifications, and the Musée de l'Ordre de la Libération, an important source of information if you're interested in the Resistance movement in France during World War II.

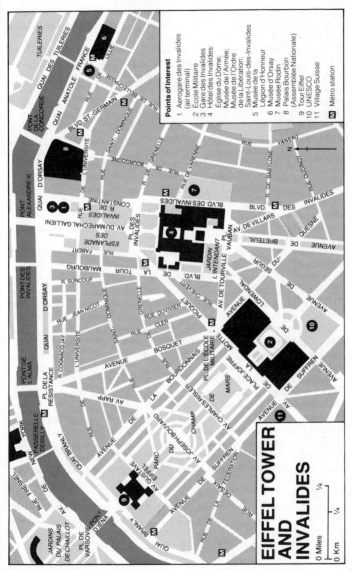

Points of Interest

1 Aerogare des Invalides (air terminal)
2 École Militaire
3 Gare des Invalides
4 Hôtel des Invalides:
  Église du Dôme;
  Musée de l'Armée;
  Musée de l'Ordre
  de la Libération;
  Saint-Louis-des-Invalides
5 Musée de la
  Legion d'Honneur
6 Musée d'Orsay
7 Musée Rodin
8 Palais Bourbon
  (Assemblée Nationale)
9 Tour Eiffel
10 UNESCO
11 Village Suisse

Ⓜ Métro station

EIFFEL TOWER AND INVALIDES

0 Miles ¼
0 Km ¼

The Invalides was built, as its name suggests, to house wounded (or "invalid") ex-soldiers, on the same principle as the Chelsea Hospital in London. It was Louis XIV who magnanimously decided to give 4,000 of these old soldiers a magnificent home, and the huge complex of buildings has been connected with the army ever since, though nowadays fewer than a hundred veterans live here. For a fine view of the harmonious 18th-century complex make your way to the north façade overlooking the Esplanade des Invalides, which is nearly 200 metres (over an eighth of a mile!) long and is dominated by a fine equestrian relief of Louis XIV flanked by reliefs of Justice and Prudence. In front of the façade an attractive garden is dotted with bronze canons pointing proudly down the Esplanade to the Seine. The Esplanade has been given a new lease of life with the creation of attractive gardens to restore something of its former glory as it sweeps down to the Seine. One of Paris's two major air terminals is to be found here, opposite the imposing Foreign Ministry. The British Council and the Canadian Cultural Center are also here, in the rue de Constantine. The Gare des Invalides is a starting-point for the express métro (RER) taking you out to Versailles.

Opposite the eastern façade of the Invalides is the Hôtel Biron, a perfect setting for the superb Rodin Museum. As well as many masterpieces by the 19th century's greatest sculptor, including *Le Penseur* and *Les Bourgeois de Calais,* the museum has preliminary drawings, plus furniture and paintings belonging to Rodin, who was allowed to use part of this beautiful 18th-century mansion as a studio in return for leaving his personal collection of his paintings to the nation. The delightful gardens, with a particularly lovely display of roses, are also adorned with his sculpture, and every two years work by promising young sculptors is exhibited here.

South and east of the Rodin Museum is the district known as the Faubourg Saint-Germain, full of palatial private mansions that now, when no individual can afford to live in such style, house ministries and embassies. For a glimpse of the façades and courtyards of these magnificent buildings, most of which date from the 18th century, walk along the rue de Grenelle or the rue de Varenne. You can visit just one, the Hôtel de Salm opposite the Musée d'Orsay close to the Seine. And that's only because it is now the Musée de la Légion d'Honneur, presenting the history of the order plus a collection of medals and decorations of various kinds.

The Musée d'Orsay was opened early in 1987, and within days was one of the most popular tourist attractions in Paris. Once a major rail station, the Gare d'Orsay, this magnificent building lost its original function when railroad electrification brought in trains too long to fit under its superbly curved roof. The building narrowly escaped demolition by being classed as an historical monument in 1978, and work on converting it into a gallery to enshrine fine and applied art from the period 1848–1914 took the next eight years. The imaginative conversion was the task of an Italian architect, Gae Aulenti, who created a limestone structure to fill up the area where the tracks once ran. It looks for all the world like the bottom half of a De Mille movie set, and makes a splendid foil for acres of historical painting and tons of dramatic sculpture. Here, too, is a fascinating model of the Opéra district that you look down on through a glass floor, and a cutaway model of the opera house itself, showing the machinery and the labyrinth of backstage rooms.

Gae Aulenti adapted the maze of rooms that used to be the station hotel, running down two sides of the great building, into a network of exhibition areas, the most striking of which is the reborn Salle des Fêtes, a miracle of polished marquetry and crystal swags. On the floor above are works by the Impressionists and other late-1800s artists, pictures known across the world through millions of reproductions—pictures by Manet, Monet, Renoir, Degas, Van Gogh, Cézanne, Toulouse Lautrec, and dozens of others. If this is your kind of painting, get there early in the day and make your way directly up to these rooms. It takes a while for the tide of visitors to rise this high, but when it does it is almost impossible to get anywhere near anything you want to study. Up here, too, is a handy coffee shop, and from this floor you can look out over the Seine through the glass face of one of the two great clocks. There is a superb internal view over the whole complex from two towers, as well, ideal for the camera buff.

On the middle level there are more paintings, furniture, sculpture, and china—a lot of it Art Nouveau—statues by Rodin, and temporary exhibitions. The excellent restaurant, once the restaurant of the station, must by reserved in advance.

Further west along the Seine is the Palais Bourbon, home of the National Assemblée Nationale, France's Parliament, but you have to get special permission to visit it.

 SIGHTSEEING CHECKLIST. Look under *Sightseeing* in the *Practical Information* section for general points on museums and other places of interest.

Eiffel Tower, Champ-de-Mars, 7e (tel. 45–50–34–56). 1st and 2nd floors open daily 10 A.M. to 11 P.M.; 3rd floor daily 10 A.M. to 10.30 P.M. Audiovisual show illustrating the history of the Tower on 1st floor, open daily 10.30 A.M. to 11 P.M. Post office open 10–7.30 only. Half-price for children under 7; no charge for children under 4. *Métro:* Bir-Hakeim. *RER:* Champ-de-Mars.

Invalides, Esplanade des Invalides, 7e. **Musée de l'Armée,** (tel. 45–55–92–30). Open daily 10–5 (10–6 Apr. through Sept.). Half-price for foreign students. Film on the two World Wars shown between 2 and 5. **Napoleon's Tomb** may be visited all year up to 7 P.M. **Musée des Plans-Reliefs,** (tel. 47–05–11–07). Closed for renovation. Check locally. **Son et Lumière** (sound-and-light show) *Le Retour des Cendres (The Return of Napoleon's Remains)* twice nightly, once in English, once in French, with extra performances in English mid-summer. Check times locally. *Métro:* Latour-Maubourg, Varenne.

Musée de la Légion d'Honneur et des Ordres de Chevalerie, 2 rue de Belle-chasse, 7e (tel. 45–55–95–16). Daily except Mon., 2–5. No admission charge on Sun. *Métro:* Solférino. *RER:* Quai d'Orsay.

Musée d'Orsay, 62 rue de Lille, 7e (tel. 45–49–48–14). Main entrance, 1 rue Bellechasse. Open Tues., Wed., Fri., and Sat., 10.30–6; Thurs., 10.30–9.45; Sun., 9–6; Closed Mon. (N). *Métro:* Solférino. *RER:* Quai d'Orsay.

Musée Rodin, 77 rue de Varenne, 7e (tel. 47–05–01–34). Open daily except Tues., 10–5.45 (4.30 Oct. through Feb.). Half-price Sun. (N). *Métro:* Varenne.

UNESCO, pl. Fontenoy (tel. 45–68–10–00). Normally open Mon. to Fri., 9–5.30. Can be closed during conferences. Data on artworks etc. is available.

Village Suisse, av. de Suffren, 7e (tel. 43–06–69–90). Open 11–7; closed Tues. and Wed. *Métro:* La Motte-Piquet.

 LUNCH SPOTS. The places given below are all moderately priced and good for a fairly speedy lunch in the middle of a sightseeing jaunt. See our regular Restaurant Listing for more expensive and leisurely spots.

Annexe du Quai, 3 rue Surcouf, 7e. A quick-service sister-restaurant to the long-established Quai d'Orsay round the corner. Bustling; goodish light cuisine. Closed weekends. AE, DC, MC, V.

Fontaine de Mars, 129 rue St.-Dominique, 7e. Plain and pleasant spot near the Eiffel Tower. Tables outside overlooking a delightful square with fountain. Smiling service, unpretentious home cooking. Closed Sun.

Jardin Impérial, 38 av. Bosquet, 7e. Good-value Vietnamese restaurant, handy for the Eiffel Tower. V.

Musée d'Orsay, quai Anatole-France, 7e. There is a café on the top floor, and a restaurant with one entrance inside the museum and another (for after hours) on the rue de Lille. Reservations are essential for the restaurant.

Parisien, first level of the Eiffel Tower. Not as good as the **Jules Verne** on the next floor up, but more suitable as a sightseeing stopoff.

Petite Chaise, 36 rue de Grenelle, 7e. An old favorite and still popular. Home cooking, lots of atmosphere. V.

Petits Oignons, 20 rue de Bellechasse, 7e. Convenient for the Musée d'Orsay and the Musée de la Légion d'Honneur. Good for light meals; pretty and refreshing decor after a hard morning's sightseeing. V.

Veggie, 38 rue de Verneuil, 7e. Good vegetarian restaurant.

The Left Bank

A short bus ride from the Rodin Museum is Montparnasse, once known as a district of poets and painters but now an area of towering skyscrapers and large modern hotels. Yet enough of the old bohemian atmosphere is left for this to be a pleasant place to spend an evening, and you'll never be short of entertainment, with movie houses, theaters and café-theaters galore. The name, in case you hadn't guessed, comes from Mount Parnassus, an ironical label adopted by the students who came to live here in the 17th century. And in the first half of this century all the world's poets tried to live up to the label.

Start your visit in the place du 18 juin 1940 (so named to commemorate General de Gaulle's famous appeal from London after the fall of France). It's overshadowed by a 59-story monster, the Tour Maine-Montparnasse, an uninspiring hunk of steel and reinforced concrete with bronze-tinted glass. The tallest skyscraper in Europe, it also has what is claimed to be the fastest elevator on the Continent, so it won't take you long to be whisked up to the top to enjoy the truly magical view of Paris. Behind the tower Montparnasse station is the terminus for trains to Chartres, Versailles and points west. This station is undergoing huge changes due to be completed by the end of 1989 when the first TGV Atlantique will leave for Britanny and Bordeaux. Beside the station, at 34 boulevard de Vaugirard, you'll find the well-designed Postal Museum, a mecca for stamp collectors.

But if, like most of those who come to Montparnasse, you're merely looking for some relaxed entertainment, head for the rue de la Gaîte, which has been crammed with dance halls, theaters, nightclubs and restaurants since the 18th century (can be a bit sleazy late at night). Or to one of the big cafés or brasseries, the Dôme or the Coupole, once the haunt of Ernest Hemingway and before him of Verlaine and Modigliani and many lesser poets and painters, as well as no less a personage than Lenin, though it's hard to imagine that he added much to the fun. At the far end of the boulevard the romantically named Closerie des Lilas is now a rather expensive restaurant, but you can still have a drink there and dream of the days when this pretty spot was a center of Montparnasse bohemianism.

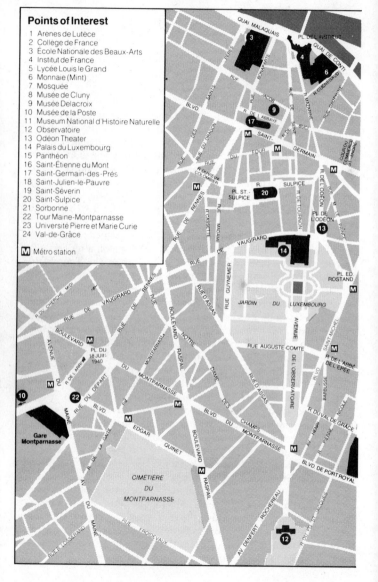

Points of Interest

1 Arènes de Lutèce
2 Collège de France
3 École Nationale des Beaux-Arts
4 Institut de France
5 Lycée Louis le Grand
6 Monnaie (Mint)
7 Mosquée
8 Musée de Cluny
9 Musée Delacroix
10 Musée de la Poste
11 Museum National d'Histoire Naturelle
12 Observatoire
13 Odéon Theater
14 Palais du Luxembourg
15 Panthéon
16 Saint-Étienne du Mont
17 Saint-Germain-des-Prés
18 Saint-Julien-le-Pauvre
19 Saint-Séverin
20 Saint-Sulpice
21 Sorbonne
22 Tour Maine-Montparnasse
23 Université Pierre et Marie Curie
24 Val-de-Grâce

Ⓜ Métro station

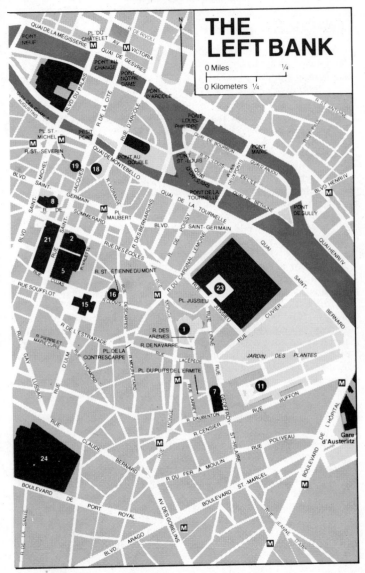

THE LEFT BANK

0 Miles ¼

0 Kilometers ¼

Saint-Germain-des-Prés

Long the mecca of intellectuals and would-be intellectuals, Saint-Germain-des-Prés has been somewhat eclipsed by the rebirth of the Les Halles and Beaubourg areas, where the avant-garde now tend to congregate. But we're sure you'll fall for this delightful part of Paris, with its lively little streets, good bookshops, tiny art galleries and antique shops. Many of the city's attractive little restaurants are to be found here and you'll find plenty of jazz cellars and discos, too, if that's what you're after. Those on the lookout for a fashionable outfit would do well to investigate the possibilities of the myriad of fashion boutiques nestling among the many narrow little shops selling everything from pomanders to antique nautical instruments.

The church of Saint-Germain-des-Prés, once part of a Benedictine abbey that was destroyed during the Revolution, is the focal point of this district and the best place to start your visit. It was a Romanesque bell tower, the only one of the original three to have survived, and the east end is still basically as it was in the 12th century. Good concerts are held here. Opposite the church the Deux-Magots café (the name comes from a pair of grotesque Chinese figures inside—*magots* in French) is still thronged at all times of the day and night, though nowadays you won't rub shoulders with the intellectual giants of France, as you might have in the heyday of existentialism. The people at the next table are more likely to be up from the provinces or foreign tourists. But it's still great fun to sit here, and even if the conversations aren't as highbrow as they once were, there's plenty of alternative entertainment in the form of street acrobats, fire eaters, musicians and the like. The Café de Flore, next door, tends to be a gay mecca these days. Both cafés have recently changed hands (for fabulous sums, of course) but in each case the new owners had first to guarantee not to change them in any way!

On the other side of the boulevard Saint-Germain the Brasserie Lipp is still the haunt of politicians and movie people. You won't get a table on the ground floor here unless you're really somebody (or the guest of someone who's really somebody). The Drugstore next door is less rarefied, and a good place for shopping into the early hours.

This isn't primarily a sightseeing area and most visitors are well content with soaking up the atmosphere and peering into the pretty little shops in the narrow streets running down to the Seine or up to the Luxembourg Gardens. But there are one or two places to visit. The most attractive is the delightful little place Fürstemberg, which you can find by taking the rue de l'Abbaye behind the church. With its white globe lamps and catalpa trees it looks almost like a stage set and is a paradise for the amateur photographer. In one corner, at no.6, the painter Delacroix had his studio; you can visit the charming little museum that has been opened here. Then in the narrow rue des Saints-Pères, on the other side of the boulevard, you'll find, alongside smart little shops and restaurants, the little-known Museum of French Protestantism, at no.54. Running parallel to it, the rue du Dragon houses the American Cultural Center.

From the southern end of the rue du Dragon, the rue du Vieux-Colombier, once the home of a famous avant-garde theater dedicated to a "natural" style of acting, brings you to the church of Saint-Sulpice, fronted by a large square. The square is surrounded by little shops selling prayer books, rosaries, holy pictures and other ecclesiastical objects, and adorned by an elaborate fountain with statues of four great bishops and preachers. The church, originally the parish church of Saint-Germain-des-Prés, was started in the mid-17th century but not completed until nearly 150 years later. It is best known for its beautiful wall paintings by Delacroix (you'll find them in the first chapel on the right leading off the nave), and for its fine organ.

At the river end of the rue Bonaparte is the Ecole Nationale des Beaux-Arts, Paris's fine arts academy, which has a number of fragments and copies of sculptural and architectural elements. Good temporary exhibits are now held here. A short walk along the quai Malaquais and you come to the place de l'Institut, once the site of a tower called the Tour de Nesle, round which Alexandre Dumas centered his melodrama of the same name. But the *place* is now famous for the Académie Française (in fact one of five academies that together form the Institut de France) with its 40 "immortal" members and its enormous prestige—to be elected to the academy is the highest literary honor France can bestow. The majestic building with its glittering cupola dates from the 17th century and was built with funds left by Cardinal Mazarin in his will. A little further along, the Monnaie (the 18th-century Mint) includes a coin museum. You can also visit the workshops.

The street beside the Monnaie, the rue Guénégaud, has several attractive little shops and galleries, as does the rue Mazarine on the left, a book-publishing stronghold. This area is also good for fashion boutiques, and for buying an enticing picnic meal in the mouthwatering rue de Buci street market, just before the rue Mazarine becomes the rue de l'Ancienne Comédie. In the rue de l'Ancienne Comédie the Café Procope was *the* literary meeting-place in earlier centuries and you can still see the table where Voltaire used to sit. Just behind here the picturesque Cour du Commerce Saint-André has seen its fair share of history in the making: Marat printed his revolutionary newspaper *L'Ami du Peuple* here, and a gentleman called Dr. Guillotin experimented on sheep to perfect the "humane" new method of execution that was to be so much in demand during the Revolution and remained France's method of execution right down to its abolition by President Mitterrand in 1981.

You will now come to the bustling Odéon crossroads, surrounded by small movie houses. Ahead in the distance appears the subsidized Odéon theater, set in a semicircular *place* and surrounded by streets named after major French playwrights and authors (Corneille, Racine etc.). In the middle of this century it was famous as the home of the Jean-Louis Barrault and Madeleine Renaud theater company, until they fell out with the authorities for allegedly spurring on the student revolutionaries in May 1968. Foreign companies now perform here regularly. On the far side the theater overlooks the Luxembourg Gardens.

The Luxembourg Gardens

This oasis of greenery in the middle of traffic-thronged streets, with its ornamental ponds and dozens of statues (watch out for Mary, Queen of Scots), is one of the pleasantest places to stroll in the whole of Paris. If you've got your children with you, they'll love the puppet and Punch and Judy shows that are given here. The Luxembourg Palace was built by Queen Marie de Médicis and was supposed to look like the Pitti Palace in Florence, where she had been born and brought up, though the architect opted for a pretty free interpretation of that rather severe building. After serving as a prison during the Revolution it became the seat of the Directory and the Consulate and is now the Senate (France's parliamentary "Upper House"). There is little of interest inside except for some famous wall paintings by Delacroix in the former library (the finest shows Dante and Virgil in Limbo), and anyway it's only open on Sundays, so best make the most of the delightful gardens.

South of the gardens, the avenue de l'Observatoire, laid out with lawns and flowerbeds, leads to the Observatory. Before reaching it you come to the boulevard de Port Royal, with Paris's best-known maternity hospital, a highly appropriate site because the convent church of Val-de-Grâce on the other side of the boulevard owes its existence to the unhoped-for birth of a child—later to be Louis XIV—to Anne of Austria after 23 years of marriage. The delighted queen built the church in thanksgiving. The convent, incidentally, is now a military hospital.

The Latin Quarter

You have now skirted round the Latin Quarter, Paris's student district since the days of the great scholar Pierre Abelard in the 12th century and one of the most interesting parts of Paris. To visit it you can either make your way back to the edge of the Luxembourg Gardens and the boulevard Saint-Michel, or, better still, start afresh from the place Saint-Michel opposite the Ile de la Cité.

The boulevard Saint-Michel (popularly abbreviated to the "Boul' Mich") is the highway of the Latin Quarter—Latin, by the way, because in the Middle Ages Latin was the students' *lingua franca,* and indeed it remained the official language for the university down to the Revolution. Then as now it was thronged with students of all nationalities and with its dozens of itinerant street sellers it enjoys a lively bustle at all times of the day and night. It's hard, though, to remember that it was the scene of violent clashes between police and demonstrators in the May 1968 upheavals. The surrounding streets are full of jazz cellars, experimental movie houses and picturesque little restaurants, while the boulevard itself is best known for bookshops and—for some reason—shoe shops.

The narrow rue de la Harpe, lined with Tunisian pastry shops and Greek restaurants nowadays, leads off the *place* to the rue Saint-Séverin, which brings you to Saint-Séverin church, a good example of the Gothic style as it changed and developed, and which has a beautiful double ambulatory. A side door leads to a 15th-century charnel house. Continue along the rue Saint-Séverin and you come to another church, Saint-Julien-le-Pauvre, best known for the not-to-be-missed view of Notre Dame from the garden surrounding it, and for the false acacia tree in the garden, the oldest tree in Paris, so they say. The church belongs to a Greek Orthodox order and has a screen hung with dozens of icons.

Now take the rue Saint-Jacques, running behind Saint-Séverin, until you reach the rue de Sommerard. Turn right and you are in the leafy place Paul Painlevé, facing the entrance to the Musée de Cluny, in a 15th-century mansion belonging once to the monks of Cluny Abbey in Burgundy. It was built on the site of the city's Roman baths, the ruins of which can be seen in the museum. But it's better known for its collection of medieval art and applied art, and especially for its tapestries, the jewel in the collection being the superb *Dame à la Licorne* (Lady with a Unicorn) series, with allegorical scenes that have never been fully understood woven in beautifully-soft colors on a red background and full of animals and flowers depicted down to the tiniest detail. Here too now are the 13th-century heads of the kings of Judah that were hacked off the façade of Notre Dame during the Revolution.

On the other side of the rue des Ecoles runs the north wing of the Sorbonne, Paris's main university building. It takes its name from Robert de Sorbon, a medieval canon who founded a theological college here, and is crammed with lecture halls, examination rooms, laboratories, even though many of the students have now been moved out to brand-new buildings in other parts of the city and the suburbs. When you've had a look inside at the splendid staircase and (if a lecture isn't in progress) at the mural by Puvis de Chavannes in the main lecture hall, continue round the building and up the boulevard Saint-Michel to the Sorbonne church, a good example of French classical architecture. Behind the Sorbonne buildings are many important academic institutions, such as the Lycée Louis-le-Grand, where Molière and Voltaire studied, and the élite Collège de France.

More interesting to the tourist, however, is the mighty Panthéon, which can be reached via the rue Victor-Cousin and the rue Soufflot. Beneath its huge dome are buried such illustrious figures as Voltaire, Jean-Jacques Rousseau and Victor Hugo (their tombs can be visited in the crypt). This rather cold and gloomy building also has some interesting murals, the most famous illustrating the story of Ste. Geneviève, patron saint of Paris, on whose hill (the Montagne Sainte-Geneviève) the Panthéon stands. And behind the Panthéon, the place Sainte-Geneviève is dominated by the church of Saint-Etienne du Mont, where the former shepherdess is specially venerated. Inside the church you can see a magnificent shrine containing relics of the saint, but the most interesting piece of decoration is the beautiful 16th-century rood screen, the only one left in Paris, though they were once a common feature.

The rue Mouffetard Area

Beside the church, the rue Clovis leads to the Ecole Polytechnique, where France's *crème de la crème* are educated (former students include ex-President Valéry Giscard d'Estaing), though most of its activities have been moved out to the suburbs. Take the rue Descartes on the right until you come to the pretty place de la Contrescarpe, almost provincial by day, but a lively center of Parisian night life, with dozens of restaurants, cafés and cabarets. In the Middle Ages this whole area was full of student hostels and colleges, and it still has something of a medieval feel, especially now that many of the buildings in the narrow streets have been restored and the old inn signs are swinging cheerfully on their iron hooks once again. The continuation of the rue Descartes, the rue Mouffetard, is famous for the picturesque market that has been held here for centuries—a must if you're fond of local color.

From the place de la Contrescarpe, the rue Lacépède takes you to the rue Monge. Turn left and the first turning on the right brings you to the entrance to the Arènes de Lutèce, the ruins of Paris's Roman arena. Apart from the remains of the baths in the Musée de Cluny, this rather neglected-looking ruins is all that is left of the powerful Roman city of Lutetia, and is well worth visiting for that reason. The peaceful gardens round it and the lively children playing there also make this a charming spot for a quiet sit-down or even a picnic lunch—particularly as you're bound to have succumbed to the temptation of the market stalls in the rue Mouffetard.

Close to here, in the place Jussieu, are the somewhat faceless modern buildings of the Pierre and Marie Curie University. They recently replaced the old Halle aux Vins, where millions of gallons of wine had been stored since Napoleonic times. Follow the rue Jussieu and you come to one entrance of the Jardin des Plantes, Paris's botanical gardens, attractively laid out and popular with Parisians, but curiously little known to tourists. Here you'll find the excellent Natural History Museum, plus an aquarium, a reptile house and a charming, if rather old-fashioned, zoo. If you're interested in mushrooms and fungi and are here in October, don't miss the popular Salon du Champignon. The Austerlitz rail station is just east of the gardens.

Just behind the gardens, in the place du Puits-de-l'Hermite, you may well rub your eyes in surprise as you suddenly find yourself gazing at a mosque with a tall minaret. This is the center of Moslem life in Paris, which has a large Moslem population; it can be visited every day except Friday, the holy day. A refreshing visit to the little tearoom in the gardens would be a good way to round off your visit to this very varied part of Paris.

 SIGHTSEEING CHECKLIST. Look under *Sightseeing* in the *Practical Information* section for general points on museums and other places of interest.

Arènes de Lutece (Lutetia Arena), rue des Arènes. Permanently open. *Métro:* Jussieu.

Ecole Nationale supérieure des Beaux-Arts, 17 quai Malaquais, 6e (tel. 42–60–34–57). Special exhibits only, open daily except Tues., 1–7. *Métro:* St.-Germain-des-Prés.

Galeries Nationales du Luxembourg, 19 rue de Vaugirard, 6e (tel. 42–34–25–95). Open daily except Mon., 11–6; Thurs. 11–10. Reduced admission charge on Sat. *Métro:* St.-Sulpice. *RER:* Luxembourg.

Monnaie de Paris (The Mint), 11 quai de Conti, 6e (tel. 43–29–12–48). Open daily 11–5, except weekends. No admission charge. Workshops can usually be visited Mon. and Wed. at 2.15. Special exhibits generally open same times. No admission charge for children under 13. *Métro and RER:* St.-Michel.

Musée de Cluny (Musée National des Thermes), 6 pl. Paul-Painlevé, 5e (tel. 43–25–62–00). Open daily except Tues., 9.45–12.30, 2–5.15 (no admittance after 11.45 and 4.30). Guided visit with lecturer Wed. at 3. Half-price on Sun. (N). *Métro:* Odéon, St.-Michel. *RER:* Pont-St. Michel.

Musée Delacroix, 6 pl. de Furstemberg, 6e (tel. 43–54–04–87). Open 9.45–5.15; closed Tues. Half-price admission on Sun. (N). *Métro:* St.-Germain-des-Prés.

Musée de la Poste, 34 blvd. de Vaugirard, 15e (tel. 43–20–15–30). Open 10–5; closed Sun. and public holidays. No admission charge for under-18s; half price for those between 18 and 25 and over-65s. *Métro:* Falguière, Montparnasse-Bienvenue, Pasteur.

Muséum National d'Histoire Naturelle, 57 rue Cuvier, 5e (tel. 43–36–54–26). Open daily except Tues. and public holidays. *Anatomy* and *Mineralogy* departments, 1.30–4.50; 10–4.50 on Sun. *Entomology* department 2–5. *Temporary exhibits* 10–5. *Menagerie* open daily 9–5 (9–7 in summer). *Métro:* Censier, Gare d'Austerlitz, Jussieu, Monge.

Observatoire, rue du Faubourg-St.-Jacques, 14e (tel. 43–20–12–10). Guided tours on 1st Sat. of the month at 2.30 P.M., or on application.

Panthéon, pl. du Panthéon, 5e (tel. 43–54–34–51). Open daily 10–12, 2–4. Half-price Sun. and holidays. *RER:* Luxembourg.

Puppet and Punch-and-Judy Shows in Luxembourg Gardens (tel. 43–26–46–47). Generally Wed. and Sun. at 2.30, 3.30 and 4.30; Sat. at 3 and 4, but always check locally. *Métro:* Notre-Dame-des-Champs, Vavin.

Rue Mouffetard Market. Held Tues. through Sun., mornings.

Tour Montparnasse, pl. R. Dautry, 15e (tel. 45–38–52–56). Open 9.30–11.30, April to Sept.; 10–10, Oct. to Mar. *Métro:* Montparnasse-Bienvenue.

LUNCH SPOTS. Once again, an area absolutely bursting with restaurants of every kind. Apart from the fairly easy, and moderately priced, places below, you might look at our regular Restaurant Listing to find other possibilities.

Bistro de la Gare, 59 blvd. Montparnasse, 14e. Genuine art-nouveau decor; fast service; good "formula" meals.

Les Classiques, passage Dauphine 6e. Good salads as well as hot *plats du jours.* Wide range of teas as well as wines.

Comptoir de l'Ecluse, 2 rue Christine, 6e. Chic if rather bare-looking restaurant now belongs to Ecluse wine-bar chain and is a good place for sampling wine by the glass to accompany a tasty dish. Closed Sun. v.

A la Cour de Rohan, 59 rue St.-André-des-Arts, 6e. Rather elegant tearoom in a covered arcade; good light meals. Closed Sun.

Deux-Magots, 170 blvd. St.-Germain, 6e. Paris's most famous café, good for people watching. Sandwiches, snacks, wine by the glass, good icecreams.

L'Ecluse, 15 quai des Grands-Augustins, 6e. Rather chic wine bar. v.

Le Flore, 172 blvd. St.-Germain, 6e. Another famous café, though not as good as the Deux-Magots with its prized corner location.

Village Voice, 6 rue Princesse, 6e. Lively American bookshop with tables at the back for delicious health-food meals. Closed Sun.

Yvan, 44 rue de la Montagne Ste.-Geneviève, 5e. New restaurant with reasonable prices, especially good-value *menu* for lunch.

Montmartre

High up in the north of Paris, on a hill roughly 400 feet high, is the district known as Montmartre, a name familiar to tourists and redolent of a delightfully free-and-easy bohemian life with a typically French flavor. Alas the presence of so many foreign tourists means that the atmosphere can be more cosmopolitan than French these days. But that being said, Montmartre still has a great deal to offer if you can close your eyes to the most glaring manifestations of tourist exploitation. And away from the overcrowded place du Tertre and the gleaming white Sacré Coeur basilica, in the narrow streets and picturesque little squares, you'll still find ordinary people going about their business and be able to imagine how it was when the area was peopled by genuine artists and poets rather than the pseudo variety who are liable to offer to paint your portrait or sell you knick-knacks or entice you into overpriced restaurants. With this warning firmly in mind, you'll be able to enjoy what is still after all a highly romantic place. The name, by the way, allegedly comes from a corruption of *mont des martyrs,* the martyrs' mountain, because it was here that St Denis and two of his priests died a martyr's death by beheading in A.D. 272. According to the legend, the redoubtable saint promptly picked up his head and walked off northwards to the place where the town and basilica of Saint-Denis stand today. Be that as it may—and there are other theories—the fact that Montmartre is perched high up on a hill has always seemed to set it apart from the rest of Paris, and it was no doubt partly this that attracted so many artists here in the 19th and early-20th centuries.

A good place to start a walk around Montmartre is the place des Abbesses. It's surrounded by picturesque streets, in one of which, the rue Yvonne-le-Tac, St. Denis is said to have suffered his martyrdom (to be precise, where a chapel now stands at no. 9). Strangely enough, it was on this very same spot, though nearly 1,300 years later, that Ignatius Loyola and his companions took the vows that eventually led to the founding of the powerful order of the Jesuits.

Climb up the rue Ravignan and you come to the delightful place Emile Goudeau, peaceful except at the height of the tourist season—when it turns into a combat zone. This little square is firmly on the map of art history because it was here, at no. 13, that Picasso and Braque and other giants of modern painting had their studios. Alas, the rickety wooden building in which they lived and worked was destroyed by a fire in 1970 and has now been replaced by a concrete structure, far less romantic, though no doubt a better insurance risk. And at least it is still divided into artists' studios. The rue Orchampt around the corner leads to the steep and winding rue Lepic, where the Dutch painter Vincent Van Gogh and his devoted and long-suffering brother Theo once lived (at no. 54). Around the corner in the rue Girardon is the centuries-old Moulin de la Galette, immortalized in one of Renoir's paintings and one of only two windmills left in Montmartre (there were once dozens of them, used for grinding flour to make, among other things, the flat waffles or biscuits known as *galettes* that gave the mill its name). In the 19th century the mill was a popular dance hall and cabaret frequented by painters and lovers of the bohemian life for which Montmartre was so famous. And we're glad to say that after extensive rebuilding work this area has been restored to its former attractiveness, with a restaurant and a theater-cum-cabaret.

If you're one of the many people who find cemeteries romantic, don't miss Montmartre Cemetery, easily reached from the bottom of the rue Lepic via the rue Joseph-de-Maistre. Appropriately enough for an area with such a reputation for the arts, you'll find the graves of writers and poets (Stendhal, de Vigny, the Goncourts and Heinrich Heine), musicians (Berlioz and Offenbach), as well as painters (Fragonard, Greuze and Degas), and Henri Murger, whose *Scenes of Bohemian Life* formed the basis of Puccini's opera *La Bohème*.

If you prefer your reminders of the past in museums rather than graveyards, or indeed if you like them both, follow the rue Caulaincourt up past another little cemetery to the rue des Saules (or if you've got the time, meander pleasantly back up through the winding streets and squares). At no. 42 you'll find the interesting little Museum of Jewish Art, which includes paintings by Chagall and Pissarro, and then if you turn left into the rue Cortot (at no. 12), the Montmartre Museum, with hundreds of exhibits painting a vivid picture of old Montmartre. Near the museum is, believe it or not, a vineyard, which still produces enough white wine to keep the local bars and restaurants merry at grape harvest time in October, when all sorts of colorful festivities are held. One such bar-cabaret is the famous Lapin Agile, where you can sit on wooden benches and listen to lively French songs sung (sometimes surprisingly well) on the very spot where Picasso and Vlaminck and their friends once congregated. (The name, which means "The Nimble Rabbit," is a pun based on a sign outside which used to say *Là peint A. Gill*—"A. Gill paints here.") At the bottom of the rue des Saules is another well-known cabaret with a lively past, La Bonne Franquette.

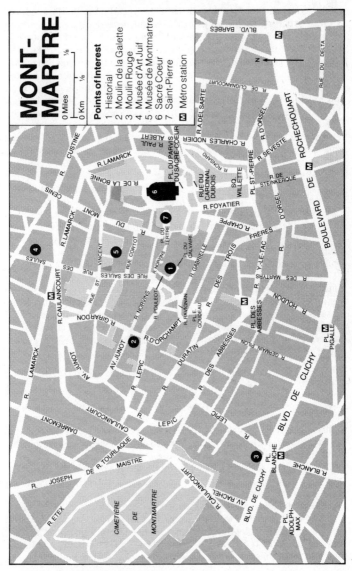

MONT-MARTRE

Points of Interest

1 Historial
2 Moulin de la Galette
3 Moulin Rouge
4 Musée d'Art Juif
5 Musée de Montmartre
6 Sacré Coeur
7 Saint-Pierre
M Métro station

0 Miles   1/8
0 Km   1/8

Cross over the rue Norvins and you come to the rue Poulbot (called after an artist whose drawings of delightful little street urchins you'll see everywhere) and the little waxworks museum called the Historial, with tableaux illustrating the history of Montmartre. The tiny place du Calvaire is a good place for admiring the sweeping view over Paris and catching your breath before launching into the famous place du Tertre, jam-packed at the height of the tourist season but still picturesque. If you feel like having your portrait painted by a "contemporary artist," this is the place, but don't expect it to be a work of art—or inexpensive. During the day in the winter months some of the village atmosphere returns and you'll find it easier to remember that this was once a village square like those all over France, with the obligatory town hall (which used to be at no. 3).

Moving on from the place du Tertre you come first to Saint-Pierre, once part of a mighty abbey and one of Paris's oldest churches (parts of it date from the 12th century), and then to the massive structure often likened to a wedding cake that you'll undoubtedly see many times gleaming like a snowcap in the distance as you travel round Paris. This, then, is the Sacré Coeur, built by public subscription as a symbol of national revival after the disastrous Franco-Prussian War in 1870. Opinions are divided on its aesthetic merits but, like the Eiffel Tower, it's so familiar a landmark that the carping of art historians is really neither here nor there. And the view is unrivaled, especially if you go up to the top of the cupola. The inside of the basilica is decorated with mosaics and there's some interesting modern stained glass too.

You can either take the little funicular down to the bottom of the gardens, or saunter slowly down the many flights of steps before returning to the less rarefied air of central Paris.

Pigalle

You may like to combine your visit to Montmartre with an evening in one of the nightclubs in Pigalle or Clichy, where the air isn't rarefied in any sense of the word. If so, take the rue Steinkerque at the bottom of the gardens, turn right into the boulevard Rochechouart and walk on until you come to the place Pigalle.

This is one of *the* centers of Parisian nightlife (though the Parisians themselves mostly steer clear of it). By daylight the district is frankly seedy and rather depressing, with gloomy prostitutes in the doorways and the clubs and bars looking as if they belonged to a tawdry fairground. But at night, with the crowds and the glittering lights the sleaziness isn't so obvious, and it does still have something of the romantic glamor so grippingly captured by Toulouse-Lautrec's drawings and paintings. Nowadays, inevitably, the strip-tease clubs and dubious hotels are almost outnumbered by movie houses showing soft porn and sex shops, many of them with blacked-out windows to conform with a ban on overtly pornographic window displays, so that some streets round here look like rows of teeth with gaps in them. This is quite a place for gay night life too, with both sexes well catered for.

If your knowledge of French and things French is good you'll enjoy the *chansonniers* with their witty patter and topical allusions, but the beaten tourist track mostly ends in such well-known names as the Moulin Rouge or the Folies-Bergère, where the shows are good enough, but are more international than typically Parisian.

At no. 14 in rue Rochefoucauld, not far from the place Pigalle, is the house of the painter Gustave Moreau, an excellent illustration of the homes of the prosperous bourgeoisie who were so shocked by Baudelaire's scandalous life—and who succeeded in getting his masterpiece *Les Fleurs du Mal* condemned by the censor (believe it or not, this sentence wasn't quashed until 1949!). Moreau left the house, where he lived from 1852 to his death in 1898, to the nation, along with hundreds of his strange mystical and allegorical paintings and literally thousands of drawings—the fruits, he said in his will, of 50 years' work. The resulting museum is a little old-fashioned but full of charm with its art-nouveau spiral staircase leading up to a large studio at the top of the house.

 SIGHTSEEING CHECKLIST. Look under *Sightseeing* in the *Practical Information* section for general points on museums and other places of interest.

Historial (Historical Waxworks), rue Poulbot, 18e (tel. 46–06–78–92). Easter to Nov. 12, 10.30–12.30, 2.30–5.30; same times on Wed., Sat., Sun. and holidays rest of year.

Montmartre Cemetery, av. Rachel, 18e. Open 7.30–4.30 (7.30–6 in summer). *Métro:* Blanche, pl. de Clichy.

Musée d'Art Juif (Museum of Jewish Art), 42 rue des Saules, 18e (tel. 42–57–84–15). Open 3–6; closed Fri. and Sat. *Métro:* Lamarck-Caulaincourt.

Musée Gustave Moreau, 14 rue de la Rochefoucauld, 9e (tel. 48–74–38–50). 10–12.45 and 2–5.15; closed Tues. Half price for students and on Sun. (N). *Métro:* Trinité.

Musée de Montmartre, 12 rue Cortot, 18e (tel. 46–06–61–11). Open Tues. to Sat., 2.30–5.30; Sun. 11–5.30; closed Mon. Half-price admission for students and over-60s. *Métro:* Lamarck-Caulaincourt.

 LUNCH SPOTS. All the places we give in our main restaurant listing for Montmartre would be suitable for lunch—they are capable of producing a fast meal if you need it in the middle of a busy sightseeing day. Apart from them, here are a few extra ones:

Bateau-Lavoir, 8 rue Garreau, 18e. Basic home cooking just by the spot where Picasso and Co used to hang out. Modest; good value. Closed in June.

Le Melrose, 5 pl. Clichy, 9e. Fun mock-art-nouveau decor; fast service; good value food in *nouvelle cuisine* style.

Au Pichet du Tertre, 10 rue Norvins, 18e. Villagey atmosphere; good choice of *menus.* Closed Tues.

Relais Normand, 32bis rue d'Orsel, 18e. Good-value *menu* Specialty dishes from Normandy. Closed Sat., and Aug.

Tartempion, 15bis rue du Mont-Cenis, 18e. Surprisingly peaceful, considering that this is the touristy part of Montmartre. Closed Wed. and Dec.

On the Fringe

So far in this chapter the accent has been on what might loosely be called "central" Paris, but the fringes of the city offer many interesting places to explore once you have absorbed the main sights. We have divided these into two sections—a few close in, which we deal with below, and more farther away, which we cover in the *Days out from Paris* chapter.

Passy and Auteuil

These pleasant, prosperous residential districts in western Paris near the Bois de Boulogne have few tourist sights but are a good illustration of the way Paris has developed from a series of separate villages. Both Passy and Auteuil did not officially become part of Paris until the time of Napoleon III in the second half of the 19th century, and in spite of many modern apartment blocks they still have something of a separate feel, with their peaceful cul de sacs (strangely known as "villas") surrounded by trees and gardens, their villagey squares and their chic little shops. The rue de Passy in particular, easily reached from the Trocadéro, is an excellent shopping street for the discriminating—by no means inexpensive, but always good quality.

One of the most interesting streets in the area, rue Rayounard, has seen many famous residents, including Jean-Jacques Rousseau and Benjamin Franklin. At no. 47 is the attractive pavilion where the 19th-century novelist Honoré de Balzac lived in the 1840s, set delightfully in a little garden. Here he followed the eccentric régime that seemed to suit his genius, working from midnight to 8 in the morning to trace the lives of the unforgettable characters who people the stage of his *Human Comedy*. Wrapped in his celebrated dressing-gown, he drank gallons of black coffee, then ate the equivalent of a midday meal before working frantically on to 5 P.M., his dinner and bed time.

A visit to the charming little museum that is now housed here will soon show you why he needed to work such long hours and ruin his health on sleep-banishing coffee. As well as his coffee pot you'll see a pile of unpaid bills—for the sad truth is that this prolific author was constantly in debt. Indeed the whole point of his living in what was then an out-of-the-way part of Paris was to keep out of the way of his creditors. You'll even be shown the hidden rear exit that enabled him to slip secretly out into the rue Berton if unwelcome visitors turned up. And by the way, don't miss a walk along this strange little street with its ivy-covered walls and old gas lamps. It can scarcely have changed since Balzac's day and it won't take much of an effort of the imagination to picture the heavy, thick-set figure creeping pathetically down here to escape the dreaded knock on his front door.

The western end of the rue de Passy leads to the Ranelagh Gardens (once a popular spot for *al fresco* dancing and dining) with the Musée Marmottan, formerly a collection of Renaissance tapestries and sculpture plus mementos of the Napoleonic era, but recently greatly enriched by a superb collection of paintings by Claude Monet and some of his contemporaries, donated by his son. The museum had already included the famous painting called *Impression—Sunrise* that gave the Impressionists their label, so this museum is essential visiting if you like their work. Close to the museum are the buildings of the OECD (the international Organization for Economic Cooperation and Development), originally built by a member of the Rothschild banking family. And on the far side of the place de Colombie, with its statues of Peter I of Serbia and his son Alexander I of Yugoslavia, is the Bois de Boulogne.

The Bois de Boulogne

"The Bois," as it is generally known, is an appropriately lung-shaped oasis of greenery covering 900 hectares (nearly 2,250 acres) on the western edge of the city. It is very popular with the Parisians, who live at such close quarters in the densely-populated streets and apartment blocks that they badly need some space to breathe fresh air and take exercise when leisure time permits. And in spite of the traffic thundering through it, the Bois is surprisingly relaxing and even more surprisingly full of wild life, many more species of birds than you can see in a London park, for instance. But because it is still fairly wild, a word of warning: it isn't wise to wander on your own at any time, except around the lakes where there are always plenty of strollers, and even couples or groups should steer well clear of the Bois at night.

The Bois was laid out on the instructions of Napoleon III, a great admirer of London's parks, and his planner Baron Haussmann, who did so much to create Paris as it is today. In the Belle Epoque it was an ultra-fashionable place to see and be seen, with elaborately-dressed ladies promenading in their carriages or on horseback. But nowadays the elegant ladies and their escorts have been replaced by joggers in unisex tracksuits and the Bois is best known for its sports opportunities, which are legion: tennis courts, riding, boating lakes, bikes for hire, a pigeon-shooting area, fishing, even a polo ground. And of course walking—you can walk for miles in relative peace. There are several good restaurants too, all chic and expensive.

Perhaps the pleasantest spot is Bagatelle, a delightful little château set in grounds famous for their flower displays—a mass of spring blooms, waterlilies, a splendid rose garden and so on. Special exhibits related to the art and history of Paris are staged in the pretty little château, built at lightning speed in the 18th century for a wager. At one stage Bagatelle belonged to Sir Richard Wallace, founder of the Wallace Collection in London and best known in Paris for the delightful drinking fountains adorned by graceful female figures a few of which can still be seen in the streets.

The Bois also has a museum, the Musée des Arts et Traditions Populaires, an ideal place to take children because the modern presentation is designed to encourage participation—which basically means there are plenty of knobs for them to press. The museum is at the Sablons end, near the once-aristocratic "inner suburb" of Neuilly which is increasingly being dominated by modern office blocks. Next door is the Jardin d'Acclimatation, a children's zoo and amusement park that can be reached by a little train running from the Porte Maillot (a sure-fire hit with children).

But for many people the main interest of the Bois is its two racecourses, Auteuil and Longchamp, which attract a chic cosmopolitan crowd to the major races of the season. Little known to tourists is the Jardin des Serres d'Auteil, best visited in the morning or early afternoon. This garden has hothouses and unusual trees, including Chinese gingkos.

The Bois de Vincennes

To be honest, the Bois de Vincennes, most of which is just outside the Paris boundary, on the opposite, eastern, side of the city, has a more plebeian reputation in general, in spite of its royal past. But don't let this put you off, as there's plenty to see and do there—a large zoo, an excellent museum of African and Australasian art, a Transport Museum, two artificial lakes, a magnificent flower garden, a cycle track, plus many restaurants and cafés. What's more, it has a full-scale royal castle, the château de Vincennes.

A guided visit of the castle includes the 14th-century keep, with a museum illustrating its history; the Gothic chapel with beautiful stained glass; and the twin royal pavilions in the imposing Cour d'Honneur (Louis XIV spent his honeymoon in the king's pavilion). One other historical fact among the many you'll learn here: Henry V of

England, victor at Agincourt and Shakespeare's Prince Hal, died on the second floor of the keep, in 1422.

Next to the château is the Parc Floral de Paris (Floral Garden), which will be fascinating to the dedicated gardener, specializing as it does in dahlias, irises, water plants, orchids, rhododendrons and azaleas—each in their correct season. There are also exhibitions, a children's garden and some modern sculpture.

The Cité Universitaire

On the southern edge of Paris is the Cité Universitaire, a well-planned series of hostels for students of all nationalities set in attractive grounds and with many amenities such as tennis courts, swimming pool and a good theater. 37 buildings or "houses" belong to the various countries (the Swiss House, the Japanese House and so on) or are foundations called after philanthropists. The first dates from 1925, while others are very recent. Two of them (the Swiss Foundation and the Franco-Brazilian Foundation, both on the eastern side) were designed by Le Corbusier.

Opposite here is the Parc de Montsouris, little known to foreign tourists but quite delightful, with a lake, a waterfall, even a Chinese-style pavilion, built for the 1930 Exposition Coloniale, which makes a charming setting for a restaurant. The streets round about are unusual in present-day Paris in having many little houses—most Parisians live in apartments. For instance east of the park and quickly reached via the rue Liard, across the rue de l'Amiral Mouchez and along the rue Auguste-Lançon you'll find the peaceful little Cité Floréale, a series of tiny paved streets and squares all named after flowers and seeming to belong to another age, with their little two-story houses and tiny gardens, a far cry from the looming tower blocks being put up all around, and fortunately protected by a preservation order.

The long avenue René-Coty leads north to the place Denfert-Rochereau, with its large statue of a lion commemorating the successful withstanding of a Prussian siege at the fortress of Belfort in 1870–1 by the colonel who gave his name to the square. But it's best known to tourists as the entrance to the rather sinister Catacombs, originally quarries in the Roman period but used as an ossuary since the end of the 18th century. If you're in a macabre frame of mind you'll delight in the bones piled along the walls—and you won't be the first. In the 19th century visiting the catacombs was quite the thing to do for fashionable and important visitors to Paris. During World War II the Resistance movement used them as their HQ.

Parc Monceau

Another delightful park that is rather closer to the center is the smart Parc Monceau, north-east of the Arc de Triomphe (take the avenue Hoche). Popular with the old-established families living in the large and rather grand apartments in the 17th *arrondissement,* it's always full of children, and you can still occasionally see smartly uniformed nannies wheeling their charges. This is a good place for observing the *grande bourgeoisie* in their natural habitat, except in July and August, when they desert the capital for their country houses.

This pleasant spot, with its statues, pyramids and pagodas, its artistically arranged ruins, its waterfalls and little lakes, and even a windmill, was masterminded by the same Philippe Egalité who planned the Palais-Royal gardens. It stands out like an oasis in this overcrowded city. Close to the park are two interesting museums, standing side by side: the Musée Nissim-de-Camondo, with 18th-century furniture, paintings, silver and tapestries arranged so as to give the impression that you're visiting a private house; and the Musée Cernuschi, devoted to Far Eastern art.

Père-Lachaise Cemetery

Paris's largest and most interesting cemetery, Père-Lachaise in eastern Paris, is well worth a visit both for the romantic setting, with the typically French tombs looking like little houses and the weeping willows, and of course for the many well-known people buried here. (There's a map at the main entrance in the boulevard de Menilmontant to help you find your way about.)

Here you'll find the tombs of Edith Piaf, Isadora Duncan, Gertrude Stein, Alfred de Musset, buried beneath a weeping willow as he had asked, Molière and Beaumarchais, Modigliani, Marcel Proust and Guillaume Apollinaire, Jean-Paul Sartre, Balzac and Victor Hugo, and Chopin too, though not George Sand.

The oldest inhabitants are no doubt the great philosopher and author Pierre Abelard and his beloved Héloïse, the protagonists of that moving love story of 12th-century Paris that ended so tragically. Apparently their remains were transferred here in 1817 to "popularize" the new cemetery, which had originally been a large garden on land belonging to the Jesuits (the Father de la Chaise who gave the cemetery its name was a Jesuit priest and father confessor to Louis XIV). You can spend many a fascinating hour here, tracking down the famous graves. Interestingly, one of those most frequently visited is that of the Irish writer and wit Oscar Wilde, who died in poverty in a room in the rue des

Beaux-Arts in Saint-Germain-des-Prés that is now part of a fashionable and expensive hotel. Another much-visited grave is that of the tragic actress Sarah Bernhardt, one of whose greatest roles was Doña Sol in Hugo's *Hernani*.

SIGHTSEEING CHECKLIST. Look under *Sightseeing* in the *Practical Information* section for general points on museums and other places of interest.

Bagatelle, Route de Sèvres-à-Neuilly, 6e. Château open only for special exhibits, usually May to Oct. Check locally. Gardens open on a seasonal basis, with admission charge depending on the flower displays currently available. *Métro:* Les Sablons, Pont de Neuilly, then a 15–20-minute walk.

Catacombs, pl. Denfert-Rochereau, 14e (tel. 43–22–47–63). Open Tues. to Fri., 2–4; weekends 9–11 and 2–4; closed Mon. Guided tours Wed. at 3. *Bring a flashlight.* (CP). *Métro* and *RER:* Denfert-Rochereau.

Château de Vincennes, av. de Paris, Vincennes (tel. 43–28–15–48). Guided tours 10–5, 5.30 or 6 depending on season. **Parc Floral,** open June to Sept., 9.30–8; other months it closes roughly at dusk—April to May, 7; Mar. and Oct., 6; Nov. and Dec., 5.30; Jan. and Feb., 5. *Métro:* Château de Vincennes.

Jardin d'Acclimatation, Porte des Sablons, 16e (tel. 46–24–10–80). Open daily 9–5.30. Some activities available only Wed., Sat. and Sun. *Métro:* Les Sablons.

Jardin des Serres d'Auteuil, 3 ave. de la Porte d'Auteuil, 16e. Open daily 10–6.

Maison de Balzac, 47 rue Raynouard, 16e (tel. 42–24–56–38). Daily 10–5.40; closed Mon. No admission charge on Sun. (except for temporary exhibits). (CP). *Métro:* La Muette, Passy.

Musée Cernuschi, 7 av. Velasquez, 8e (tel. 45–63–50–75). Open usually 10–5.40; closed Mon. and public holidays. Opening times sometimes change when temporary exhibits are on, so check locally. Half-price for students. No admission charge for permanent collections on Sun. (CP). *Métro:* Monceau, Villiers.

Musée des Arts et Traditions Populaires, 6. av. du Mahatma-Gandhi, 16e (tel. 47–47–69–80). Open 10–5.15; closed Tues. Half-price on Sun. (N). *Métro:* Les Sablons.

Musée Marmottan, 2 rue Louis-Boilly, 16e (tel. 42–24–07–02). Open daily 10–5.30, except Mon. Half-price admission for students. *Métro:* La Muette.

Musée national des Arts africains et océaniens (Museum of African and Australasian Art), 293 av. Daumesnil, 12e (tel. 43–43–14–54). Open daily 9.45–12, 1.30–5.20; closed Tues. Half price on Sun. (N). *Métro:* Porte Dorée.

Musée Nissim-de-Camondo, 63 rue de Monceau, 8e (tel. 45–63–26–32). Open 10–12, 2–5; closed Mon., Tues, and public holidays. Half-price admission for students and over-65s. *Métro:* Villiers.

Père Lachaise Cemetery, blvd. Ménilmontant, 20e (tel. 43–70–70–33). Open Mon. to Sat., 7.30–6, 16 Mar. to 5 Nov.; 8.30–5.30, 6 Nov. to 15 Mar.; Sun. 9–5.30 (winter), 9–6 (summer). *Métro:* Père-Lachaise, Philippe-Auguste.

LUNCH SPOTS. The following restaurants are all notable for their settings in some way, and moderately priced as well. You will find a few other possibilities in our regular Restaurant Listing, but they may be in a higher price grade.

L'Amanguier, av. de Madrid, Neuilly. Convenient for the Bois de Boulogne and Bagatelle. Good value meals and efficient service.

Bagatelle. Delightful open-air restaurant in the grounds, open roughly April through Sept. Rather chic clientele, lovely setting beneath venerable trees, good cold meats, melons, wine—perfect for a summer's day.

Le Châlet des Iles, on island in the middle of Lac Inférieur in the Bois de Boulogne, reached by a mini-ferry service. Charming leafy setting, plenty of wildlife to enliven your after-lunch stroll—peacocks, squirrels, ducks—and open-air tables for sandwiches and drinks. Also restaurant inside, pleasant atmosphere, but overpriced.

Drugstore de Neuilly, 14 pl. du Marché, Neuilly. Rather better food than in most drugstores. Pretty leafy courtyard for summer meals, colorful open-air market three times a week to add zest to your meal.

Le Mors aux Dents, 8 blvd. Delessert, Passy. Classical cuisine with good lunch *menu.* Terrace.

DAYS OUT FROM PARIS

Cathedrals and Castles

Paris, for so many centuries the focal point of French political and artistic life, has attracted to the countryside around it a multitude of historically-interesting, attractively-sited buildings. By using Paris as a base, and taking advantage of the excellent transport available, you can embark on a series of day-trips that will take in many of the most beautiful and interesting places the region has to offer. In this chapter we list alphabetically a few of the more important, giving some hints as to travel and where you might like to have lunch in the middle of a day's sightseeing. Naturally, in such a short chapter we cannot cover all the possibilities, but we hope that the following ideas will serve as a springboard.

Opening times of châteaux and restaurants change frequently, so we advise you to double-check locally.

BRETEUIL

Although France in general and the area round Paris in particular have many historic châteaux open to the public, an excursion to the château de Breteuil makes a specially interesting day or half-day out because it is one of the very few where you will most probably find the owner or his wife greeting you in person (they speak excellent English), and where you will feel more like a guest than a tourist.

In fact the château has been owned and lived in by the same family, that of the marquis of Breteuil, ever since it was built in the early 17th century. The current owner, the enterprising young Henri-François de Breteuil, and his wife have not only restored the château more or less single-handed but have also reacted energetically to the problem of upkeep (they have won an award for their dynamism). From May through October they stage cultural events of all kinds (plays, concerts, exhibits) to attract visitors, as well as keeping the château open for guided visits every day of the year. Groups can be shown over at any time by previous arrangement, and certain rooms can be rented for receptions, seminars, weddings and the like.

Only the central core of the château dates from the 17th century, the wings on either side were built in the 18th century, while the pavilions are 19th-century additions. Inside, the history of the château and the Breteuil family is brought to life by means of lifesize wax figures dressed in period costume and arranged to form historical tableaux. You'll see the fifth marquis in the library talking to Louis XVIII, and the Baron de Breteuil presenting Louis XVI and Marie Antoinette with the Treaty of Teschen. (Among the many fine pieces of furniture on display is the magnificent "Teschen table" inlaid with precious stones given to the baron, then France's ambassador in Austria, by the Empress Maria Theresa to commemorate this diplomatic coup.)

Also here is the languidly-reclining figure of the great 20th-century novelist, Marcel Proust, who based one of his characters on the eighth marquis. More important for the course of European history was the meeting arranged by the eighth marquis between the prince's grandfather, Edward VII, and the French statesman Léon Gambetta. This historic encounter, which was to lead to the Entente Cordiale, is again commemorated in a wax tableau.

The presence of these lifelike figures takes away the dead feeling that sadly permeates so many historic châteaux, so that the beautiful furniture, the tapestries and paintings and porcelain, seem much more than museum pieces. You will also be shown the old kitchens with their gleaming copper pans, and the chapel with wax wedding figures.

Be sure to leave enough time to visit the beautiful grounds (which incidentally are open in the morning too). Directly behind the château is an elaborate *jardin à la française* laid out Le Nôtre-style with ornamental ponds, smooth lawns and neatly-trimmed cypresses, but the rest of the grounds are a sort of nature reserve, with many species of birds and animals allowed to roam wild, and such delights as tiny wild cyclamen. And—a great plus point in France—no one, but no one will try to stop you walking on the grass! You can even bring your own picnic and eat it in the well-organized picnic areas. Children will enjoy the "doll's house" in the grounds with figures from Perrault's much-loved fairy stories, Red Riding Hood et al.

 GETTING THERE. By Express Métro. Take the B4 line of the RER southwards to St.-Rémy-les-Chevreuse. From here you must either take a taxi or you might like to walk at least one way—it's a pretty route of about 7 km (4½ miles).

By Car. Take the F18 feeder road (labeled Chartres) from the Pont de Sèvres on the western edge of Paris. Leave it at Saclay and then take the N306 road to St. Rémy-les-Chevreuse; from there on the château is signposted.

 SIGHTSEEING CHECKLIST. Château de Breteuil, (tel. 30–52–05–11). Open daily, year-round. July and Aug.: 11–6 daily. The rest of the year: Mon. to Sat., 2.30–5.30, Sun. and public holidays 11–5.30. The grounds are open year-round 10–6.

 LUNCH SPOTS. There is a pancake house (crêperie) in the château grounds open on Sun. and public holidays only, from May 1 through Sept.

CHEVREUSE. Auberge du Moulin (M), 56 rue de la Porte-de-Paris (tel. 30–52–16–45). Attractive, creeper-covered building, adequate food. Closed Tues., mid-Aug. to mid-Sept. v.

La Puszta (M), carrefour St.-Laurent (tel. 34–61–18–35). Good-value *menu* made up of Hungarian specialties. Ambience is Hungarian too, and you can eat outside in the attractive garden on fine days. Closed Tues. v.

Lou Basquou (I), 18 route de la Madeleine (tel. 30–52–15–77). Specialties from the Basque country. Closed Thurs. and mid-Aug. to early Sept. v.

ST.-RÉMY-LÈS-CHEVREUSE. La Cressonnière (E), 46 route de Port-Royal (tel. 30–52–00–41). Looks like a country inn, but serves very chic *nouvelle cuisine,* plus a few more classical dishes. Outdoor meals in summer. Closed Tues., Wed. and during mid-semester vacations in Feb. AE, DC, V.

FONTAINEBLEAU

Though the château of Fontainebleau was once the home of kings, its Napoleonic associations are more familiar to the French. Being only 64 km. (40 miles) out of Paris and surrounded by a huge forest, it is a favorite place for excursions.

The history of Fontainebleau is tightly woven into the history of France and her kings, thanks primarily to the forest, in which the monarchs loved to hunt. In the 10th and 11th centuries there was a hunting lodge where the palace stands today. The name Fontainebleau appears for the first time in the chronicles as early as 1137. The name itself is derived from "source" or "well"—*fontaine* in French; the *bleau* part is a corruption of Blaud, the owner of the well. A chapel was built here in 1169 and consecrated by Thomas à Becket, who fled here from England to escape the wrath of his own king, Henry II of England. The legendary Saint Louis, Louis IX, enlarged the hunting lodge; it was here that he sat beneath an oak tree listening to the pleas of his people and dispensing justice. Philip the Fair was born in Fontainebleau, and also died here. Charles V established a library, but François I, whose

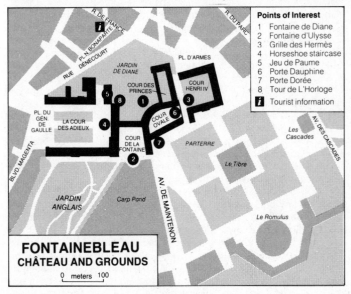

Points of Interest

1 Fontaine de Diane
2 Fontaine d'Ulysse
3 Grille des Hermès
4 Horseshoe staircase
5 Jeu de Paume
6 Porte Dauphine
7 Porte Dorée
8 Tour de L'Horloge
i Tourist information

FONTAINEBLEAU
CHÂTEAU AND GROUNDS

0 meters 100

name is so closely linked with the Renaissance in France, demolished the modest medieval home of his predecessors and began building a new royal residence in accordance with the taste of the age. The work was continued by Henry IV. By the end of the 16th century two-and-a-half million francs from the royal treasury had been spent on the building and its lavishly decorated interior.

In the middle of the 17th century, Queen Christina of Sweden lived in the château after her abdication, while in the Deer Gallery the ex-Queen's favorite, Monaldeschi, was assassinated. Though the Sun King was primarily interested in Versailles, he didn't neglect Fontainebleau: he commissioned Mansart to design some new pavilions and had Le Nôtre replan the gardens. Peter the Great, Christian VIII of Denmark and many other royal personages were guests at the château, which was also the scene of Louis XV's wedding.

But it was Napoleon who made a Versailles, as it were, of Fontainebleau, spending 12 million francs restoring it to its former glory. During his rule the château was the scene of many historic events: Pope Pius VII was held prisoner here, and it was at Fontainebleau that the Emperor signed the Concordat. Napoleon was in the château when he heard that Paris had fallen to the Allies and signed his abdication document. The large cobbled courtyard is known as La Cour des Adieux (Farewell Court) for it was here that on 20 April 1814, Napoleon bade farewell to his Old Guard, many of whom wept to see their Emperor go into exile.

Nearer to the present, Fontainebleau was the headquarters of Field Marshal von Brauchitsch during the Nazi occupation; later Field Marshal Montgomery had his headquarters here when serving with the infant North Atlantic Treaty Organization. Still later, by an irony of fate, German officers returned to Fontainebleau as West German representatives of NATO. When NATO found a new home the French Army occupied a wing that is closed to visitors.

Today the château is a museum, and the monumental buildings themselves could be considered to be a museum too, since the various wings and pavilions represent so many architectural styles from the Renaissance onwards. The main building was constructed during the reign of François I, but has been modified many times. Five of the pavilions are of two stories, the connecting buildings of one story only. The famous "horseshoe" staircase was built by Du Cerceau under Louis XIII. The François I wing, on the left-hand side, though less grandiose, is actually Renaissance. Road and gateways pass through the great complex of buildings. One gateway near the circular staircase gives access to the Courtyard of the Well, named after a well depicting Ulysses which was commissioned by Napoleon in 1812. This courtyard overlooks the Carp Pond. Very old carp are said to swim in this pool—centuries old! This must be something of an exaggeration as the Allied soldiers drained the lake in 1915 and ate all the fish; then in 1940 Hitler's soldiers did exactly the same thing. Still Parisians like to feed the admittedly large fish under the illusion that they were swimming there in the days of the Emperor . . .

The Porte Dauphine is the most beautiful gateway in the château and was designed by the Italian artist Primaticcio, court architect to François I, and court sculptor and court painter, too. The cupola above the gateway dates from the reign of Henri IV. The name Porte Dauphine derives from the fact that the Dauphin, later to become Louis XIII, was christened under this particular gateway when he was 5 years old.

As far as the château as a museum is concerned, you'll find Napoleon's apartments on the first floor. Here you'll see the hat he wore on his return from Elba, and a lock of his hair, too. The bedchamber has the bed on which he really and truly slept. (It's necessary to emphasize this because you will come across "imperial beds" in almost every small town in France where the Emperor is supposed to have spent a night.) His Légion d'Honneur medal and his imperial uniform are among the many mementoes of Napoleon on display.

There's also a throne room. Napoleon seemed particularly anxious to have one here, though the kings were satisfied with one at Versailles. The queen's bedroom is called the "Room of the Six Maries"—and six there were: Marie de Médicis, Marie-Thérèse, Marie Leczinska, Marie-Antoinette, Marie-Louise and Marie-Amélie. The Diana Gallery was built during the reign of Henri IV; it's a seemingly endless room, which was finally used as a library. Salon follows salon, the most interesting decorations being the 17th-century tapestries, the frescos by Primaticcio and the marble reliefs by Jacquet de Grenoble, who molded a likeness of Henry IV in 1599.

The ballroom has dazzlingly rich Renaissance ornamentation and gilding. Here you'll see the coat of arms of Henri II and Diane de Poitiers. Most spectacular are the eight huge paintings by Primaticcio and Niccolo dell' Abbate, begun in 1552. The smaller apartments were the bedchambers of the Queen Mothers; the Deer Gallery opens on to those occupied by Pope Pius VII.

The Forest

The forest is remarkable for its size: 42,000 acres in area, 60 miles in circumference, crossed by about 50 miles of made-up road and 200 miles of woodland tracks. You'll notice cliffs where budding mountaineers practice rock climbing. Some of the rock formations and ravines have romantic names such as "Wolf Gorge," "Eagle's Nest," or "The Young Ladies' Cliffs." There's an atmosphere of mystery, and even terror, about some of these places, and grim events are said to have taken place in the depths of the forest. But there are lovely clearings among the trees, too, and the forest can be an enchanted and enchanting place. Unless you wander far off the beaten track, you're unlikely to lose your way, since there are many well-placed signposts. If you have a car the forest is ideal for a picnic; the area also has campsites.

Barbizon

This village of about 1,000 inhabitants lies on the western edge of the forest, close to the motorway. Barbizon found itself world-famous in the Romantic period when artists such as Michallon, Bertin, Aligny, followed by Théodore Rousseau and Jean-François Millet, settled here. In the mid-19th century Père Ganne's inn became the artists' meeting-place, and it still stands today. It is now a gallery with many paintings of the Barbizon School. You can buy reproductions of the work of Corot, Decamps, Diaz or Barye or, to get nearer to the spirit of the place as it was, you can visit Millet's studio and also Rousseau's, which is now a memorial museum.

GETTING THERE. By Train. Trains from the Gare de Lyon take 35–50 mins.

By Bus. Excursions are covered under *Traveling outside Paris* in the *Practical Information* section.

By Car. Take either the A6 motorway (around 1 hour, but can be a lot more on Sun. and public holiday mornings) or the N7 (around 1½ hours, but again very crowded at peak times).

SIGHTSEEING CHECKLIST. Auberge de Père Ganne, rue Grande, Barbizon (tel. 60–66–46–73). Open daily except Tues., 10–6.

Château de Fontainebleau (tel. 64–22–27–40 or 64–22–34–39). Open daily except Tues., 9.30–12.30, 2–5. No admission after 11.45 or 4.15; *petits appartements* closed on weekends. Reduced admission charge on Sun. Visit without guides, but cassettes in French or English available for extra charge. (N).

Millet's Studio, rue Grande, Barbizon. Open daily except Tues., 10.15–12, 2–6.

Rousseau Museum, rue Grande, Barbizon (tel. 60–66–22–38). Open daily except Tues., 10–12, 2–6.

LUNCH SPOTS. BARBIZON. Bas-Bréau (E), 22 rue Grande, (tel. 60–66–40–05). Delightful *Relais et Chateaux* hotel with beautiful garden and excellent restaurant specializing in game with wild mushrooms in season. Tables outside in summer. Closed Jan. to mid-Feb. AE, MC, V.

Le Relais de Barbizon (I), 2 av. du Général-de-Gaulle (tel. 60–66–40–28). Good home cooking, outdoor meals in summer; gets very crowded. Closed Tues. and Wed., last half of Aug. and over Christmas and New Year. V.

FONTAINEBLEAU. Beauharnais (E), in *Aigle Noir* hotel, 27 pl. Bonaparte —opposite the château (tel. 64–22–32–65). Grand restaurant in very grand hotel, but the cuisine is far from stuffy, with *nouvelle cuisine* specialties as well as light versions of classical cuisine. AE, DC, MC, V.

Bivouac (M), again in the *Aigle Noir* hotel (see above), but more modest. Good-value newish cuisine. AE, DC, V.

Filet de Sole (M), 5 rue du Coq-Gris (tel. 64–22–25–05). Attractive old building, good-value cuisine. Closed Tues., Wed., and July. AE, DC, MC, V.

Dauphin (I), 24 rue Grande (tel. 64–22–27–04). Modest, but with some good home-style cooking. Closed Wed., Feb. and first half of Sept. MC, V.

Ile de France (I), 128 rue de France (tel. 64–22–21–17). Attractive, typically French provincial building, but the restaurant in this pleasant hotel serves Chinese cuisine! AE, DC, V.

GIVERNY

Visiting Giverny is in many ways like witnessing a miracle. This charming little village in southern Normandy has become a place of pilgrimage for art-lovers from all over the world, for it was here that Claude Monet, greatest of the Impressionist painters, lived for 43 years, and here, too, that he died in 1926, at the age of 86. But the miracle is that after decades of neglect his pretty pink-washed house with its green shutters, his studios and most of all his wonderful garden with the lily pond he so magically captured on canvas have all been lovingly restored to their former glory, thanks to generous gifts from many patrons of the arts, including Americans, and are now open to the public for much of the year. The spring is perhaps the best time to visit, when the Norman apple trees are in blossom and the spring flowers offer a riot of color, but right through to the fall (it's closed in winter) Giverny is a worthy goal for a stimulating day out from Paris.

Monet was a Norman by birth and when, like all the Impressionists, he set out to look for the ideal spot to paint light effects, and the play of light on water, he was drawn to the very edge of his native region, in the verdant Seine valley. He moved to Giverny in 1883 with his two sons and his mistress Alice Hoschedé, whom he later married, and her six children. They rented the house at the end of the village with a large piece of land that Monet was soon busy turning into a wonderfully flower-filled garden.

Giverny seems to have brought him luck, for it was here that he first began to enjoy real success as a painter and after many years of privations to earn considerable sums. By 1890 he was able to buy the house and in 1893 purchased another piece of land the other side of the railway line, subsequently obtaining permission to divert a tributary of the river Epte to make a small lake or pond. The "Japanese bridge" that features in many of his best-loved paintings was added a couple of years later.

There is a delightful family feel about the house that may well come as something of a relief if you have been visiting formal châteaux. The small rooms have all been faithfully restored so that they are exactly as Monet planned them. The blue kitchen with its decorative tiles and the fabulous buttercup-yellow dining room are particularly charming and everywhere you'll see the Japanese prints Monet collected so avidly. You can visit his bedroom on the second floor and his studio on the first floor, plus another studio in the grounds that has been converted into a reception area for visitors. Here you can buy books and postcards, and some beautiful china and table linen copying the designs you've seen inside the house.

The garden is quite breathtaking, every corner bringing to mind yet another of Monet's light-filled canvases. Unlike the formal *jardins à la française* you'll have seen so often in France, this is an informal cottage-style garden, with flowers spilling over the paths wherever you look. The lily pond is yet another delight, with the waterlilies blooming once again, faithfully mirroring Monet's series of paintings displayed in the Orangerie in Paris. A generous donation from Walter Annenberg, one-time U.S. ambassador to London, has ensured that you can reach this enchanting water garden without breaking the spell via an attractively decorated tunnel, instead of having to cross a busy road.

GETTING THERE. By Train. Trains from the Gare St. Lazare (the Rouen line) will take you to Vernon in around 50 mins. From there Giverny is a taxi-ride or a 45-min. walk away.

By Bus. Guided excursions are run by *American Express, Cityrama, Europabus, Paris-Vision* and the *RATP,* either half-day or a whole-day combined with Rouen.

By Car. Take the A13 motorway westwards out of Paris, then the D181 to Vernon, followed by the D55 (watch out for the signposts when you're by the river in Vernon). This excursion can easily be combined with Thoiry (q.v.).

SIGHTSEEING CHECKLIST. Claude Monet's house, studio and garden (tel. 32–51–28–21). Open daily except Mon. from 1 April through Oct.; garden 10–6, house and studio 10–12, 2–6. Reduced admission for children between 7 and 12, students and the over-65s. No admission charge for children under 7.

LUNCH SPOTS. Beau Rivage (M), 13 av. Maréchal-Leclerc, Vernon (tel. 32–51–17–27). Just beside the river, good-value *menus carte* is more expensive. Closed Mon., first half of Feb. and of Oct. AE, MC, V.

Relais Normand (M), in *Evreux* hotel, 7 pl d'Evreux, Vernon (tel. 32–21–16–12). Closed Sun. and Aug. Attractive old building. AE, DC, MC, V.

Les Fleurs (I), 71 rue Carnot, Vernon (tel. 32–51–16–80). Friendly family-run place, offering good food and a warm welcome. Closed Mon., and mid-Aug. to mid-Sept. V.

Château de Brécourt (M), 10 km. away at **Douains**, near Pacy-sur-Eure (tel. 32–52–40–50). A member of the Relais et Châteaux association, with huge grounds around a 17th-century building. Goodish food and a particularly pleasant atmosphere. Must reserve, as this is a popular spot for motorized visitors to Giverny. AE, DC, MC, V.

MALMAISON

Just outside Paris, in the pleasant residential district now called Rueil-Malmaison, is the château of Malmaison, the country house where Napoleon Bonaparte and his beloved Josephine lived during the early 1800s. Although in later years Napoleon lived at both Compiègne and Fontainebleau, it was here at Malmaison that he was happiest.

There is a feeling of enchantment about this pretty house with its rose gardens and stone basins which makes it the most moving of all the Napoleonic museums. All the rooms are furnished with Napoleonic period furniture, and many of the pieces actually belonged to the Emperor and to Josephine. Her bedroom on the first floor is exactly what a *nouveau riche* young woman would have liked in 1799, and the tent-draped ceiling must have seemed the last word to this young couple very much on their way up in the world. Fascinating also are the library, game-room, and dining-room with their handsome furnishings, as well as the display of Josephine's gowns and jewels. Here she spent her remaining years following her divorce from Napoleon, and here too she died, in 1814, while her ex-husband was still in exile on Elba. Less than a year later, after his escape from Elba, Napoleon came back to Malmaison on a melancholy pilgrimage during which he apparently remembered their happy years together. And he came back again after the Battle of Waterloo, before the final exile to St. Helena.

As well as visiting the château and its collections, don't miss the Carriage Pavilion in the grounds, with a fine selection of vehicles including Josephine's attractively named carriage *L'Opale* (The Opal), which took her on her sad journey from the Tuileries to Malmaison when she knew at last that Napoleon would never return to her.

Another pavilion in the grounds is known as the Osiris Pavilion from the pen-name of the man who rescued Malmaison from neglect by buying the château at the end of the 19th century, restoring it and giving it to the nation a few years later. The pavilion houses his collection of "Napoleana," including popular items such as snuff boxes that bear witness to the Napoleonic cult that lasted long after the ex-emperor's death.

The grounds are attractive at any time of year, but are particularly lovely in the rose season and when the spring flowers are out. After visiting them you can do as the empress herself used to do and stroll to the adjoining grounds of the château of Bois-Préau, which Josephine bought in 1809 and which is now used as a sort of annex to Malmaison, housing many relics of the imperial family, including Napoleon's famous triangular hat and frock coat. The exhibits associated with the exile on St Helena are particularly moving. Bois-Préau was bought in 1920 by the former American consul in Paris, Edward Tuck, who bequeathed it to the French nation.

You can continue along the N13 to Bougival and Marly, both of which offer many pretty walks, and combine your excursion with a visit to Saint-Germain-en-Laye. Lunch at one of the restaurants overlooking the Seine at Bougival or Louveciennes would be a pleasant way of beginning or ending your visit to Malmaison, though here you will be moving ahead of the Napoleonic era to the time of the Impressionists: Renoir and Manet often came here, as did Hector Berlioz. In fact this delightfully peaceful area once echoed to the sound of much bohemian merrymaking centered on a series of *auberges* and lively dance halls. One of them is currently being restored and by the end of the decade may well be echoing once again to the sounds of highjinx-by-the-river.

GETTING THERE. By RER. Take the line C of the express metro to Rueil-Malmaison, then about 10 mins. walk to the château.

By Regular Bus. Take the RER or the 73 bus to La Défense, then the 158A bus, which drops you right outside the château grounds. The same bus continues to Bougival, Louveciennes and Marly.

By Excursion Bus. Guided tours, some combined with Versailles, are covered in *Traveling outside Paris* in the *Practical Information* section.

By Car. Take the N13 road westwards out of Paris. The same road continues on to Bougival, Louveciennes and Marly.

SIGHTSEEING CHECKLIST. Château de Bois-Préau, av. de l'Imperatrice Joséphine (tel. 47–49–20–07). Same opening times as Malmaison, but admission charge is lower. (N).

Château de Malmaison (tel. 47–49–20–07), av. du Château. Open daily except Tues., 10–12.30, 1.30–5 (may be later in summer months); no admission after 12 and 4.30. Audiovisual presentation included in admission charge. Reduced fee on Sun. (N).

Parc de Marly (tel. 49–69–06–26). Visits with cassette guides 2–6, Wed. to Sat., closed Mon., Tues. and public holidays. For hire of cassettes go to the *Grille Royale.* The park itself is open till dusk.

LUNCH SPOTS. BOUGIVAL. Le Camélia (E), 7 quai Georges-Clemenceau (tel. 39–69–03–02). A very chic roadside inn close to the river, serving superb *nouvelle cuisine* in delightful setting. Popular with well-heeled Parisians, especially on Sun. Good-value *menu.* Closed Mon. AE, DC, V.

Château de la Jonchère (E), 10 côte de la Jonchère (tel. 39–18–57–03). Once a private château bought by Napoleon for one of Joséphine's brothers, now converted with no expense spared as a hotel-restaurant; startling decor, lots of style, good *nouvelle cuisine* too. Set in lovely grounds. Closed Mon. AE, DC, MC, V.

L'Huître et la Tarte (M), 6 quai Georges-Clémenceau (tel. 39–18–45–55). New place with tasty, imaginative cooking at good-value prices. Closed Mon., and Aug. V.

LOUVECIENNES. Aux Chandelles (M), 12 pl. de l'Eglise (tel. 39–69–08–40). Prettily set on a villagey square up the hill from the river. Relaxed atmosphere, garden, *nouvelle cuisine* versions of good home cooking. Closed Wed. and Sat. V.

La Hulotte (M), 17 route de Versailles (tel. 39–69–05–97). Tasty *nouvelle cuisine* and excellent *menu* on weekdays. Terrace and garden. Closed Sat. AE, V.

MALMAISON. Pavillon Joséphine (M), 191 av. Napoléon-Bonaparte (tel. 47–51–01–62). Just by the château entrance. Good value *menus,* interesting *nouvelle cuisine.* Closed most of Aug. AE, DC, V.

Relais de Saint-Cucufa (M), 114 rue du Général-de-Miribel (tel. 47–49–79–05). Attractive terrace for summer eating, lots of excellent fish, but good meat dishes, too. Closed Mon. and most of Aug. AE, DC, MC, V.

SAINT-DENIS

Saint-Denis is a not particularly attractive industrial town on the northern edge of Paris but it is well worth a visit for its splendid cathedral housing the tombs of most of France's monarchs.

It did not in fact become a cathedral until 1966. It started life as an abbey church, built on the site of a much earlier Carolingian church. The plans were drawn up by the famous Abbot Suger of Saint-Denis, who was an adviser to both Louis VI and Louis VII—indeed he effectively governed the country at frequent intervals, when his royal master was out of the kingdom on a major crusade. Work started in 1137 and continued for over a century, Abbot Suger's role being taken over in due course by Pierre de Montereau, Saint-Louis's architect. On completion it was the most richly decorated church in France and many of its treasures have happily survived the injuries of long years, though they are now on display not in Saint-Denis itself but in the Apollo Gallery in the Louvre.

At the end of the 13th century the abbey church was promoted to the rank of basilica and it is still frequently referred to as such (even in the name of the métro station that was built well after the basilica became a cathedral!).

With the passing centuries the building was neglected and suffered much damage. Before the Revolution there was even a plan afoot to demolish the old church and build a completely new cathedral better suited to the taste of the age. Then during the Revolution the royal tombs were desecrated and the royal bones dumped in mass graves. The tombs themselves were left unharmed, though for a time they were removed to the newly founded Museum of Monumental Arts. During the Restoration they were returned to the cathedral. Much of the statuary in the precincts was removed during the Revolution. Because of the long years of neglect some restoration work was attempted during the 19th century. But it was carried out so inexpertly that the structure of the building itself was impaired and one of the towers had to be demolished. The nave, shorter but wider than that of Notre-Dame, is divided by a railing. On one side is the burial place of the kings, a truly astonishing sight.

All but three French kings were buried in the cathedral, though the tombs are empty today. The first laid to rest here was Dagobert, five centuries ago, in what was then a new church. But twelve centuries of French monarchy are recorded on the monuments. Kings, queens and royal children—and a few particularly noteworthy servants of the Crown—were also buried here. When a king was buried, his heart was first removed and buried elsewhere.

The cathedral is therefore a museum of French sculpture of the Middle Ages and the Renaissance, and you can trace the development of the art from the time of Saint-Louis, who commissioned monuments to all his royal ancestors, down to the reign of Philip the Bold. From then until the Renaissance it was the custom to take a death-mask of the monarch and make a copy in stone. After the Renaissance richly-adorned mausoleums enshrined the memory of the rulers. For these mausoleums it was customary to make two sets of images of the royal couples. In the lower section the figures lie naked, symbolizing the reality of death, while above, the effigies are clad in all the splendor of their royal robes. Catherine de Médicis, who outlived her husband by 30 years, wanted to order the funeral monuments for both Henri II and herself, but when she saw the likeness the sculptor had made of her she was so horrified that she ordered another one—this time depicting her, as it were, in gentle sleep. Both monuments are on view so you can draw an interesting comparison. The first was designed by Primaticcio, the second by Germain Pilon.

In the choir you'll see the famous *oriflamme,* the battle standard of the French kings, originally the personal banner of Abbot Suger. Until the Revolution it was traditional for the leaders of the troops to go to Saint-Denis to receive this sacred flag before going to war.

Also worth visiting in Saint-Denis is the Musée Municipal d'Art et d'Histoire, now housed in a restored 17th-century Carmelite monastery. This rich museum uses paintings and early engravings to illustrate the life of the French working classes and the history of the town. It also has many fine canvases, by Picasso, Matisse, Fernand Léger, Albert Marquet and Frans Masereel among many others, as well as nearly four thousand lithographs and woodcuts by Henri Daumier. A special room is devoted to the poet Paul Eluard, who was born in Saint-Denis and donated to the town a large number of his manuscripts and personal possessions in his lifetime; then, after his death in 1952, his widow added many more items to the collections. There is also an important section devoted to that key period in French history, the Paris Commune.

Those interested in modern architecture might like to visit a housing complex called the Cité Paul-Eluard in Saint-Denis, a world-famous example of "social housing." Theater-lovers should also know that the town has an excellent company playing at a theater named after that much-loved actor Gérard Philipe.

GETTING THERE. By Métro. Take the no. 13 line northwards to St.-Denis-Basilique.

By Car. Take the A1 motorway or the N14 from the Porte de Clignancourt, then the N310A. As Saint-Denis is only 10 km. from Paris, you might like to drive on to Chantilly.

SIGHTSEEING CHECKLIST. Cathedral, pl. de l'Hôtel de Ville (tel. 42–43–00–71). Open daily 10–4; no visits during Sun. morning masses. Half-price admission charge on Sun. and public holidays.

Musée d'Art et d'Histoire de la Ville de Saint-Denis, 22bis rue Gabriel-Péri (tel. 42–43–05–10). Open Mon. and Wed. to Sat., 10–5.30; Sun. 2–6.30; closed Tues. No admission charge on Sun., under-16s always free. Guided visits on weekends (tel. 42–43–33–55).

LUNCH SPOTS. Melody (E), 15 rue Gabriel-Péri (tel. 48–20–87–73). Conveniently near the museum; interesting *nouvelle cuisine* with specialties from southwestern France. Closed Sun., school Easter vacation and Aug. V.

Grill St.-Denis (M), 59 rue Strasbourg (tel. 48–27–61–98). Adequate, specializing in grilled meat. Closed Sun. and public holidays, Aug. and during Feb. mid-semester break. AE, DC, MC, V.

Les Mets du Roy (M), 4 rue de la Boulangerie (tel. 48–20–89–74). Right opposite the basilica, reliable cuisine. Closed weekends, Easter period and most of July. AE, DC, V.

THOIRY

As a day out from Paris, a visit to Thoiry is hard to beat, especially if you are traveling with children. It really does have everything you could want for a full and varied excursion: a beautiful château designed by Philibert de l'Orme in the 16th century and lived in continuously by the same family for 400 years; a series of treasures including priceless letters from French monarchs; a magnificent safari park with over 800 animals living together in conditions as close as possible to their natural habitat; a Museum of Gastronomy; and a pleasant self-service restaurant in what was once the château's 16th-century stables.

The chateau was built in 1564 and was carefully designed, in the Knights Templar tradition, to face due south—the designs follow exactly the points of the compass. This means that at the solstices a truly magical effect is created—the sun seems to rise or set in the Great Hall, creating a dramatic impression of total transparency. The Renaissance façades are set off by gardens landscaped by Le Nôtre, in the true *jardins à la française* style, but there is a *jardin à l'anglaise* too, less formal and creating a good contrast.

The château is now the home of Vicomte Paul de La Panouse, whose family can be traced back to the 11th century, and his dynamic American wife, Vicomtesse Annabelle. Together they have restored the family fortunes and saved the château and garden by attracting hundreds of thousands of visitors to Thoiry every year. They have even been awarded a medal for "services to tourism."

The family history of the Comtes de La Panouse frequently was involved with great national events—a Comte César even fought in the American Revolution—and many leading political figures were invited to Thoiry over the centuries. Thanks to these energetic men (and their strong-minded womenfolk, too) the château's collections of furniture and documents are quite enthralling. In the Archive Museum you can pore over papal bulls, letters from such great figures as Napoleon, Thomas Jefferson and Benjamin Franklin, and the only known copy of the official document annexing Alsace and Lorraine. Two manuscript waltzes by Chopin were discovered in one of the attics in 1973 by the American pianist, Byron Janis, in a trunk misleadingly labeled "old clothes." They were apparently given by the composer to the present Vicomte's great-grandmother.

Many of the fine pieces of furniture and tapestries that you'll see were also discovered recently in the attics and have been lovingly restored. You can visit the dining-room with a fabulous 18th-century Gobelins tapestry series of the adventures of Don Quixote; the lovely Green-and-White Salon housing a wealth of portraits, more tapestries, and furniture that includes a rare harpsichord; and the Grand Staircase.

A temporary exhibit from Paris which celebrated the 1984 bi-centenary of the birth of the great French chef, Antonin Carême, has found a permanent home in the former pantries as the basis of a Museum of Gastronomy. Amongst much else it contains a magnificent array of *pièces montées,* ornate confections dreamed up to adorn elaborate banquets, recreated in spun sugar to Carême's designs by modern practitioners—one of these masterpieces is over 15 feet high and took 8 months to make! There are also beautiful old copper and lead molds for terrines and desserts, early recipe books, and some fascinating engravings.

Thoiry's "African Reserve" made the world's headlines when the first ever "ligrans" were born here, confounding experts who didn't believe that lions and tigers would ever mate. You can get a bird's eye view of these majestic creatures in the Tiger Park, with its ingeniously raised footbridge (with a safety parapet).

But the ligrans are only one feature of the Safari Park that has made the Vicomte one of the world's leading experts on wildlife conservation. Apart from the lions, tigers and bears, you can see bison, antelope, zebra all grazing together, or watch emus and elegant pink flamingo hunting for food. There is an "exploratory play area" where children can clamber in and out of giant burrows and climb up huge spiders' webs, meeting birds and animals on the way.

GETTING THERE. By Train. Train from Gare Montparnasse to Montfort-l'Amaury (around 30 mins.), then taxi (around 10 mins.).

By Bus. Departure from the Porte de St.-Cloud on the western edge of Paris at 9 A.M. and 1 P.M. weekdays only (takes around 1½ hrs.). Return journey around 4.15 P.M. to Versailles Rive Gauche station, from where you can get a train or express métro into central Paris.

By Car. Take the A13 motorway westwards out of Paris, leaving it at Bois d'Arcy; drive towards Dreux, following the signs, and at Pontchartrain take the D11 to Thoiry. Total distance: 45 km. from central Paris.

 SIGHTSEEING CHECKLIST. Château et Réserve africaine de Thoiry, 78770 Thoiry (tel. 34–87–40–67). Open year-round, every day of the week. 1 April through Oct., 9.45–6, Mon. to Sat.; 9.45–6.30 Sun. and public holidays. 1 Nov. through Mar., 10–5, Mon. to Sat.; 10–5.30 Sun. and public holidays.

Château: for guided visits reservation is essential; otherwise you will be given explanatory leaflets for the various rooms, the Archives, the Gastronomy Museum, and so on. *Safari Park:* cassettes explaining the animals' behavior are on loan free of charge; audiovisual presentation for children; two marked itineraries (8 km. by car or 3 km. on foot). Reduced admission charge for children, students, over-65s and the handicapped; safari park free for children under 2, château free for children under 4.

 LUNCH SPOTS. Self-service restaurant (I) in converted 16th-cent. stables in the château grounds; open during Safari Park opening hours. Good choice of fixed-price menus.

Etoile (I), in hotel of the same name across the village green from the château (tel. 34–87–40–21). Closed Mon. and Jan.

In **Montfort l'Amaury: Les Préjugés (E),** 18 pl. Robert-Brault (tel. 34–86–92 –65). An old building, elegantly converted, with equally elegant *nouvelle cuisine.* Pretty garden too. Closed Tues. and Jan. AE, DC, V.

In **Pontchartrain: L'Aubergade (M),** on the N12 road (tel. 34–89–02–63). Classical cuisine served in attractive diningroom with open fire; lovely garden. Closed Wed. and Aug. V.

Auberge de la Dauberie (M), 53 rue Dauberie in **Les Mousseaux-Pontchartrain,** 3 km. (2 miles) south via D13 (tel. 34–87–80–57). Delightful, villagey spot, good *nouvelle cuisine,* too. Closed Mon., Tues., and in Feb. AE, DC, V.

Château de Brécourt (M), at Douains, near Pacy-sur-Eure (tel. 32–52–40– 50). If you are car-bound, try this Relais et Châteaux spot and combine your trip with one to Giverny (q.v.). A popular spot, so reservations essential. Closed Wed. AE, DC, MC, V.

VERSAILLES

At Versailles you will find the most convincing proof of *la grandeur* and *la gloire,* the splendor that was France, personified in the Sun King and the palace he built. Lying to the southwest of Paris, Versailles attracts tens of thousands of visitors every year, and it is inconceivable that any visitor to Paris should leave the palace and its gardens—both incomparable masterpieces—out of his itinerary.

In the early 17th century the only building here was an insignificant settlement, surrounded by a forest—Crown property—in which Louis XIII used to hunt, and where he had a modest hunting-lodge. It was here that his son, Louis XIV, the absolute monarch *par excellence,* decided he would build a palace the like of which had never been seen in France, or anywhere else in all Europe. Le Vau was commissioned as architect; Le Nôtre was made responsible for the grounds, which were to be on a scale worthy of the palace. The gigantic undertaking began in 1661. Records show that 30,000 men worked on the château itself, and on the terraces, pools and canals. Six thousand horses had

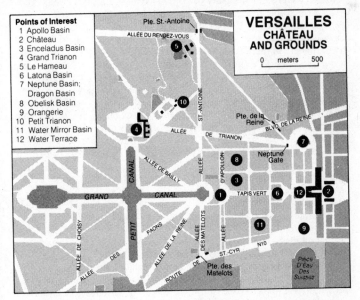

Points of Interest
1 Apollo Basin
2 Château
3 Enceladus Basin
4 Grand Trianon
5 Le Hameau
6 Latona Basin
7 Neptune Basin;
  Dragon Basin
8 Obelisk Basin
9 Orangerie
10 Petit Trianon
11 Water Mirror Basin
12 Water Terrace

VERSAILLES CHÂTEAU AND GROUNDS

0   meters   500

to be used to transport building materials. The cost of the enterprise was over 65 million francs, at that time an astronomical figure. The gulf between the extravagance of royal pomp and the poverty of the common people was so wide that it was undoubtedly a factor in the discontent that brought France to revolution and expelled a king from his glittering palace.

Focus of History

Versailles in fact represents the work of several generations who labored here. Architect replaced architect. On the death of Le Vau his place was taken by Mansart, but he, too, failed to live long enough to complete the work. His brother-in-law Robert de Cotte finished the chapel, while the opera was built by Gabriel.

Yet Louis himself managed to derive a great deal of pleasure from his palace, since he lived for 77 years. When he died in 1715 the palace was the home of many thousand persons. The king was surrounded by innumerable lords and ladies, not to mention politicians and advisers, and general hangers-on, all revolving like satellites around his sun. The Court was served by an army of 10,000—cooks, assistant cooks, lackeys, maids, stablemen, gardeners and engineers to look after the 1,400 fountains designed by Le Nôtre and see that their mechanism was kept in good working order. (Only around 600 function today.) Every year the gardeners planted 150,000 flowers. No wonder Louis XIV left his successor, Louis XV (born in the palace), such enormous debts. Here at the palace, incidentally, were signed the treaties with Austria in 1756, 1757 and 1759 that changed the political organization of Europe.

In 1774 the palace and the country had a new ruler in the 20-year-old Louis XVI. Already the omens were bad, though the treaty that marked the end of the American War of Independence was signed at Versailles in 1783. Six years later, in 1789, the storm was breaking. On 5 May, the Estates General formulated moderate demands. On 20 June the representatives of the people refused to leave the Jeu de Paume until a new document was drawn up on oath limiting the powers of the Crown. Three days later, on 23 June, Mirabeau declared, "We are here by the will of the people and only the power of spears can remove us!" On 25 October the people of Paris demonstrated outside the palace. The following day they occupied it. Louis XVI, Marie-Antoinette and all the members of the royal family in the palace were seized and taken into custody, to perish finally under the blade of the guillotine.

Though the Revolution destroyed many palaces, Versailles remained untouched, only the magnificent furnishings were put up for auction. But when the monarchy was finally restored the new rulers did not dare to return to Versailles. Louis Philippe was happy for it to become a museum. Yet the palace continued to play a part in history. In 1871, in the Hall of Mirrors at Versailles, Wilhelm, King of Prussia, was declared Emperor of Germany. The palace had been the headquarters of the Prussian High Command during the war, and this no doubt saved it from destruction. It was also from Versailles that Thiers sent his troops to crush the Paris Commune. The Third Republic was established at Versailles and the new parliament had its seat at the palace for four years. Eighty years later, in 1958, members of the National Assembly and the Senate, meeting in this regal palace, nominated as head of state General Charles de Gaulle, a man who performed his presidential duties in a regal manner.

The name Versailles became famous all over the world at the end of World War I, for it was here, in the Hall of Mirrors, where half-a-century earlier the German Empire was born, that France and her Allies forced Germany to sign a treaty designed to humble the Fatherland into the dust.

Between the two great wars, the palace was neglected and fell into decay. The roof leaked, walls peeled, woodworm and dryrot attacked the fabric. At last the government decided to vote funds and, with a generous gift from the American millionaire John D. Rockefeller, given after World War I, a start could be made on the work of restoration. The project gained new impetus in the '50s when the Fifth Republic—possibly motivated once again by the ideals of *gloire* and *grandeur*—voted large sums to enable Versailles to glitter again with its old brilliance. In 1966, the Grand Trianon was refurbished so that it could provide suitable accommodation for visiting heads of state. Since then much has been restored, including the famous Hall of Mirrors in the main block of the palace.

Most importantly, in 1980 President Giscard d'Estaing ceremonially reopened the King's Bedroom, which has recovered all its former splendor. Unfortunately the new rooms devoted to the Napoleonic era opened a couple of years earlier were badly damaged by a terrorist bomb planted by Breton separatists and will not reopen in the foreseeable future.

The Main Palace

The main palace, or château as it is called in French, overlooks the 17th-century place d'Armes. The richly-gilded wrought iron railings are crescent-shaped and through them you can see the courtyard. An immense gate leads into what is, in fact, the first of three courtyards, all at different levels, separated in royal days by different sets of railings. The first and largest is the Ministerial Courtyard; the second the King's Courtyard; the third the Marble Courtyard, at the level of the royal bedchambers. In the Royal Courtyard stands a rather commonplace statue of Louis XIV, which was erected during the reign of Louis Philippe. The wing to the right is the work of the architect Gabriel, the wing to the left is the earliest part of the palace, designed by Le Vau. To reach the grounds go through the right wing, which is also the entrance to the museum.

The palace is at its most beautiful when seen from the grounds, and its huge size also seems most impressive from here—it is nearly 680 meters (2,230 feet) long. The middle section is Le Vau's work, though it was completed by Mansart, who also built the south and north wings, in 1682 and 1684 respectively. It was also Mansart, together with the sculptor Coustou, who created the royal chapel. The projecting central section of the palace contains the celebrated Hall of Mirrors. The interior was designed by Mansart, aided by Le Brun. The statues are by the two most celebrated sculptors of the period, Coysevox and Tuby, while the immense frescos depicting the Sun King's victories are by Le Brun.

The king's bedchamber is the work of Mansart. After 10 years of painstaking restoration, it was reopened to the public in 1980 and is now just as it was when Louis XIV slept here in the early 18th century. The anteroom to the bedchamber is the famous "Oeil-de-Boeuf (Bullseye) Room," so named because of the architectural term for its large round window. Here courtiers awaited the king's pleasure, and here many Court intrigues were hatched. Gabriel designed Marie-Antoinette's bedchamber. The Queen's Staircase, the most beautiful in the palace, was again Mansart's work.

The north wing contains the former opera house, designed by Gabriel and restored between 1952 and 1957 by André Japy. Since the restoration special performances of operas of the Louis XV period have been staged here for distinguished visitors. The congress hall is in the south wing.

It is difficult to offer guidance about the art-treasures the palace contains. The collection spreading through the various rooms and galleries is so vast that you can easily become tired of the seemingly endless portraits of kings, queens, courtiers, noble ladies, favorites, generals—and the statues. In the "Gallery of Battles" on the upper floor of the south wing only battle pictures are to be seen: Delacroix's canvas of the *Battle of Taillebourg* is definitely worth a look, as is Gérard's *Battle of Austerlitz*. Then too, the painting of the celebrated meeting of François I and the English King Henry VIII on the Field of the Cloth of Gold, with its rich coloring and extraordinary attention to detail has much to say about the whole "royal scene" of the 16th century. Of the portraits, one of the most remarkable on view (among the queens) is by an unknown artist of the 16th century: it is a likeness of Claude de France, wife of François I, executed with deceptive simplicity. Interesting too, is the portrait of the architect Mansart himself, a dignified bewigged figure. In a portrait by Nattier of another queen, Marie Leczinska, the royal lady seems to be smiling forgivingly. Perhaps she needed to be forgiving, for Nattier's portrait of Madame de Pompadour, the king's celebrated mistress, is graceful but triumphant. The portrait of Louis XV himself is by Carle Vanloo—a soft, full, almost girlish face, yet with the slightly aquiline nose and sensuous lower lip characteristic of the dynasty.

The Grounds

The grounds are dotted with many somewhat pompous statues, some of genuine artistic merit. The fountains, the pools on their various terraces, all functioning on hydraulic principles worked out during Louis XIV's reign, are well worth exploration. The best time to see them is on *Grandes Eaux* days, when vast quantities of water leap and cascade in a glittering display. In these days of belt-tightening, the huge expense of having the great fountains play means that you can see them only a few times a year. Also a must, if you are lucky enough to be around then, are the magnificent *Fêtes de Nuit,* with floodlighting and fireworks.

In the mid-'80s, several smaller fountains were refurbished and the formal gardens replenished to create an even more attractive circuit. The best place to start your fountain tour is, as Louis XIV himself advised, on the main terrace: "Leave the palace by the entrance hall to the marble courtyard (Cour de Marbre), then stop at the top of the steps to take in the view of the flowerbeds, pools and fountains. Then continue straight on to the top of the Latona Parterre, and pause to gaze at Latona, the amphibians, the grassy slopes and statues, the Royal Avenue, Apollo and the Canal, before turning round to view the Parterre and the Palace." In restoring Louis' beloved fountain displays to something approaching their former glory, the designers have followed his instructions as closely as possible. A well-illustrated plan will guide you as you visit such delights as the Dragon Fountain, the Apollo Pool, the Colonnade, the Water Avenue or the Bathing Nymphs. The largest ornamental pool of all is the Pool of Neptune, which has a huge sculptured group depicting Neptune and Amphitrite and no fewer than 99 different fountains and spraying jets of water. This is where the "Evening Festivities in the Pool of Neptune" and "Triumph of Neptune" are held, enhanced by lighting effects, music and fireworks.

Another major feature of the vast park are the smaller outlying palaces, the Trianons, and the tiny toy farm, Le Hameau. The Grand Trianon is a palace just for play, one of the loveliest in France. Only one story high with a colonnade linking its two sections, this pink marble fantasy was erected in six months by Mansart. Its very size makes it ideal for a guest house, as the roster of its famous visiting list—including Peter the Great and Madame de Pompadour—indicates.

The Petit Trianon, ordered by Louis XV and built by Gabriel, designer of the place de la Concorde in Paris, owes its fame to its last owner, ill-starred Marie-Antoinette. She came to this grey stone mansion nearly every day to flee the noxious atmosphere of the court. Close by she built the village, with dairy and mill where, dressed as shepherdesses, she and her companions lived a make-believe bucolic life and most visitors are more fascinated by the village and its setting.

 GETTING THERE. By Train. Trains run from Montparnasse and Saint-Lazare stations, taking from 15–30 mins.

By Express Métro. Line C of the RER will take you from the Gare d'Austerlitz, Gare des Invalides and all other stations on that line. Take trains with names starting with "V," such as Vick; there are large explanatory notices posted up on all stations, in French and English. The trip takes about 25–30 mins. from central Paris.

By Bus. Whole-day or half-day guided visits to Versailles, some of them combined with Chartres, Malmaison or Fontainebleau, are covered in *Traveling outside Paris* in the *Practical Information* section.

By Car. Take the N10 or the A13 motorway *(autoroute de Normandie)*, which will get you there in around 20 mins., more on weekends.

 SIGHTSEEING CHECKLIST. Château et Musée de Versailles (tel. 39–50–58–32). Open Tues. to Sun., 9.45–5.30 (no admittance after 5); closed Mon. and public holidays. Basic entry fee (around 18 frs) entitles you to visit the *grands appartements* and the *Galerie des Glaces* (Hall of Mirrors) without a guide. For the *private apartments* and the *Royal Opera House* you must take a special ticket in the second hall and will be accompanied by a guide; guided tours in English available at intervals. For the *Chambre du Roi* (King's Bedroom) you must again have a guide and it is usually open only 10.15–11.30 and 2–4.20. (N).

The *Grand Trianon* (open 9.45–5.30, no admission after 4.30) requires an extra admission fee of about 10 frs, as does the *Petit Trianon* (open 2–5.30 only, closed weekends, Mon. and public holidays). Combined tickets for the two Trianons cost around 14 frs. (N).

Half-price for everyone on Sun. Under-18s are free at all times, people between 18 and 25 plus the over-60s pay half-price at all times.

The grounds are free from sunrise to sunset.

The *Fountains* play two or three Sun. per month from May through Sept, usually at 3.30 for around 1½ hours. The schedule varies, so best check at the Paris or Versailles Tourist Offices (for the latter, tel. 39–50–36–22). The same applies to the *Fêtes de Nuit,* with floodlighting and fireworks, which are held three or four times a year, in June and Sept., at around 9 P.M. Admission charge for the *Grandes Eaux* around 14 frs, for the *Fêtes de Nuit* around 22 frs.

LUNCH SPOTS. Les Trois Marches (E), 3 rue Colbert (tel. 39–50–13–21). One of the best-known restaurants in the Paris area, now housed in a lovely 18th-century mansion. Superb *nouvelle cuisine,* deluxe atmosphere. Closed Sun. and Mon. AE, DC, MC, V.

La Boule d'Or (M), 25 rue du Marechal-Foch (tel. 39–50–22–97). Boasts of being the oldest inn in Versailles (it dates from 1696) and specializes in recipes invented by famous French chefs of earlier centuries; also has a good selection of dishes from the current chef's native region of Franche-Comté in eastern France. Closed Mon. AE, DC, V.

Rescatore (M), 27 ave. de St.-Cloud (tel. 39–50–23–60). A fish restaurant close to the château, in an attractive old building. AE, V.

Londres (I), 7 rue Colbert (tel. 39–50–05–79). Right by the château, with tables outside in fine weather; also good for reviving teas after a long visit to the palace. Closed Mon. and mid-Jan. to mid-Feb.

Le Potager du Roy (I), 1 rue du Marechal-Joffre (tel. 39–50–35–34). Under the same ownership as *Les Trois Marches* and also very good, though less elaborate. Good value. V.

DISTANT DAYS OUT

In this chapter we have picked out a few places that we think you'll particularly enjoy visiting for a day out during your stay in Paris. But if you have the time to visit further afield and prefer to base yourself in one spot rather than keep changing hotels, there are many other places open to you on a longish day's trip from Paris. They are largely opened up by the excellent rail network.

For instance—thanks to the high-speed train service (TGV)—you can get all the way to **Lyon** in only two hours now. Other possibilities are **Dijon, Orléans, Rheims, Rouen** and **Tours,** all of which can be reached by train in no more than two hours. For some useful data see under *Traveling outside Paris* in the *Practical Information* section. For descriptions of these places and details about visiting them, please see our annually-revised *Guide to France.*

Index

The letters H and R indicate hotel and restaurant listings.

FODOR'S TRAVEL GUIDES

ailable in a

n)
Travel Values)
ee Belgium)
ng Kong)

Mexico's Baja)

Travel Values)
Acapulco
& Puerto
zatlan,
Copper Canyon
in)

ia)

(see Canada's
ovinces)
e Continent

kholm)

olic of China

ebec
a (see Mexico's
Stockholm)

un on)

Maarten

Beijing)

ravel Values)
e India)